Triple Decker

Triple Decker

A Novel

D-L Nelson

D-L Nelson

The characters in this book are fictious. Any similarity to real persons,
living or dead, is coincidental and not intended by the author.

©D-L Nelson

If you would like permission to use material from this book other than material for
review purposes, please contact
dlnelson7@hotmail.com
or
Perspectives Publishing
30, rue Vermeille
66700 Argelès-sur-mer
France

First Edition July 2019

Paperback ISBN-13: 978-1-7332696-1-2
Kindle-13: 978-1-7332696-0-5
ePub ISBN-13: 978-1-7332696-2-9

*For Llara, who shared a Triple Decker with me
and is one of the best parts of my life.*

PROLOGUE

MISSION HILL
BOSTON, MASSACHUSETTS

The Flanagan's triple decker on Delle Street in the Mission Hill section of Boston was a deep, serious sea green. The bay windows on each floor brightened the three apartments. An estate agent's advertisement, if the apartments were for sale which they were not, would describe each unit as having three spacious bedrooms, living room, dining room, kitchen and good-sized pantry.

The front had privet hedges. Latticework hid the basement windows. Six stairs, always repainted before they showed the wear of footsteps, led to the entrance, a double door each with a scene of swans swimming on cat-o-nine tail filled ponds etched in the oval panes. The windows let light flood into the hall even during the most depressing Boston weather.

Behind the house was a fenced-in back yard, large enough for barbecues and for small children to play but not large enough for a rowdy football game.

The color and slight architectural variations marked the differences of the Flanagan's triple decker from the neighbors' identically constructed houses, which were painted blue, grey and yellow.

The houses stood in hand-shaking distance of their neighbors, as did all the houses on The Hill.

Most Mission Hill houses had been occupied since the mid-1880s by the Boston Irish. Even after they were welcomed throughout the city instead of being shunned they stayed on The Hill rather than move to Back Bay or the North End. More often than not, extended families occupied the three flats of the triple deckers, with children not really caring if it were Aunt Mary's and not their own place where they played. If they were there at dinner, they ate and perhaps the next night their cousins would eat at their table.

Until the last decade, when rising prices caused some residents to sell, the same families occupied the houses for generations. Condos had begun to replace single ownership.

The Flanagans didn't know or care about the history of The Hill – how in pre-Revolutionary days it was John Parker's prosperous farm, how the long-gone Stony Brook provided fish, and the area was lush with vegetation despite the rocky soil and boulders dropped by departing glaciers. Some boulders were larger than the houses. Nor did they know that over the years the farm was broken up or that an influx of immigrants made practical the construction of a station of the Boston-Providence Railroad, which in turn led to the opening of a brewery where there were no signs reading "Irish need not apply." So they did. And because of shared backgrounds and beliefs the Irish became a community of families without knowing that was what they were doing.

The Flanagans knew only their own history of how they had purchased the house at 40 Delle Avenue in 1955 when it was colored brown. That was the year Bridget Riley and Patrick Flanagan, himself an Irish immigrant, married. The price was $15,595.

The couple took a 25-year mortgage. They gave birth to four children one after another.

The first floor was occupied by Bridget's mother, another Irish immigrant, until she died, the middle floor rented to the spinster lay teacher at the Catholic school attached to the Mission Hill Church. When she retired, she moved to Florida.

When each of their two daughters married, they moved into one of the apartments. One son became a priest, another a State Rep, who lived close enough to come to dinner every Sunday. Their family's history was like their neighbors who hadn't sold to condo developers ... until Operation Iraqi Freedom began March 20, 2003. After that nothing was ever the same.

CHAPTER 1

Long ago, Bridget Riley Flanagan had learned to talk with her mouth full of multi-colored, round-headed pins. This day was no exception.

"Hold still." She sat cross-legged on her workroom floor, surrounded by stray threads, pinning the hem of a violet linen dress. The dress had only one Juliet sleeve tapering to an eight-inch cuff. The other sleeve was on the long blue-painted table supported by matching sawhorses.

On the other side of the room was her sewing machine, her buttonhole maker and the machine that let her stitch-finish seams. Folded bolts of silks, velvets, brocade and linen fabric were stacked on floor-to-ceiling shelves opposite the bay window.

Three headless dummies wore unfinished bridal gowns. A fourth wore a suit with chalk marks on brown herringbone wool. "You were a wiggle worm when I made your bridal gown and you're worse when I'm making your mother-of-the-bride dress."

Bridget swept a strand of white hair that fell from the coil pinned to the top of her head. It fell again. The length was her rebellion against the short-permed cuts decreed for women of her age and class. No Irish Afro sported by most of her friends for her.

Her client, Jeanne, was in her late 40s, far younger than Bridget's 70 years. Jeanne's black hair was streaked with grey, but her skin had only laugh lines around the eyes. "I'm fatter now."

"I didn't say that." Bridget stabbed the hem with the last pin in her mouth and plucked three more from the red velvet cushion strapped to her wrist. She'd thought it, though. "Turn. Not that much. Back half a step. Good."

"I'm sorry the bridesmaids didn't have you make their dresses, but at least April wants you to make her gown." Jeanne rolled her eyes at the fecklessness of bridesmaids.

Bitch, you're not sorry at all. "Just as well. I'm swamped with work." Snowflakes flickered by the three curtainless bay windows.

Bridget's daughters in the two apartments downstairs used their equivalent rooms as living rooms. She couldn't even remember what year she'd converted hers into her workroom, overruling the protests of her kids, unhappy about losing the biggest room in the flat.

"It pays for your school." That shut them up. Fees for four children in Catholic school, books and uniforms added up, and although Patrick earned a good salary once he started at Polaroid, it wasn't enough for four tuitions on top of their other living expenses.

Thus, the Flanagan family began the game of musical rooms with the living room accommodating Bridget's clients and the dining room becoming the living room. Everyone ate in the kitchen anyway except for Thanksgiving, Christmas and Easter. She saw no sense in wasting the space just for three meals a year.

When the boys left, the living room moved to their former bedroom. Bridget's sewing took over the old dining room too.

"Now what's new with your family?" Jeanne shifted position. The hem dipped on one side.

She's asking so she can brag about her family, Bridget thought. She'll mention how well April is doing in her job but won't say anything about her Tommy's divorce.

When it came to showing-off trophy children and grandchildren, Bridget was unbeatable although she had to do it verbally. The trophies her boys won for Pop Warner and Little League were stored away: high school and university diplomas hung above the TV out of client sight. Years of practice let her slip in at just the right moment some accomplishment of one of her babies or grandbabies.

"Connor is fine. Still up at the State House." Bridget stabbed a pin into the material.

"He's been a good rep for Newton. I read about him all the time in *The Globe*. I just saw a photo of him, his wife and daughter, not the …"Jeanne started to say.

"That was Jamie. She's applying for colleges." Bridget wasn't going to say that she knew the reason Jeanne paused was that she didn't want to say the handicapped one. Ashley was doing well in her special school for kids with Cerebral Palsy.

Not that she was ashamed. Ashley's progress was nothing short of a miracle, and she took some credit with her own contribution of daily prayer. Of course, her daughter-in-law Rachel had been nothing short of a saint in working with the child. For a moment, Bridget felt a flash of regret, as she thought how shocked she'd been when Connor had brought home the Jewess. Sympathy replaced regret when Rachel's Orthodox family disowned her.

Jeanne shifted position and again the hem moved. "Too bad he isn't going for bigger things."

"Stand still unless you want an uneven hem. He'd love to run for Congress, but Barney Frank will never give up his seat." She imagined her son on C-span giving a speech from the House floor, then as a senator questioning some presidential appointee and finally standing with his hand on the family Bible saying, "I do solemnly swear that I will faithfully execute the Office of President of the United States."

The picture vanished. At 70 she wouldn't live long enough to see it. And if she were to examine her thoughts closely, she knew he would not make a good president – too much of a bully.

So much for imagination. I've the real clincher, Bridget thought. "I wish Desmond would write more."

"What's he doing?"

"Something in public relations. At the Vatican." That'll show her. Not only had Bridget produced a priest but one assigned to the Vatican.

Dreams surpassed had drawbacks. She had always thought her kids would live near Mission Hill where she and Patrick grew up. Her mother came from Ireland in her teens and settled here. Bridget's girls stayed home, but her sons wandered. A son will be a son until he takes himself a wife, but your daughters will be your daughters all of your life. No, that wasn't true in her case.

Rachel had been a daughter-in-law from heaven, probably because she felt the need to replace her family. The town of Newton wasn't all that far. Rome was.

"Desmond sent me a rosary blessed by the Pope himself. 'Out of his hands and into yours,' his card said." She wouldn't tell her that he hadn't uttered a word about what the Vatican was like. He was her silent child.

Others told her about his Little League runs or she heard it from Patrick if it were a game she couldn't attend because she had a dress to finish. One thing you could say about her husband, he never missed any game when the boys played. The only way she knew that Desmond was a top student was when she signed his report card.

"He invited us to visit him in Rome." Rome! If Patrick wouldn't go vegetable shopping at Haymarket only a short T-ride away, she would never get him on a plane.

"Go alone, Ma," her daughters said. They said it again last Sunday after she cooked a New England boiled dinner for the family. Patrick, the Old Goat, told them to leave some. He wanted leftovers for red flannel hash. He was getting increasingly cranky, and she wasn't sure what to do about it. Today she'd thrown him out of the house rather than have him grouse around while she had a client.

Her girls were close emotionally, close physically: Peggy downstairs, Katie two flights down. Katie said they should switch apartments now that Patrick's leg gave him so much trouble. Katie's Bill wasn't pleased. He'd worked too hard on their flat to change to his in-laws' old-fashioned one, but he offered to buy one of those chairs that climbed stairs.

Patrick hit the roof. The Old Goat refused to admit he was old. He hadn't been looking well, but he refused to visit the doctor saying it cost too much. How much of her life had she spent making her man feel important, while supplementing the money they needed first for the kids' school and now for medicine not covered by Medicare? Too much, she thought. The McDonald's theme, "You deserve a break today," ran through her head.

The client grimaced as a pin scratched her leg. "And Peggy? It's hard to be laid off."

Bridget stood in one graceful motion. Peggy worked harder to find a job than she had when she was the Mission Hill loan manager for a branch of yet another defunct bank. This bitch might think her daughter a failure, but Bridget didn't: raising two boys as a widow, going to Northeastern University nights, graduating cum laude, getting all the promotions possible without changing work location. No, her daughter wasn't a failure in any sense of the word. "The bank that merged with Peggy's promised not to cut jobs and then made 3,000 people redundant."

"And her son? The one in Iraq?"

"I'm on my knees every morning at the Church." If Bridget added up all the hours she spent on her knees between hemming and praying, half her life would have been spent at half mast, as Patrick claimed.

"Ever think of retiring?" the woman asked.

Bridget's knees hurt. Her hands hurt. Probably arthritis or maybe that new-fangled disease called metacarpal syndrome. What would she do if she didn't sew for half the people on The Hill? She used to sew for her kids' education, now she sewed for the Old Goat's medicine. Her days without the challenge of how to put darts in somebody's dress to make some cow look thinner would be dull. She was too old to develop the habit of sitting on the couch and eating bonbons.

Her clientele had changed as the Irish moved out. Now she made more business suits using photos torn from fashion magazines brought by briefcase-carrying women who wanted designer knock-offs.

Sometimes she thought that moving someplace else like Florida might be refreshing, but she discarded the idea each time. She would miss running in and out of her daughters' flats much too much. What would she do with all that sunshine and not being able to complain about the cold and snow? Anyway, Patrick would never agree, but it was an idea that she still took out to examine from time to time just for the fun of it.

"And did you hear about Marie O'Reilly?"

"What about her?" She hoped it wasn't another death. Marie's husband had dropped dead just six months before. There were too many old friends who had died recently.

"She sold her house and is taking a cruise. On a tramp steamer of all things, and then will move to Arizona."

Bridget sank back on her heels. When she was young, old women didn't do things like that, much less good Irish girls from The Hill. They stayed to take care of their grandchildren. She thought of a National Geographic Special she'd seen with a three-armed cactus twice as tall as the narrator standing next to it. There was so much to see that she would never see, so much to experience that she would never experience, not Rome, not Ireland, not even New York City. Although she would never let on, it made her sad.

She took the pincushion from her wrist and set it on her work table so she could glance at her watch. Patrick was probably at Flann O'Brien's Pub eating what he shouldn't and driving everyone there crazy.

"Done. You can change."

CHAPTER 2

Patrick Flanagan needed to decide, one of the piddling ones he made every day. The first was to get up. Going out wasn't much of a decision. Bridget had been on his back, again. Who would think a 70-year-old woman could nag so much? His new choice was should he drink a beer at the American Legion or at Flann O'Brien's Pub.

His cane tapped against the brick sidewalk in what he hoped was the jaunty confident beat of a man that ruled his world rather than that of an old man trying to stay upright on ice. Stupid bricks. Treacherous. They rose and fell in uneven patterns just waiting to trip him.

Brick sidewalks: another example of gentrification ruining his childhood neighborhood. What was wrong with plain old cement? And fake gas lamps – who needed them? Okay, he admitted, he grew crotchetier with each passing day, but he didn't like today's world one little bit.

He'd worked hard all his life. Where was the respect he deserved as a patriarch of four grown children? Patriarch, now that was a funny word. All the titles he had in his life, but when his son Connor called him a patriarch last week, that was a new one. He'd been called lots of things: a mick, Mr., Private, PFC, and finally Sarge. He had been a tester for Polaroid then a testing manager. His kids called him Da, his grandkids Gramps or Grampy and his wife called him her Old Goat. The government called him a senior citizen.

Senior citizens had too much time to think about a past they couldn't change. When they were young enough to change it, they didn't have time. Strange world, but one which had been better than bad to him, he had to admit that. It was a bitch to admit that his body wasn't keeping up with his mind. Damn, he had outlived his usefulness.

When he was in a good mood, he thought of himself as the king, albeit of a very small kingdom. Instead of a country, he ruled a family. Instead of a castle, he had a house with his queen. He'd produced two princes and two princesses, one a year for four years, bang-bang-bang-bang. When he compared his children with the bland Charles, Anne, Andrew and what's-his-face of England, his kids were superior in every way. They worked harder. They weren't running around sleeping hither and yon.

When he poked his head into the Legion no one was in the musty hall, so he crossed Wigglesworth Street to Flann's. Even on the brightest day, which today wasn't, it was dark inside this pub that tried but failed to imitate the kind his parents had frequented back in Ireland in the early part of the last century. It took him a minute to see Janie washing glasses behind the bar.

The picture on the large screen TV hanging over the bar was soundless. Words appeared on the bottom of the screen in white letters against a black background and looked like those strips produced by the hand-held whatchamacallits that tapped out plastic labels. *News at Noon.* Not real news, nothing about what counted – just fires and murders. Didn't any of those reporters ever check out city hall?

"Hey Janie." His speech, with a hint of the brogue carried from the old country when he moved to Boston at age 10, was woven into the Boston accent acquired during his next 65 years.

The stool was a challenge. He draped his cane on the edge of the bar and using its long black plank hoisted himself onto the seat. At least his arms still worked.

"Hey yourself."

Patrick guessed she was about 30, no older, but he didn't need to guess she was pretty. Probably was a natural blond considering her skin and eyebrows – however, with his girls dyeing everything, there was no guarantee of natural. At least Bridget had let her hair go snow white. When they put their heads together, they made a blizzard.

Janie wore jeans and a pink sweater tight enough to be appealing – not so tight to make her look like a tramp. He liked looking, but look was all he did.

Never had he cheated on Bridget with his body. He never understood why people were shocked when Jimmy Carter said he lusted in his heart. All male hearts lust – even kings. If he were a real king, he would be King Arthur faithful, not like some of those English kings, but what did anyone expect from the English anyway?

"Whatcha havin'?"

"Guinness and a barbecued chicken sandwich. On a roll. No sissy wrap thingies."

"I wouldn't dare serve you a wrap, sissy or otherwise." Janie winked.

Patrick turned on his stool to admire the portraits of Joyce and Beckett hanging over the windows. Not that he ever read them, but he knew they were good Irish writers who, like himself, left Ireland not for the good old U.S. of A., but France of all places to live with the froggies.

When he read, it was the sport pages of *The Boston Globe* and since Jason left anything about Iraq.

He needed new glasses, but they were expensive. That was the problem with growing old – one part went then another – worse than an old car. Cars went to a garage. They never had a car – didn't need one in the city, although his son-in-law had a truck and a car. They drove him someplace if he needed transportation, usually only to the doctor.

His medical costs seemed to keep going up and up far beyond what Medicare covered. Goddamn Polaroid for cutting back on their promise to provide their retirees with health insurance. Loyalty seemed to go only one way. Edward Land must be spinning in his grave at what those young Turks did to his company. Sure, Land had made mistakes – too crazy about technology and not enough into marketing – but he never made a mistake in the way he treated his workers.

Nothing lasts forever. *The Globe* said moving companies were swamped shipping Irish immigrants' stuff back to Ireland – something he would never do. He was American now, 100% or maybe 90% considering he had spent his first years in Ireland. The States had been kinder to him than the old country. Changing your nationality was like changing your religion – not done easily. No, a person should choose his path and stick to it like he had.

Two young men, one with a stethoscope around his neck and the other with a grey knit sweater under his white doctor's coat, sat at one of the small square black wooden tables – nothing unusual about wearing a stethoscope with all those hospitals in walking distance not to mention Harvard Medical School. Kids showing off, letting everyone know "I'm a doctor I'm a doctor," Patrick thought.

"What happened to the blanket?" Stethoscope referred to the heavy brown blanket that had hung over the entry to cut drafts.

Patrick hadn't noticed it was gone. Not like the old days when he'd been a tester for Polaroid – noticing every little detail made him a valued worker. He carried it into his daily life. Sometimes he wished he could witness a crime so he could give the police a good description of the perp.

Perp was a word they used on detective shows. He liked thinking it. Showed he wasn't totally out of touch with the times. Imagine watching their faces when he said the robber was wearing a sweater with red and blue stripes, had blond hair parted on the left. Now he would probably ask what robbery.

"Fire department made us take it down, said it was a hazard," Janie said. She turned back to Patrick. "Coming down for the Pats-Steelers playoff?"

"Depends on Bridget. She's on the warpath these days. Can't do anything to please her. I threatened to turn her in for two thirty-five-year olds, but all she does is tell me to get out." That wasn't true, but he liked the joke. Henry VIII kept changing his wives. However, none of old Hank's wives had produced two strapping sons as Bridget had done. So what if one became a priest? The rest of his children had children of their own, insuring his dynasty or at least his DNA when he wasn't feeling grandiose. Grandiose was harder with each passing day.

"Imagine," Stethoscope said, "the Pats and the Sox, champions the same year."

"Fries with that sandwich?" Jamie wiped down the bar. The grey rag was frayed. "Since Bridget isn't here to yell about your cholesterol."

What the hell? Since he paid so much for his Goddamned medicine, he might as well give it something to work on. "Sure."

"We should wipe those towel-heads out," Sweater drawled.

Patrick swiveled on his stool. Only a kid from the South would sound like that. Probably from a good family – one that let others fight their battles. That attitude pissed him off. Big time. Sure, he felt the war was a mistake, but in for a penny in for a dime. "You for us being there?"

Janie walked over to the hole in the wall leading to the kitchen and reached for a plate the cook handed out. "Be good, Patrick," she said over her shoulder.

"Sure am. Even if they didn't do 9/11, they would've if they could've," White Coat said. Nine eleven sounded like nahn ah-levahn.

Janie glowered as she gave Patrick his sandwich.

Stethoscope put down his wrap. "We have to show the rest of the world…"

"Sign up then," Patrick said. Pissed him off how so many people said they were for the war from the comfort of their chairs. Including the president, but it was his president, and he would support him, right or wrong.

"I'm in the middle of my internship," Stethoscope said.

"Join the medical corps then," Patrick said. Maybe Stethoscope would save his grandson, if he were wounded. Just the thought that Jason might be hurt made him shudder.

17

"I'm getting married," White Coat said.

"Lots of those guys are married. If you want the war, fight it. Sign up."

The doctors turned away from him.

"Sign up."

"Let's get out of here," Stethoscope said. He wrapped his sandwich in his napkin and grabbed his navy-colored down ski jacket. He and White Coat started towards the door.

"If you change your mind and want to sign up, I'll take you down to the recruiting office. Janie here knows where to find me. And if you don't wanta sign up, stop saying you're for the war."

The door of the pub slammed.

"You gotta stop doing that, Patrick. It's bad for business."

"War is bad." His left leg still ached when it rained from the shrapnel it caught in Korea. He remembered Vietnam – not that he was there – but the government lied from the time they sent the first soldier until that skunk Nixon declared peace with honor. "I'm getting too old to stomach all this again."

On the other hand, if you lived in a country you did what the country asked of you. My country right or wrong was as good a slogan in 2005 as it was in the sixties. He saw no dichotomy in the contradictory point of view. We were there, now we should finish the job and get the hell out. Those snot-nose brats had no idea that being an American meant sacrifice. He wondered if they'd ever heard Kennedy's speech, ask not what your country can do for you but what you can do for your country.

He wanted to go home – take a nap instead of sitting in Flann's listening to idiots who still hadn't learned to tell their ass from their elbow. Life as an old king was hard.

CHAPTER 3

The message, "You have an e-mail from jason.doherty20120@hotmail.com," popped up on the lower left corner of her laptop just as the phone rang. Peggy Doherty, née Mary-Margaret Flanagan, was torn between reading it and answering the telephone.

She had heard nothing from her elder son for three days. The first day she imagined him asleep on his U.S. Marine Corps cot covered with a fatigue-green thick wool blanket. The second day he was listening to music with friends. By the third she saw him driving down a palm tree-lined Baghdad street like those shown on CNN as a sniper climbed a bullet-marked stucco wall and took aim. That image disappeared the second she saw his name on her screen. At least she knew a couple of minutes before when he had hit the send button, he was alive and well. Another day to check off before his assignment was up.

Although he told her what he was doing wasn't all that dangerous, she shouldn't worry, she did. She'd worried about him from the day he was born; stopping was not possible.

It seemed he went directly from her womb into scrapes. When she thought he had straightened himself out by joining the Marines and learning to accept responsibility, that was when he ended up in a war. Why couldn't they have left him stationed at his first assignment, the Embassy in Oslo where he might have found a nice Norwegian girl who would bear her grandbabies?

The phone was in its base next to a file folder, labeled "Jobs to apply for, January 2005." Eleven files marked for the months of January 2004 to November 2004 were in her file cabinet. December's was in her follow-up pile.

The dining room was her office. Her laptop and printer nudged out the candelabra. A file cabinet, found in the trash, like all her furniture, had been refinished with Da helping until they matched the table, chairs and sideboard. Da had taught her all she knew about paints and varnishes, allowing her to build a cozy home while spending almost no money.

Although she would have preferred to leave her dining room as just that, she needed someplace to plan her attack to find work.

Peggy had always taken pride in her organizational ability. It had helped her when she started at First New England Bank as a teller two days after her Elizabeth Seaton High School graduation. She worked up to loan manager through three bank mergers. It helped her earn a degree at Northeastern nights, and on the way, marry a drunken fool and raise two sons after he wrapped himself around a tree. Only the tree had survived.

These activities all happened within five square miles. Peggy would have been promoted to branch manager if she'd been willing to change locations. When her boys were little she wanted to be near home for emergencies. After they were older, she'd told herself she liked working where she knew people.

She loved not commuting. Even her Northeastern classes were only three T stops away. She liked walking the same route, stopping at the same Dunkin Donuts for the coffee and blueberry muffins each day that was as much of a ritual as dipping her fingers in holy water when she entered the yellow stone walls of Mission Hill Church. Not even to herself would she admit that going far from her own territory left her heart racing.

Only to herself would she let on that she worried about everything possible to worry about and a few things that she probably shouldn't waste worry time on.

When she was working and as she lay in bed at night, she was sure that she hadn't checked a last loan reference. When she left home in the morning, she worried if she had shut off the stove. The list started with her kids, money, her kids, menstrual cramps, her kids, what she would buy Ma and Da for their anniversary, her kids …

Jason was excellent at providing her with worry subjects: teacher conference after teacher conference were filled with words like "underachiever" and "class cut-up." He dropped out of school, drank and used drugs. She remembered him telling her he "accidentally broke" 20 windows in a deserted triple decker across from Brigham & Women's only it was Peter Bent Hospital then. It seemed every day when she drove by that hospital it bore a new name.

Change was okay if she didn't have to travel to it. She rushed to learn the latest computer program or at least she did until change cost her a job that she loved.

She worried about Sean too, although he never seemed to do anything wrong. He was too good, as if he had looked at his older brother and knew at some level that his mother couldn't handle two problem boys.

The phone stopped ringing. My God, it was as if she had been frozen. Jason's being in danger did that to her. The worry she felt for him alternated with the worry about finding work, although she knew living under her parents meant she would always have food in her belly and a roof over her head, but she didn't want to burden them.

Her sense of organization would help her find a new job quickly, or so she thought when the new management decided to close what it claimed was its unprofitable Mission Hill branch. How wrong she had been.

Her methodology allowed her to keep a cover on her fear, shoving it down when it rose too high. If she was doing something towards her goal, she maintained a modicum of control rather than giving in to hovering fates waiting to knock her flat. This didn't stop the nights when images of never again bringing in money scared her awake. During the day, the fears melted. If she couldn't find work, if she couldn't even temp and her parents were gone, because at their ages there was no guarantee that some illness would not bear them away, her sister and brother-in-law would help: even her sons would help, but she didn't want that.

When she first learned that her branch was closing after Customers First America bought her bank even before her cards had been printed from the last merger, she took 24 hours to mourn. Then she got busy contacting recruiters.

She regretted not attending American Bank Association meetings. She hated schmoozing, although she'd been told she was good at it when she gave in and went to a luncheon that had a particularly interesting speaker. But not going, not schmoozing meant she had few industry contacts.

Although she filled out her 1099-G form to qualify for unemployment, she hadn't expected to be out of work long enough for her benefits to run out. They had.

What she missed was not just the certainty of a paycheck. Her co-workers had been a second family. Over the years, they had cheered each other on as much as if they wore cheerleading uniforms at a high school football game.

Last week she learned Maddy O'Brien was dating again after being widowed. Bobby Harris, Jackie's son, was having trouble making it through Lowell University, not just because of money but because he was basically stupid. She had watched him grow up pushing himself beyond his capabilities in everything he did.

If her co-workers were her professional family, customers coming into the lobby of the bank year in and year out were like distant relatives, seen more at funerals and weddings but well-known all the same.

Her several interviews that she thought went well resulted in no job offer. She wondered why every human resource person asked why she had stayed at one branch her entire working life.

Although 47 didn't seem old to her, she manipulated her résumé, dropping her high school information. Since she had taken 12 years to get her college degree, people might think her younger from that graduation date. She dyed her hair to its original chestnut.

At Macy's, a sales clerk, whom Peggy thought might still be in kindergarten, modernized her make-up.

The phone rang again. Peggy picked it up on the second ring.

"Hi, it's me, Mary Ann." When Peggy said nothing, the voice continued, "Hutchinson, your old colleague."

Peggy hadn't seen Mary Ann, who went from the HR department in their old bank to the new with nary a blink. Mary Ann was the one who fired her, but it was Mary Ann who broke down during the meeting until Peggy found herself comforting her colleague.

They'd been friends, as much of a friend as any HR person could be, having started together and seeing several bank changes. They had gone to Northeastern together, but they were not so close that they went out together socially.

Mary Ann said, "Come see me this morning about eleven if you can. We'll grab a bite. We've things to talk about."

Although Mary Ann's invitation was for lunch, Peggy allowed the couple of hours between the call and her leaving the house to hope it was a job. She traded the jeans for a suit and trundled downtown to the bank's Arch Street headquarters. In the cavernous lobby, water cascaded over a floor-to-ceiling black marble wall with two-foot gold letters embedded in it reading CFA Customers First America.

Employees, people with paychecks and health insurance, scuttled back and forth. The plastic receptionist behind the black marble counter directed Peggy to a bank of mauve sofas grouped around a black marble table decorated with a vase of flowers as tall as a four-year-old child and a big one at that. The running fountain made Peggy want to pee. The flowers' scent reminded her of funerals.

Mary Ann stepped from the elevator with open arms. As soon as they were in her office, she said. "I've good news and bad news." She blushed as she offered Peggy a job at three quarters of her former earnings. Her seniority was wiped out.

Small paychecks were better than none, and if she had to pay double for health insurance than she did before, at least she would have it.

"When do I start?" Peggy asked.

"Monday."

* * * * *

Back home, her last jobless Friday, Peggy turned her work area back into her dining table. She put her laptop on the small table in the corner. Waves of gratitude swept through her that she could use the computer for emails and games and not spend hours searching recruiting sites and sending out résumés.

For the first time since she'd begun her job search, she put the dried flower centerpiece on the table. As she stood back to admire it her laptop dinged, signaling an email. Let it be from Jason, she thought. When several days went by without any word from him, her imagination always went into overdrive picturing him in the hospital or worse. It was.

> From: Jason (jason.doherty20120@hotmail.com)
> To: peggy.doherty338@hotmail.com
> CC: sean.doherty20120@hotmail.com,
> lawyer.to.be.jess@yahoo.com
> Date: January 21, 2005
> Subject: checking in
>
> Yours and Grandma's prayers have been working. I'm still ok. I'm almost afraid to count the days until I rotate out of here, because of extensions that have happened, but if all goes well, I'll see U in early March.
>
> Love ya,
> Jason
> P.S. My buddy took the attached photo. Look at the dog that's become our mascot. We call him Bullet.

The downloaded photo showed her son decked out in Marine gear and fatigues with his goofy grin. He held a mangy yellow dog. They never had a dog, although both boys wanted one. She hadn't had the time to handle an animal along with everything else.

The phone rang.

"Aunt Peggy, we have to do something."

"What about, Jess?" As long as Peggy could remember, her niece was doing something about something: picking up street trash, collecting money for the homeless, calling city hall about a woman who had her heat shut off. This was before she started Boston Latin in seventh grade. Had her niece rushed into a phone booth to fly out wearing a cape, she wouldn't have been surprised.

"Jason."

Peggy twiddled the phone cord around her hand and she could hear traffic sounds. "Where are you?"

"Heading to Fill a Buster."

"Sorry?"

"A restaurant near the State House. I'm meeting a rep there on legislation about ... it doesn't matter. What's important is making Jason safe."

Peggy wanted Jason safe. Every minute of every day she tried to throw the boomerang of fear away. Like all good boomerangs it returned, soaring on her guilt. If she hadn't encouraged him to join the Marines, he wouldn't be in Iraq. "He doesn't have much longer."

"They'll extend him, I know they will. If he could only get a leave home, I'll drive him to Canada."

That wasn't realistic even for I'm-going-to-save-the-world Jessica Kelly. "Our family doesn't desert." She could just imagine Da's reaction to his grandson being a military deserter. Peggy dreaded the tirade about the government, illegal wars, etc. that was sure to come in the next few seconds.

"Oops. My lunch date is here. See you Sunday, if not before."

Saved by the bell. She and her sister Katie talked about the advantages of daughters versus sons. Her boys jumped off furniture. Jess sat still. Her boys played cops and robbers, Indians and cowboys. Jess and her friends huddled in conversation while the boys wrestled. Jess was safe. Jason wasn't.

CHAPTER 4

The real estate agent's four-inch heels clicked across the polished wood floor. Katherine Marie Flanagan Kelly and her husband Bill followed the woman like ducklings waddling after their mother.

"Just sit on the bed." The agent directed the couple to the four-poster with the white bedspread and matching dust ruffle. Ten pillows in various shapes and shades of off-white linens, silks and brocades were stacked against the headboard in a failed attempt to look casual. Katie suspected their positioning was a ritual. She couldn't imagine coming in from work and flopping on this bed. She couldn't even imagine sleeping in this room. However, she and Bill obeyed, slipped off their shoes and lowered themselves onto the spread.

The agent looked about Katie's age, somewhere in the mid-40s. Comparing herself with other women was something Katie had done from the time she wore school uniforms.

The agent was thinner in her grey pleated skirt. Katie's hips wouldn't support pleats. As Katie glimpsed her reflection in the mirror on the wall, she knew she'd lost the pound battle; but she'd won the wrinkles war.

"Imagine waking each morning to this." The agent pulled the white drapes to reveal a small pond down the pine tree-covered slope where the house perched.

Bill whistled. "That's a hundred percent different from our view in the city."

"Well, you said you wanted something that gave you the impression of the country," the agent said.

He does, I don't, Katie thought. By now they should have been blacklisted as time-wasters by the New England Realtors Association, if any such group existed. At least two weekends a month for the last five years Bill dragged her to look at houses all over: Arlington, Brookline, Cambridge, Concord, Jamaica Plain, Malden, Medford, Newton, Reading, Stoneham, Stowe, Sudbury, Wakefield, Waltham, Watertown, Winchester, Woburn. The list read like the no-school announcements on a snow day.

Lately the distances became greater and greater from the city, which made no sense to her. Bill's plumbing clients were all in the city. Her secretarial job at Harvard Medical was a 10-minute walk from her front door.

And Jess, what about Jess?

She could just imagine Bill saying that it was time Jess was out on her own. Her daughter had lived at home during her four years at Boston University, where she won a full scholarship after graduating from Boston Latin. Now she was in her last year at Suffolk Law. Soon she would be working, but with her plans to become a storefront lawyer, she would be living in poverty. Besides, Katie loved having her only child at home. She loved having her sister and parents upstairs.

Her life was exactly as she wanted it, except her husband wanted more distance from his in-laws. Not that he didn't love her family – he'd been the boy in their living room so much so that Da and Ma called him their third son. Katie couldn't remember many evening meals when he hadn't been at their table. Ma even helped him with his homework. But now he wanted something different.

Each week Katie oohed and aahed over a different feature: a wall refrigerator, a large deck, a built-in barbecue or a fish pond. On the way back home, she would point out something wrong, a damp floor in the cellar, commuting hassles, possible termites.

As she rolled off the bed, the wind gusted through the pine trees, moving the curtains. Drafty, Katie thought. That'll be what I'll point out to Bill. "Let's look at the kitchen again," she said. As she walked by her husband, she patted his pot belly without being aware that she did so.

CHAPTER 5

Jess Kelly shifted her weight as she waited at the kitchen door of the slate blue Cape Cod house. Unlike her Mission Hill house, where she could enter at will through open doors, her Uncle Connor and Aunt Rachel's house was locked, but then they lived in the suburb of Newton.

She didn't want to ring the bell, an old-fashioned zzzz rather than a modern melody, a second time. She knew someone was home because her aunt's Escort was parked in the garage. Buy American, her politician uncle insisted but not too grandiose so his constituents wouldn't think he was on the take.

If she were honest, Jess would admit she didn't like her Uncle Connor all that much, or maybe it was just she found he lived the definition of pompous. Aunt Rachel, now that was something else. Rachel was warm and loving and always had time to listen when Jess couldn't talk with her own mother, which was often and when Aunt Peggy was too busy, which was less often.

Peeking over the ruffled yellow curtain half covering the kitchen door window, she saw her Aunt Rachel leaning against the fridge talking on the phone and motioning to her daughter Jamie to answer the door. A second later the door opened, and Rachel waved as Jamie rolled her eyes at her older cousin.

A smell of beef roasting greeted Jess. A Friday night dinner invitation to her aunt and uncle's was a wonderful meal guarantee. She eyed a newly frosted chocolate cake on the table. Glancing through to the dining room she saw the table set with a hand-embroidered, olive-green linen tablecloth and the best dishes, tableware and crystal making up five places.

"Governor's receptions don't get called at the last minute," Rachel said into the telephone as she moved to the sink to run water into the kettle.

"Daddy's in deep shi ... er ... doo-doo," Jamie mouthed.

"Dinner is already being cooked, and I was going to go get Ashley," Rachel said.

Pause.

"I don't see why he can't skip it: the governor is a Republican for God's sake," Jaime said.

A long pause as Rachel hushed her daughter with her finger against her mouth. "Connor, Friday night is family night, you know that."

"Daddy'll win," Jamie mouthed.

Jess also knew her aunt would give in: she always did. She knew Aunt Rachel knew she would. Uncle Connor knew she would. The question was when.

"Yes, my black dress is just back from the cleaner's." Rachel cradled the phone under her chin.

A long pause. "What time?"

Rachel hung up. "Forty-five is too old to cry about a missed dinner. Children can scream their lungs out. Adults can't."

"Guess it's part of being the wife of State Rep Flanagan," Jess said.

"But Daddy must have known about the reception for weeks. You don't think Governor Romney called Daddy and said, 'Why don't you drop by tonight?'"

Rachel gave her the look which all mothers master that said, "Don't push it."

Jamie pulled both arms downward and smirked. "YES! I'm free tonight."

Jess understood her cousin. At 17 and in her senior year of high school, Jamie chafed to be more independent and not deal with the family, but when they left her out, she sulked.

As much as her uncle annoyed her, she had to agree when she heard him tell her aunt, "Be grateful seventeen lasts only a year." She'd also heard him say the same about 16, 15, 14 and 13. Once he'd suggested deep-freezing children from 13 to 20, but never where a constituent might overhear.

Before she had turned into a teenager, Jamie had been a sweet little girl, not acting resentful at the extra attention her younger sister Ashley needed. Jamie was never difficult with Jess, however.

Rachel looked at the blue slate clock hanging between the kitchen windows. "Let me call Ashley. She should be in her room at this hour." Instead of picking up the phone she poured hot water into a tea cup and gave it to Jess. Then she called St. Andrew's. "Honey, your dad and I will be going out tonight. We can't pick you up until tomorrow." Pause. "Yes, you can spend the weekend with Tiffany."

Jess could hear her cousin's thick speech through the receiver, but it was clearer than when she started at the boarding school for youngsters with Cerebral Palsy. How often she had wondered if she had a child like Ashley would she be able to handle it like her Aunt Rachel did. The woman was incredible the way she'd taken the little girl as far as she could before realizing neither mother love nor public school special-ed classes replaced experts.

"Have fun, but have her mother call me to confirm."

After hanging up she sat with her niece and daughter.

"That's great. It's a normal weekend for a fifteen-year old," Jess said.

"If someone had asked me two years ago if that would happen, I'd have said no," Rachel said.

"I'm going to Deanna's," Jamie said, "now that I'm a free woman."

"Be home by nine, and I *will* check," Rachel said. "The house phone: not your cell."

Jamie sighed. "Did you have to put up with this crap from your mother?"

"We're talking about St. Katie, here." Jess said. "My mother not only cares about where my physical body is, she is convinced my immortal soul is in constant jeopardy. You have it easy."

When Jamie had left, Rachel said, "Thanks for the back up." She glanced at her watch. "I'm sorry about cancelling dinner on you."

"I've a lot of studying anyway." Jess didn't miss the expression when her aunt glanced at the set table. Only last year she'd admitted to her niece that the candlelight Friday night dinners were her secret ritual although her family took them as humoring-the-mom events. Rachel used minutes before the family sat down to light candles and say the Jewish prayers from childhood but only in her mind.

"There's next Friday," Jess said. She wasn't sure how her own mother would react if she left the Church to marry. Probably not as strongly as Rachel's parents who considered her dead to them. Although she'd always wanted to ask Aunt Rachel what it was like to be totally cut off from her childhood, she'd refrained. She played the scene in her mind, as if watching a movie, a young Rachel standing outside her childhood home two steps down from her father making him look like a giant in his black suit. "I'm marrying Connor."

"You're dead to us if you do."

"Let me in for my clothes."

He had turned his back. She started to follow. The door slammed in her face.

"Jamie wants to go to Brandeis and says she wants to get back to her Jewish roots," Rachel said.

"She's pulling your chain," Jess said.

"It is just so expensive. We budgeted for U Mass."

"If she really wanted it, she would get a job." Jess had said in an earlier conversation when Rachel told her about Brandeis. Jess had suggested a job to Jamie.

"Do you expect me to like flip hamburgers at McDonald's?" her cousin had asked.

"If that's what you have to do." Jess had said.

"Why can't Daddy take, you know, graft like other politicians?"

"I'll assume that's a joke," Jess had said. She could just imagine her grandmother finding out her son was corrupt. Hell would be good in comparison.

"Don't worry about Jamie, Auntie Rachel, she'll be fine."

CHAPTER 6

Snow fell so fast Bridget could barely see the house across the street. Cars parked on the street were white humps with antennas. She left her sewing room to join her husband.

Patrick sat in his red cracked-leather chair, his throne he called it. He flicked the remote through the channels. The *Meet the Press* host Tim Russert asked the American Ambassador to Iraq about the security of voting stations.

"The security measures are very well in hand and in place, and the expectation is that there will be large voter participation ..." Negroponte said.

Bridget turned from the window. "I hope Jason is all right." She crossed herself. The storm had kept her from church. She would light an extra candle tomorrow. If they got out tomorrow, that is. Right now, it was time to make lunch.

Bridget clicked on the kitchen radio perched on the second shelf of her spice rack, not that she used many spices. Simple food was best, but food was more than food. Each meal was a link in the chain that bound her family together. No matter how much sewing she had to do, she cooked dinner. When the kids were little, the family ate together every night come hell or high water. Even now that they were grown, she prepared Sunday dinner for everyone.

Desmond, of course, couldn't pop in from the Vatican, but when he'd been in a local parish they ate later after his Sunday duties.

When he went to work for Cardinal Law, he made it to what meals he could.

Bridget had mixed feelings about the cardinal. He should never have covered up for those priests molesting those poor little children. And the Pope should never have rewarded him with a post in Rome. But the Church was made up of men: men were fallible.

Women, too, although sometimes she thought women could run the world a lot better than men. However, God was God, and even if a few bad apples were in the Church, it would never change the depth of her faith.

"Parts of New England are expecting up to three feet of snow with the drifting. In Boston, Mayor Menino is asking people to stay inside …" She switched the radio off.

Before she began cooking, she said her rosary, willing the Pope's blessing into every Hail Mary. When finished, she dropped her beads into their case and put it in her apron pocket.

Her refrigerator was arranged with military precision: Bridget believed she could tell a lot about someone by looking at their refrigerator. Just the idea that one of her clients might march through the house and open the fridge made her smile. However, her kitchen proved that working didn't cause her to shirk her wifely and motherly duties. If she were guilty of any sin, it was pride.

When she met her mother in heaven, she could report she had lived up to all her responsibilities just as she had been taught. She could even add that she had done it for the total love of her family and could count the times she resented the amount of work on one hand and have a couple of fingers left over.

She glanced at her food processor. For the first year after Katie and Bill gave it to her for Christmas, it sat in pristine condition taking up space. Then Jess showed her how to use it for the garbage soup Bridget made every Saturday lunch from the week's leftovers. Jess threw everything in, added hot water, a bullion cube and cream at the end turning it into a thick liquid. The processor was good for smooshing things, but Bridget never used the different cutters and graters. Too high-faultin'.

Things coming too easily were worthless. When she cut onions, her tears were a gift to her family. And thinking of onions, she started chopping one before dropping it in her big cast iron pot that had simmered her soups and New England boiled dinners, pot roasts and chickens for decades.

As the onions sizzled, Bridget tried to trim the beef, bought on sale. Her knife made little progress through the flesh. Rather than ask Patrick to go to the basement to use the professional waist-high sharpener they had found in the house when they bought the place in the 1950s, she telephoned her grandson downstairs. No sense putting more stress on the Old Goat's leg.

"Aw Gran," Sean said.

"Whatever she wants, do it." Peggy's voice in the background came through the receiver. In seconds Sean was at the back door.

The phone rang.

Bridget picked it up.

"Hey Ma," Connor said.

"How much snow have you got in Newton?"

"Too much to drive into town." Sometimes Connor and the family had other things to do. Almost always Peggy and her sons and Katie, Bill and Jess were there. The best Sundays were when the grandkids had been little: five little ones playing or more likely screaming at each other. It reminded her of why she didn't mind that her thumb and forefinger of her right hand had permanent indentations from holding her needle.

Connor filled her in on Ashley's progress in boarding school. Jamie was still waiting to hear what colleges had accepted her, but her heart was set on Brandeis. Over the years Bridget had grown closer to Rachel, although the idea of having a Jewess in the family had upset her at first. She was more bothered by Rachel's family disowning. Imagine not speaking to your own child.

Their loss, Bridget thought. They missed out on their grandchildren. Okay, she wasn't happy when they'd become Unitarians, of all things, to bridge the gap between their religious disparities. Whenever Bridget recited her rosary for Jason, she added another for Connor's soul.

For all the negatives Bridget had heard about Jewish American Princesses, her daughter-in-law was a good wife, daughter-in-law and incredible mother. No lion protected her cub more than Rachel protected Ashley. Rachel found the right combination between pushing a damaged child to be the best she could and accepting her limitations. Strange thing about prejudice, once you meet an individual, old ideas fly out the window.

Snow and beef stew create nostalgia attacks, she thought. Flour stuck to her fingers as she rolled the meat before browning it in onion-flavored fat. She left out carrots and potatoes for Jess. In her day no one had ever heard of a vegetarian. Even if she sympathized with the animal's suffering, meat was too scarce in her childhood not to appreciate a good cut or even a bad one cooked well.

* * * * *

"Run Harrison." The Flanagans, Dohertys and Kellys screamed at the Patriot racing down the snowy Pittsburgh field. Sean and Jess high-fived each other.

"We're going to the Super Bowl again," Bill Kelly said.

"And win it," Patrick said. "The Sox, now that was a miracle. We expect good things from the Pats."

Bridget slipped out of the room to load the dishwasher. Peggy followed her.

"While you're out there, how about another beer," Bill called.

Peggy went to the refrigerator. Together she and her mother said, "Men."

CHAPTER 7

The smell of hot cotton melded with that of the coffee gurgling in the percolator as Peggy stood in her kitchen ironing the sleeves of her Victorian white blouse for her first day at her new job. One of the few constructive things her late husband had done was to make this built-in closet for the ironing board with a smaller shelf for the iron.

Her blue power suit hung on the kitchen door. Her boots were polished although the snow would mess those up fast enough. Her good blue pumps were in her briefcase, which was devoid of work papers, although probably not for long. She looked forward to being able to immerse herself in work again.

The phone rang. Who would call that early? Not Jason, oh dear God, please don't let anything have happened to Jason.

A headhunter apologized for calling so early. 'We've an opening for a loan officer at a credit union in Brookline.'

Last week Peggy would have blathered on about how, when, where. "I just took a job with the reincarnation of my old bank." The recruiter wished her luck. Wasn't that always the way, she thought. Once you get a job, other chances pop up.

The kitchen was toasty warm. An advantage of the middle apartment was that heat rose from her sister's while her parents' place kept it from escaping. Peggy's oil bill was the smallest of the three. She undid the buttons of her faded pink-quilted bathrobe and wiped sweat from her forehead. Today wasn't the day to be burdened with hot flashes.

Sean wandered into the kitchen wearing pajamas and his U Mass sweatshirt.

"Why aren't you dressed?" she asked.

"They'll close the campus as the storm gets worse. You going to work?"

"What kind of impression would it make to be absent my first day?"

"Good point." Unlike his older brother, her baby if you could call a boy six feet a baby, never had to be reminded to do his homework. He juggled sports and honor roll. He'd cashiered at Star Market in Brookline since he turned 16. If he were out later than he'd said he would, he called balancing out the nights she'd paced the floor waiting for Jason.

"Better hurry. The radio says the T is running very slow," he said.

* * * * *

Peggy sat in her small grey cubicle in a mouse maze of grey cubicles. The rug was grey. The walls were grey. At least the ceiling was white. Voices and telephones babbled in the background. No windows were visible. When she looked up, she imagined the walls marched toward her narrowing the space.

The training director sat next to Peggy. Up to this moment except for the training director and the person who showed her to her desk, no one had spoken to her. She knew there was life around her by the sounds of clicking computer keys and muffled phone conversations.

"You catch on really fast," the trainer said.

Peggy didn't reveal the system was an update of her old one. At 11:00 the training director led her to her new boss then melted away. His office had floor-to-ceiling walls and a door that was closed. For a second Peggy's hand hovered, then she knocked.

"Enter."

His space wasn't much bigger than her cubby and was only a slightly lighter grey. His coat hung from a bentwood coat rack. Boots dried on *The Boston Globe* editorial page. He stayed seated, leaning back in his chair and pointing to the only other chair in the room. She sat, feeling almost as if she put out her paw, he would give her a biscuit.

"I hope you'll be happy here," he said. He handed her a piece of paper with targets for the number of loans she would be expected to process. The numbers increased steadily after her first month.

Perhaps he was 30, maybe a little more. His skin was smooth, the kind most women would kill for: he had rosy cheeks. She could imagine him as an angel on a Christmas card.

She stared over his shoulder at the snow through his half window. They were too high up to see the street. He turned to look. "Horrible weather. And to think I transferred from Georgia to work here." He ran his hand through his blond crew cut.

Peggy wanted to snap that people were laid off so he could come and complain about the weather but resisted. She wasn't sure why she felt so hostile. She should be happy.

He handed her a manual of the loan guidelines. "Tomorrow you'll get your first loan to review. Of course, you'll be working with more experienced people."

"I've many, many years' experience processing loans."

"But our standards are different," her boss said. "Your old bank ... He shook his head.

My old bank was friendlier, she thought. Then she reminded herself she had only worked in a branch. Was it possible the headquarters had been like this?

At 11:55 the woman in the next cubicle poked her head over the wall. Her short grey hair was wavy, and she had bushy eyebrows. "I'm Anita. Want to go eat?"

"Sure." Over a taco salad she listened to Anita put down everyone and everything about Customers First America. Maybe Peggy's memory was selective, but she didn't remember that many complaints from her old branch mates.

At 5:30 some people put newspapers in briefcases, tugged on boots and wrapped scarves around their necks. No one called "Drive carefully" or "Watch out for the ice." Others huddled over their desks. Peggy, who had had nothing to do for the past hour while she waited for the training person to come back, wondered if she should wait for someone to tell her to leave. As the office thinned out, she thought to hell with it, wrote a Post-it note saying she had left at 5:44, stuck it on her computer screen and wrapped up for the trek home.

The Park Street Church tower looked fuzzy in the snow. Maybe this wasn't global warming, but global cooling, Peggy thought as she descended into Park Street T-station.

Coats stuffed with people stood shoulder-to-shoulder on the platform. When a Green-line E Heath Street did stop, a solid wave of coats moved as one to board. Even if Peggy had any strength left, she couldn't have fought the sea of bodies pushing her onto the car.

"Move back, move back," the driver yelled.

"There's no place to move," a man mid-car grumbled.

The subway lurched forward. Peggy had no place to hang onto, but she couldn't have fallen even if she fainted. Visions of WWII Germany flicked through her head. At least she wasn't heading for a concentration camp. In a sense, she felt she had just left the 21st-century version of a corporate concentration camp.

At Northeastern University a few passengers pushed their way to escape. A few more people got off at the Museum of Fine Arts. However, at Longwood, the car stopped. The driver announced that the tracks were blocked.

After the T's heat, the cold hurt her face. This was the type of moment where she'd have welcomed a hot flush. She crawled up Huntington Avenue. Twice she lost her footing, her arms and legs waving until she regained her balance.

Peggy had forgotten the feeling of coming home after a long day. The second she put her key in the outside door, all of it came back. Whoosh. Her cold feet wanted fuzzy slippers; her cold hands imagined cuddling a cup of tea. To put on the radio, curl up with a book or to take out her needlework – that was joy.

CHAPTER 8

After two more days of mind-numbing training, punctuated by the boredom of periodically waiting for the trainer to return from one emergency or another, Peggy trudged home, resisting second and third thoughts about accepting the job.

When she opened her door, Sean called, "Mom? That you?"

She found him with Jess seated on the couch under the blue afghan she'd knitted during the last Olympics. The speed of her needles had matched the speed of the sport. Her television was tuned to CNN.

Sean led her to the couch. He frowned. Jess's face was blotched.

"What?" Peggy asked

"Helicopter crash in Iraq, 31 Marines killed," Jess said.

No. No. There were 150,000 service men in Iraq. Thirty-one out of 150,000. "Any names?"

"No," Jess said.

She swallowed the fear that maybe the Marines sent to families to announce the family member deaths couldn't get through the storm.

All three stared at the TV during every newscast. Jess opened two cans of chicken noodle soup. Katie and Bill came up with the look that said, "We don't want to ask, but..." Bridget joined them with her sewing bag.

"Where's Da?" Peggy asked.

"Gone to bed with a headache."

"Did he hear about the crash?"

"No need to worry him for probably nothing." Bridget ploughed her needle into the yellow silk.

At 10:00, the news said most of the dead were from Hawaii.

They made their way to bed. No one wanted to think that some of the dead were not from Hawaii. They rode a collective wave of guilt for their relief that it was not Jason but Hawaiians who were dead.

CHAPTER 9

"You're crazy." Katie Kelly stood on the front porch of their triple decker. She watched Bill and Sean lug 50-pound bags of sand from the basement. They took turns emptying the sacks into the black plastic garbage can in the parking space where Bill's baby blue truck was now double parked in front of the shoveled-out space. The sign Kelly's Plumbing with the phone number on the truck door was hidden by snow banks made by the ploughs.

"See if the mayor's men can move that," Bill said. He pounded up the five steps, crossed the porch and kissed his wife on the top of the head.

She folded her arms across her chest to stop the cold from penetrating her bones. "And don't humor me."

"Wouldn't dream of it." He dropped a second kiss on her head.

"How will you move them when you want to park your truck?"

"Sean can help, won't you?"

The boy flexed his muscles. "The mayor won't stop us protecting our space."

Katie thought it would have been easier to go along with the mayor's new edict forbidding the marking of snow-cleared parking spaces with furniture or other things no matter how dumb it was.

Bostonians had their traditions.

The mayor would have a better chance cancelling the Boston Marathon. Why he didn't concentrate on real problems, she would never understand, but politics belonged in her brother's sphere, not hers.

I'm as stupid as he is by watching his idiotic maneuver, she thought. It's like a dog peeing to mark his territory.

Her husband returned with another bag of sand on his shoulder. "Tell Jess to get a move on if she wants a ride. One more bag and I'm outta here."

Goose pimples covered Katie's body as she went into her kitchen. The breakfast bar was dusted with bagel crumbs from breakfast. Long ago she'd given up trying to convince her daughter to eat in the morning. As she wiped up the crumbs she hollered, "Jess, your crazy father is about to leave if you want a ride to the T-stop."

He could waste time securing a parking place, but not time to wait for Jess. Too many calls, he would say, and he would be partially right. Bad weather produced frozen pipes galore, a sure profit spike for the month.

It had been at five years since Katie announced she would no longer work in the family business where she kept the books. Both were in good shape when she left: the books and the business.

Two new contracts to supply plumbing for apartment buildings came in last month. He was bidding on a contract to supply the plumbing for another university. Large contracts were supplemented by individual house service. Not bad for a kid from Mission Hill who only graduated from high school.

Plumbing couldn't be outsourced to India.

Katie looked out the window at what she still called the old O'Malley house, although both senior O'Malleys had died three years before. Their kids had sold the house to developers.

She didn't know the families who bought the three condos, although they nodded as they passed, briefcases clutched in hands. When she had time, Katie intended to invite them for a cup of coffee, although that tradition seemed to be dying out. Thinking of coffee, she took a final sip of hers, now cold, and stored her cup in the dishwasher.

Jess entered the kitchen wearing her Suffolk University sweatshirt in place of pajamas. The smell of sleep rose from her skin. Even after all these years, Katie felt the same surge of love she had as when she entered the nursery and Jessie poked her head up over the crib's bumper guard. Sometimes, she peeked at her sleeping daughter now, amazed that after so many miscarriages, she had brought forth this creature.

"I was checking my e-mail." Jess pushed her hair from her eyes.

"Anything from Jason?"

"No."

"It doesn't mean that he isn't okay." Dear God, let him be alive, Katie prayed even more fervently than she prayed that Jess would find a nice Catholic boy and marry him and settle down before she lost her virginity. Having a child that was a crusader kept her from being boy crazy, but now Jess was hitting her mid-20s. It was time to settle down.

"I know. He goes days without writing, but still ..."

Katie was grateful that her daughter would never serve in the military, although if she were arrested in a peace march, she wouldn't be surprised. She glanced at her watch. "I gotta run. Dad is driving me to the Med School. I've a pokey pot going for tonight. If you get home first, set the table." Without waiting for a response, she grabbed her coat and left.

CHAPTER 10

"Why can't we watch the Super Bowl up here?" Patrick called into the kitchen from the television room.

Bridget's arms were swallowed up to the elbows in bubbles. Soapsuds were her luxury. For years, she used minimums, stretching soap, shampoo, toothpaste and toilet paper, getting the last molecule out. She still used the minimum for most things, but dish soap was different. When she washed pots and pans, for she didn't believe the dishwasher got them clean enough, she squirted until the suds reminded her of a woman taking a bath in a television commercial.

As she dried her hands she mouthed "men" at Rachel who was packaging lamb slices in Saran Wrap for Peggy, Jess and Sean to make sandwiches tomorrow. The leftover bone with meat still clinging and five large onions were boiling in the cast iron pot on the stove. Her kitchen smelled of good food and love – the way she wanted it to.

She marched into the living room. "We aren't watching the Super Bowl here because we can't fit everyone in." She didn't add, the same as last year and the year before.

Patrick, who sat in his red cracked-leather chair, picked up the remote and raised the volume. "Rodney Dangerfield and I've a lot in common. We don't get no respect."

"Except you're alive, and he isn't," Bridget snapped.

Connor came up behind his mother. He wore a parka with a furry hood. "Got a list?"

Bridget left her Old Goat to go to the kitchen. Connor followed. He read the list that he carried in his hand. "Shrimp platter, cheese platter, cold cuts, bulky rolls, chips. And beer, whatever you and Bill want. I want Coke. Jess does too, so big bottles." She retrieved her bag hanging on the door handle of the pantry, where her bags had rested since forever.

"My treat, Ma."

"Go on with you. People will see you buying all this and think, 'Aha, another rep on the take.'"

"Stop&Shop isn't in my constituency. And they won't know who is paying anyway."

"Neighborhood people know you." Not true anymore: for 20 years when she shopped at Calumet Supermarket with its raw-meat-almost-gone-bad smell she knew almost everyone pushing a cart. That store was torn down three years before. A new complex held the Stop&Shop, a bank and a Walgreens. An ice-cream store would open in spring. Imagine, a fancy-dancy ice cream store to match the trendy restaurant across the street. She knew it was trendy. It served pasta not macaroni, latte not coffee and teas from weird plants.

Bridget didn't mind the changes. In fact, she felt they expanded her world, although she could imagine Patrick's reaction if she said," Here's your latte." Now that would bring an explosion.

The new people brought her different clients, women more like Jess than her daughters. They talked about career and not just about raising their families or reading *Confidential Chat* in *The Globe* to get a new recipe to entice reluctant kids to eat. Or maybe that was her generation. Periods of time folded into each other like blending chocolate into vanilla cake batter to make marble cake. Bridget wondered what her life would be if she were young now.

She held out three twenties. Connor kissed her forehead and ignored the money. "Your husband is stubborn," she said to Rachel.

"Da, we can carry your chair downstairs if you want," she heard Connor say.

"Jesus, Mary, Joseph, now that's a stupid idea. I'll sit on one of those modern things your sister so likes." Patrick sighed.

Bridget and Rachel giggled softly so that Patrick wouldn't hear. "Go downstairs and join the others. I'll finish."

"You sure?" Rachel asked.

"Get out of here. I need quiet to do some blessing counting."

As soon as her daughter-in-law left, she ploughed her hands into the bubbles. "Thank you, God, for giving Peggy a job." She named each family member until she got to Ashley and added her thanks the child was doing so well.

* * * * *

Peggy pointed at her coffee percolator still with half a brew from the morning, but her sister-in-law shook her head.

"I'm coffeed out."

Peggy pulled three bags of popcorn from the cabinet, put one in the microwave and turned the dial. "You've lost so much weight, Rachel." The words *because you were too chunky before*, stopped at her teeth.

"Since Ashley went into that school, I've joined a gym and Weight Watchers, which I'm ignoring today."

Peggy knew what it cost Rachel, the gold-medal winner in motherhood, to send Ashley away. Peggy suspected Rachel felt she'd lost her job when Ashley left. Peggy knew what it was to look into an empty bedroom, only in Peggy's case it meant that her child was in constant danger. Ashley was safe at school.

Peggy admired Rachel's courage to walk away from her Orthodox family. There wasn't a man alive worth Peggy risking her immortal soul for.

The women in her old bank used to say if something happened to Rachel, they would be first in line applying to be her replacement. Little did they know Connor was charming only to get his way. When he didn't, he became a sulky little boy or a bully, whichever he thought would help him win faster. If Peggy thought about it, she wasn't sure she liked her brothers all that much. Her brother-in-law was okay. Katie didn't appreciate him enough.

The popcorn popped first slowly, then faster and faster. As the timer twanged the last few feeble pops gave way to nothing.

Sean stuck his head into the kitchen, his parka slung over his shoulder. "I'm leaving. Working during the Super Bowl is a capitalist plot."

"It's called paying for college." Peggy blew him a kiss which he grabbed from the air the same way he'd done when he was little. After Jason went to Iraq, they'd started the routine again. The second bag of popcorn went into the microwave.

"I'm almost afraid to ask about Jason," Rachel asked. "No one mentioned him."

The bag inflated as popping sounds provided a counterpoint to their conversation. "We talked about it before you guys arrived." She looked at Rachel. "Jess and Sean were terrified he was on that helicopter that crashed."

"We all were."

"They spooked me. Jason and Jess always had such a connection: I thought of all kind of crazy ESP things." She turned her back to her sister-in-law to regain her control and pretended to look in a drawer. "Why is it when something goes wrong, we automatically think our loved ones are there? A fire in Newton must be your house. Any soldier wounded or killed in Iraq is Jason."

Rachel put her arms around Peggy. "How much longer?"

"End of March – unless they extend him." She shivered and disengaged herself to pop the last bag of popcorn.

"How's work?"

"You'll think I'm a real complainer. It's awful. I read the personnel manual just to make sure there's no rule against smiling."

"Not like your old job."

"We were a team who cared about each other, although of course there were bad days." She stood on tiptoe to get three big bowls.

"It's a pay check. Get that Wheat Chex mix and the mini pizzas over there." Peggy pointed to the table. "We'll bake them downstairs."

"You've enough food to qualify as a Jewish mother," Rachel said.

"Irish mother, Jewish mother, Italian mother, we're all the same.

Eat, eat. She pointed to the pantry. "Grab the blue plastic tray with the ducks, and let's go down to Katie's."

* * * * *

Bill and Connor hadn't returned from their food-and-beer run when Peggy pushed Katie's door open with her right hip. Her arms held a tray. Rachel followed with a bowl in each hand.

Katie and Jess moved chairs into a circle around their large flat-screen as the men arrived. The snacks were laid out. The game started.

The front door bell rang.

"What idiot would be out during the Super Bowl?" Bill asked.

"Maybe Jamie and her boyfriend changed their minds and decided to watch the game with us instead of his parents," Rachel said.

"I'll get it." Jess got up and went into the hall. They heard her scream, "No!"

Peggy screamed, too, as two very somber young marines walked into the room.

CHAPTER 11

Patrick sank into his chair. Another step and his legs would have collapsed. His throne felt like a womb. How many games had he watched from it? How many *Globes* had he read? How many naps had he taken, claiming he was just resting his eyes? This chair was where he did his best thinking.

No one dared sit in it. His kids called it his Archie Bunker chair. It was the one thing that was his, totally his, not shared by anyone else. Even his clothes weren't free of interference. On a cold day Bridget might take his socks or borrow his sweaters. The boys raided his closets. Not that he begrudged anyone anything, but there had to be one place where a man carved out his kingdom.

Others sat in that chair, but only at his invitation. His babies and grandbabies sat in his lap watching cartoons. Little hot-pajamaed bodies, smelling like shampoo and with thumbs in their mouths, cuddled with him.

Jason. Oh God. Jason was the one most often in his lap in this chair. When his buddy from the Legion, Tom Murphy, lost his son in a car crash, people said a parent shouldn't survive their children. They certainly shouldn't survive their grandchildren.

He hadn't realized tears were streaming down his cheeks, until he saw Bridget. She looked smaller than an hour ago.

He opened his arms.

She enfolded herself in them, where they stayed until they rose as one to go to bed without saying another word.

CHAPTER 12

Jess woke to sun streaming in her window. Her laptop sat next to her multi-colored file folders: blue for courses, red for personal, green for her women's shelter work. Her bookcase held her law school texts and those from her Boston University political science courses. Back issues of *The Nation* waited for her to have time to cut out articles. Time wasn't a commodity she had much of.

Books by Noam Chomsky, Richard Clarke, Naomi Klein, Jon Stewart, and Howard Zinn were arranged alphabetically on the top shelf. The shelf below held a smaller selection of Neo-Conservative literature. Although she hated putting money in their pockets, she wanted to understand the thinking behind the Bush administration.

The Lily Tomlin quote, 'If you win the rat race, you're still a rat,' embroidered and framed by Peggy, hung over the door. Her grandmother and mother would have preferred a crucifix. Time to begin this week's rat race. Squeak.

Then as if an overweight St. Bernard jumped on her stomach, she knew this wasn't an ordinary week, day, minute.

Jason was gone.

They'd protected each other. When big kids gave her trouble at school, he beat them up. When he was in trouble, she went to Aunt Peggy, allowing the brunt of her anger to dissipate before Jason faced his mother.

When they were little their mothers dressed them in brother and sister outfits for Easter Mass. Fading Polaroids in both families' albums proved it.

The shower beat scalding water over her body. It didn't melt the pain, which was too deep to be washed away. She rubbed her skin red with the towel, wishing her mother didn't use softening products. She blew her hair dry. Instead of sweeping it back with a barrette, she forced it into a French braid so tight it hurt her scalp.

Her parents sat at the kitchen counter. Usually, they'd left by this hour. Her mother wore her grey skirt and a sweater, office clothes.

"Going to work?" Jess asked.

"I don't get days off for the death of a nephew."

"Can't you take a vacation day?"

"There are some things I need to get done."

"But Aunt Peggy needs you."

"Ma and Da are there. I'll leave early and take over."

Jess went upstairs.

Her aunt wore her faded-pink quilted bathrobe. She looked as if she hadn't slept.

"Did you take the sleeping pill Mom gave you?" Jess asked.

After what seemed like hours Peggy shook her head. "It would be unfair to Jason to dull the pain."

Without asking, Jess ran water in the coffee pot. "What else can I get you?"

Peggy made a motion with her hand.

When Jess touched her, Peggy swung around and clung to her niece. "Call the office for me? I can't face it." Peggy ruffled through her bag until she came up with a phone number.

"Oh my God," Mary Ann said. "What can I do?"

"Shoot Bush." Jess was angry. She'd been angry since she became aware of politics. She'd refused to go to Elizabeth Seaton High School. She hated wearing uniforms and girl-only classes. Her parents let her take the exam for Boston Latin, which she passed in the top one percent. One of her grandmother's clients, who worked in the school department, leaked the results, so she knew before the acceptance letter came.

That first day in the auditorium with other scrawny ninth graders she listened as they were told they were the brightest students in the city. Written on the wall were names of famous graduates: John Adams, John Quincy Adams, George Santayana, Leonard Bernstein and Joe Kennedy. She felt unworthy, a feeling compounded when the headmistress told of the number of Nobel Prize winners who were alums. She pledged to do more than her best.

In history, the teacher taught them the American Revolution from the English and the Indian points of view. She learned to look at all sides.

During that course, she developed her gang, four boys as passionate as she was about history and politics. They watched the Clinton impeachment, screaming at Hyde, Barr and the Republicans. She and her buddies rattled off legislative bill numbers as some boys knew Red Sox batting averages.

However, she never had been as angry as she was now. Her bones felt angry, her muscles felt angry, her eyes felt angry.

"I'm not sure that I can kill Bush," Mary Ann said. "Can I come over tonight?"

Jess put her hand over the mouthpiece and mouthed the question to Peggy who shook her head. "My aunt says maybe later in the week. Can you talk to her boss?"

Mary Ann inhaled so hard Jess felt she might be sucked through the telephone. "I don't know how to say this, but since your aunt is still on probation, she has no time off coming. Of course, she can take unpaid leave."

"I ..."

"Can your aunt hear you?"

"Yes."

"I hate these policies. I'll see what we can do. Don't upset her any more."

Jess hung up. She had been wrong earlier. She could be angrier.

CHAPTER 13

Peggy's living room was full. She watched her family try to care for her. They answered phones, made coffee and tea. No one could give her what she wanted – her son.

She wanted to yell at him for being in bed at one in the afternoon. She wanted to find drugs in his sock drawer. She wanted a teacher's conference about his bad report card. She wanted problems with solutions. She felt no regret for the discipline that she'd meted out with so little success until something clicked in his head.

The Marines taught him self-discipline. The Marines killed him. The Marines had offered to stay with her, offered to go to the plane when the body arrived. She had told Jess to tell them that if they came near Jason's body, she would personally kill them.

The neighbors knew without being called. Angela, who lived next door, had seen the van with United States Marine Corps written on the side. She would have missed it if her dog hadn't begged to go out during the Super Bowl. The pup peed on the vehicle that meant only one thing. She saw two Marines run out the door with Peggy throwing whatever she could grab at them. Angela went home, the football game forgotten, and started dialing. Grumbles at the game interruption gave way to anguish in one house after another of the old residents as they realized one of their own was gone. Even the new ones, Bridget's customers, heard.

When people died in Mission Hill, the old residents cooked:

casseroles, roast chickens, pies, desserts. Those who had moved to other parts of the city did the same when they heard and got in their cars to deliver the food. One by one, they rang the bell and said, "We won't disturb you, but give this to Peggy. We'll see her at the wake."

What wake, Peggy thought as she listened to familiar voices. She hadn't a clue where her son's body was. Maybe it was in some Baghdad warehouse in a government-issued coffin covered by a government-issued flag. CNN reported that two other boys died with Jason. Contacting their mothers flickered through her mind. It would take too much effort. Standing took too much effort.

Jason's body could be on a plane. No fasten your seat belt signs were needed. He couldn't sit in a seat. No one from the family would be at Logan with their arms open to scoop him up. He would arrive in the States in a box with other boxes, stashed in a warehouse and hidden from photographers as decreed by the authorities.

If she could only believe Jason died for a good reason, not for the egomaniac in the White House who lied about the WMDs. The bastard lied about the connection to 9/11. She and Jason fought about it. Although he doubted the reasons for the war as much as she did, he said a Marine obeyed. For years she couldn't get him to pick up his clothes, and when he did obey, it killed him. No one died picking up pajamas.

When he first joined the Marines, she'd been thrilled, thinking it would make him a man. She wanted to hit herself over and over in punishment for suggesting that he should join.

Someone, Rachel, yes Rachel, gave her tea. Rachel and Connor had been there all day. Her parents, Sean, Katie and Bill were in and out, in and out. Jessie, Jessie, bless Jessie, was never more than a few footsteps away.

The phone rang for the umpteenth time. If she had the strength, she'd rip it from the wall.

Jess picked it up. She put her hand over the receiver, "It's a reporter from *The Globe*."

Peggy waved her hand.

"My aunt can't come to the phone."

"Please Miss …" the male voice sounded young. "God, I hate doing these calls."

"Not as much as we hate getting them," Jess snapped.

"We would like a photo of … of …"

"My cousin? Jason Doherty? The deceased? The murdered?"

"Who …"

"… murdered him? The government which sent him into this stupid war, and if you print one word about sacrificing his life so we won't be attacked on our streets by mad Iraqis, I swear it'll be your last story."

"I won't. I promise."

"You can have your photo, but you have to come get it." No one had a digital camera. Because of Patrick's job, they were still a Polaroid family. She slammed the phone into the holder so hard that the crack startled everyone in the room.

Jess put her hands on her aunt's knee. "I'm sorry, I lost it."

Peggy touched Jessica's cheek. "I couldn't have said it better myself. You know where the album is. Don't use the one of him in uniform."

Bridget emerged from the bathroom. "I've run a hot bath."

Peggy wanted to protest that she hated baths but taking one would be easier than fighting it. At a primitive level she realized that her mother needed to do something to help her. She walked into the steamy bathroom. Someone had left a clean nightdress on the toilet. She sank into the tub filled with bubbles and the smell of roses.

The scent and the heat relaxed her muscles. She hadn't realized how tense she was. She saw herself once again as a young mother bending over this tub and putting bubbles on Jason's shoulder and calling him general. He saluted and hit the water sending suds everywhere. She jumped out of the tub as if the water burned her.

In bed, she heard the babble of voices from the living room. With the cool pillowcase against her cheek, she wondered if she would ever be pain-free.

CHAPTER 14

Jess ushered the reporter from *The Globe* into her apartment. He was lanky with Dumbo ears and a grin hiding behind a serious face. His brown hair fell in waves below his collar and into his eyes. "Ms Doherty, I am sorry, so sorry to ..."

"Kelly. My name is Kelly."

"I don't suppose your aunt would talk to ..." His voice trailed off. Her expression said, not in your lifetime.

"I've a story to write. I'd like to make it a tribute to your ..." Again, he stopped. He pushed the curly black hair out of his eyes, a useless gesture. It fell back. "I'm sure the news stations will get word of this; in fact, I'm surprised they haven't been here."

"The Pats won the Super Bowl. That's more important."

"It shouldn't be. We go on here at home as if everything's normal and people are dying under awful conditions and it sucks, Ms Kelly. It sucks a lot."

Jess looked at him. She felt his anger akin to her own, not at the same depth, because he hadn't grown up with Jason, but an abstract anger. It helped, she thought, but she wasn't sure what it helped.

"I can't prove it, but I've been on almost every anti-war demonstration when I wasn't working and a few when I was. If you want to check my screensaver on my office computer it's Truthout's homepage. In my apartment it's set to Common Dreams, and I can show you cancelled checks to Not in Our Name and ..."

Something in his intensity told her that he was speaking the truth. "Your name?"

"Aidan Pelletier."

"Aidan like the nice guy in *Sex and the City*."

"Like that Aidan. I'm a nice guy too. Truce?" He held out his hand. Jess hesitated before taking it. "You'll write an anti-war story?"

"I can quote you?" The familiarity of his face niggled at her.

"Have I seen you before?" he asked. "Where do you work?"

"I'm at Suffolk Law. Student. I work at a women's shelter. Not where you'd hang out."

Aidan snapped his fingers. "The students' march against the war. You wore a navy-blue coat and beret. You carried a Bush-Lied-so Soldiers-Died sign."

Jess moved slightly. "How ..."

"You have to believe me that I go to demonstrations, but that time I was there, half as a reporter, half as a demonstrator."

"But ..."

"It helps to report an accurate number. The police give small numbers. The people who arrange demonstrations give large. I've often thought if I averaged the two numbers, I might find reality."

Jess repressed a smile. "I've thought the same thing."

"When you got up to speak against the war, I thought how smart you were. And how pretty. I wanted to speak, but you were so involved, I gave up."

Jess blushed. Her mother told her she was pretty, but her mother was prejudiced, not that she broke any mirrors. Pretty wasn't her goal. Being effective in remaking the world was. "Let's talk about my cousin."

He took out his notepad and a royal blue fountain pen. Jess hadn't seen anyone use a fountain pen for a long time. In fact, she wasn't sure she'd ever seen anyone use one.

CHAPTER 15

Unlike most women, Bridget never minded listening to her husband's snores. She didn't like sleeping. Nights were for lying awake planning whatever there was to plan. The steady beat that Patrick put out helped her think.

The streetlamp below threw a dull glow into the bedroom. Bridget didn't need light to know where the crucifix over the door was. She knew exactly the placement of each piece of furniture. They'd been in the same position since before Connor's birth. If a kitchen was the soul of a house, then the bedroom was the heart.

She pressed her body against Patrick's. He threw his arm over her. The weight felt heavy. They were like two spoons nestled in her kitchen drawer. Because he was on his side his snoring became regular breathing tickling her ear.

How much of her bone cold was from the temperature or how much was from the loss of her grandson? Did it matter? Her face and nose were colder than the rest of her body. Normally, she liked sleeping in a cold room.

All three units turned down their heat at night to conserve fuel. The top floor was the first to cool off because heat escaped through the roof. However, when it was as cold as it was outside tonight, drafts seeped through the edges of the window. She wished that they'd put that special plastic on the windows that they blew with a hair dryer even if it looked terrible.

House sounds created a hypnotizing familiarity: the clock clicked not ticked; the fridge purred.

Most nights she planned her next day: make breakfast, start a wash, cut the violet dress, finish hemming the tweed suit, send Patrick to the supermarket, start the second load until her last chore of the day which was to brew a final tea or hot chocolate for Patrick and herself before hanging up her clothes and slipping into her flannel nightgown.

Her thoughts hip-hopped. She saw herself playing hopscotch near Mission Church. Patrick first spoke to her at a church dance. She shouldn't have been there. She was in eighth grade; it was for high school students. She saw Jason looking handsome in his uniform. Connor announced he was marrying a Jewess. Rachel told her that Ashley wasn't all right. Her boys fought over a truck. Connor hit Desmond: they'd rushed to Children's Hospital. Peggy tripped as she made her First Communion. Peggy sat with Katie after her third miscarriage. Desmond hit his first homerun. Patrick couldn't speak the next day he had cheered so hard as his son ran the bases.

All their problems had been normal, though some didn't seem so at the time. Ashley had been the worst thing that had happened to their family until now. Sure, Peggy's husband killed himself, but that was almost an answer to a prayer, although she had never prayed for anyone's death, but she preferred praying for his soul rather than watching him stagger home and listening to him scream at Peggy.

Jason hadn't been a likeable child. For his first four months his colicky screams shook the house. They gave way to tantrums whenever his will was thwarted. Funny, how Sean and Jess were easy children, but Jason was difficult. Then there was Connor's Jamie, an outsider because she didn't bounce in and out of their apartments at will.

Her four gave her almost no problems because she ruled with an iron hand. "Get in trouble in school, and it's nothing like you'll find at home," she and Patrick told them. None of them did get into trouble, not even little troubles that earned detention after school. They were kept busy with after school sports and chores.

When she was young, young being up to 45, everything was clear.

You worked, paid your bills, educated your kids and then retired. Now it was murkier than the Muddy River running through the Fenway. She couldn't even stop working if she wanted to, although she pretended she could. Patrick's medicines cost too much. Jason served his country as Patrick had done, but Patrick came back. Her clients talked about their kids finding jobs without benefits, jobs without enough salary to pay rent even in a slum.

Jess claimed the war was illegal. In her day, she wouldn't have questioned Roosevelt or Truman on World War II or Korea. When did the questioning start? Vietnam, that's when. Her boys were too young for the protests. The war ended while they were in high school. How she'd prayed it would end before they could be drafted. Politics never interested her, even though her son was a state senator. He interested her, but the blah blah was boring. Politics stole her grandson.

Bridget was not used to feeling helpless. When something needed to be done, she did it. This was so different. When Peggy was little and fell, a kiss on the wound made it better. Now no kiss would cure her daughter's pain or hers.

She had failed to protect her family.

CHAPTER 16

By Tuesday night Peggy still hadn't heard when Jason's body would be released or even where it was. Not knowing troubled her more than it had after he quit school and she had no idea where he went when he slammed out of the house. Sometimes he disappeared for days. When he was home, he skulked around, speaking in monosyllables. She would sell her soul to have him monosyllabic and skulking in front of her. No devil appeared to accept the offer.

Peggy sat at her kitchen table fingering the letter with the government seal. Sean wanted to stay with her. Since he needed to pay for books, she brushed aside his concern. He grumped as he left for work.

The cream on her coffee had congealed. Dirty dishes were piled in the sink, although her mother and her sister had offered to wash them. Peggy planned to do them later. She wanted to dip her arms into hot soapy water, to do something with a beginning, middle and end. She needed small things to control: washing dishes, putting on slacks, cooking something, although she could have fed Jason's regiment from the food that friends had brought.

For the first time since the Marines flew out the door after delivering their message, she was alone – the first of many firsts after years and years of sharing Jason's life. There'd be a first Valentine's Day. He always gave her a Valentine. Sean never did.

She would have thought it would be the other way around. A first time she wouldn't buy him a birthday present. She already had her first Christmas without him, but he'd called from Iraq. "I'll be home next year, Mom," he'd said. Well he would be, but not the way she wanted.

She wanted to ask God, why him, why her, but she knew very few people got out of life without some catastrophe raining down on them. She pictured God with an assembly line of souls, each with a predestined tragedy: cancer, hurricane, Cerebral Palsy. He must have stamped her soul with loss of a son.

Katie and Bill were working late to get ready for time off once the body was here: the body, Jason's body, the child that came screaming from her womb.

The letter from the Secretary of Defense with its characters, black squiggles on white paper, didn't bring her son back. Words didn't cover how he shouldn't have been there. The letter fascinated her. If she read it enough, she might find instructions on how to live the rest of her life. Maybe they were written in invisible ink between lines. She touched each word, each space.

Nothing penetrated her concentration – not the smell of food, not the dripping tap. She'd redecorated the kitchen with wallpaper of old-fashioned coffee pots in forest green. The old wood cabinets she repainted the same dark green. Decoration on the cheap, but she'd wanted her boys to have a cheerful home. "Mom, you're clever," Jason said as he'd watched her wallpaper. She hadn't been clever enough to protect him.

When the sun poured in, the kitchen was cheery. Only at night, like now, did the darkness feel heavy. She needed better lighting, Jason complained, but no way would she do her own wiring. She hadn't wanted to ask Bill, who did so much for her. Peggy wanted to stand on her own two feet as much as possible, so the kitchen remained badly lit.

Her son hated it and went off to war and died and she had a letter from the Secretary of Defense, one of the highest politicians in the country who could walk into the Oval Office. She bet Rumsfeld never said to Bush, "Jason Doherty was killed in Iraq. He hated his mother's dark kitchen."

The president hadn't said, "That's too bad." They didn't care despite the letter full of false sorrow.

Like her mother and sister, Peggy had never been political, despite her brother being a politician. Men wasting time while women did the work, but wasn't that always the way?

Sure, she'd voted each election. Voting was a family tradition. Her father taught them it was a privilege to be a citizen of the country. Voting was his thank you. He expected his children to say thank you for the rest of their lives.

Boston Irish voted Democrat as surely as "Full of Grace" followed "Hail Mary." Democrats would do right by people.

Peggy didn't even watch the news and just grazed the headlines in *The Globe* on her way to the comics. Her favorite was *For Better or For Worse*. She felt that the Patterson family was like her neighbors. She had watched Lizzie, Michael and April grow up in black and white ink as her own kids had grown up in living color.

For the first time in her life, she understood what made her niece so angry with the system. Until now, she thought Jess overreacted. She wished she'd paid more attention. She looked up to see Jess come over and take the letter.

Jess wet her finger and rubbed the signature. It smudged. "At least the bastard is signing it himself these days ... or using one of those signature machines."

"I'm sending it back," Peggy said.

"Sending it back?"

"Help me think of a message."

Jess poured a cup of coffee and sat next to her aunt. "This means nothing?"

Peggy shook her head.

"You're a lying war criminal."

"How about putting it back in the envelope and writing refused, return to sender?"

"All I know is I must do something. I just don't know what. The letter will be a start."

* * * * *

Mary Ann had suggested during a telephone call that Peggy return to work until the funeral. "You'll need the time later and remember you're still on probation."

Peggy Doherty, Robot Loan Officer, got up, washed, dressed, took the subway, sat at her desk, and processed, processed, processed. The woman in the next booth stammered her sympathies. No one else spoke to her, but she didn't know most of their names, why should they know hers? As soon as the head loan officer realized she was back, he deposited 20 folders in her in-box. Was this her working future with no one caring a diddly-damn about anyone else?

Jonathan Abramson's loan application tilted on the top of the pile. She opened it. He lived in Boston's South End, owned his own condo and wanted to buy an SUV. Robot Doherty pulled the credit check.

No late charges on his mortgage, credit cards or his student loans. Check.

Ratio of debt to income was fine. Check.

Length in job was fine. Check.

She pictured Mr. Abramson in his shiny black SUV pulling up to a gas pump. He filled, filled and filled it. The pipeline ran across the ocean to Iraq. Her son's body was draped across the pipeline. She marked an X in the refused box.

* * * * *

"I sympathize with your loss, Peggy." Her boss sat in his office chair, his hands forming a steeple. His blond hair was almost shaved half way up his head and longer on top, a style for the up-and-coming executive, according to a *Globe* article. "But there's lots of work, so don't take any more time than is necessary."

She stared.

He shifted under her glare. "It burdens your co-workers."

"The ones who didn't bother to say they were sorry my son was killed."

His face froze. "You're new. They're busy."

"I wonder," Peggy said, "how many have a yellow ribbon saying support our troops on their cars. Do you?"

He blushed. "I do, although I don't believe ..." He touched the steeple of his hands to his lips, "... I suppose I shouldn't say it to you."

"That you don't believe in the war?"

He nodded.

"Just what does support the troops mean to you?"

"That we give them what they need, of course."

"And that's ..."

"This isn't something we should discuss. Nor is it the time. I did want you to know how sorry I was. Although I don't have any children ..."

"You married?"

"Been too busy with my career."

Career, Peggy thought, running a lousy department for a lousy bank. Probably it paid him enough to drop in on the trendy bars and find earnest young career women who were also building careers. She imagined them sitting at the bar with Legos marked career on the side and stacking them higher and higher around their white wine spritzers or whatever the in-drink was these days. Her desire for job security kept her from slapping him. "If you really want to be supportive, pay me for the time I missed."

He leaned forward. "I'm sure Mary Ann explained the policies to you. Employees have 10 days a year for anything they want, sick time, holiday, family emergencies. The days you've taken count, even though you're on probation and won't be paid for them." He reached for the telephone. "Do you want me to have her talk to you?"

"I suppose all the years I worked for the bank you guys bought ..."

"That was a different organization. It really doesn't have anything to do with the here and now. And if we make an exception for one person ..."

"How many bank employees will lose children in Iraq, do you think? One hundred? One thousand?"

She imagined batting his head against the wall. The sound of his skull hitting the plaster had a pleasing ring. She imagined him slipping to the ground, not dead, but as hurt on the outside as she was inside.

He did not realize that Peggy was beating him up in her imagination, but his expression said he didn't want to deal with this any more.

Peggy stood. "I've a lot of loans to process." For the rest of the day she behaved as she figured a good little robot should.

CHAPTER 17

Jess claimed the small round table farthest from the door by dropping her jacket. The other nine tables in the restaurant were crammed together. At the counter, mixed macaroni and potato salads were in a refrigerator case. About half the time Jess carried her lunch to save money, but this morning she overslept. Only now did she think of Aunt Peggy's funeral stash: she could have grabbed something.

The morning was difficult. Her classmates had read *The Globe* article, "Mission Hill Loses One of Its Own," about Jason and stammered condolences. She wished that the headline had picked up her quote: "The U.S. government murdered my cousin. I'm not bitter, I'm angry." That reporter had at least quoted her on the bitter-angry part. And he hadn't put in any faux-patriotic crap.

To the "I ... ah ... um ... heards" stammered over and over she'd replied, "Thank you," and nothing more. Many of her classmates had swallowed the load of shit that we were fighting on the streets of Iraq so Americans wouldn't have to fight on the streets of Boston. Hadn't those idiots ever read any history of the Middle East?

Where were their critical-thinking skills?

Up their asses. Her mother's voice about crude language rang in her ears, but she hadn't said anything in front of her mother. Thoughts were exempt.

Two professors said they were sorry. Her best friend, Amy Kolwaski, another student with the same goal as Jess of practicing storefront domestic law, hugged her. Amy was tall. Being hugged by Amy was being enveloped in arms and breasts. Amy, like Jess, was angry at the system while equally determined to change it.

Jess had mixed feelings about her classmates. A few were dedicated to justice, while others saw the law as the road to wealth. Her friends were from the first group. Professor Dutton, professor of Constitutional Law, said he'd never seen a class so divided politically since the 1960s. "I feel as if I have red and blue rows and it has nothing to do with the way your home states voted." As an experiment with his class of 20, he put red and blue markers on an equal number of chairs and asked students to seat themselves.

"Well, I'm still in liberal Massachusetts," he said, when four red row seats were empty: five students stood after the blue seats were filled.

"Hey Jess," the kid behind the counter said. "How's it hanging?"

"Okay." She was grateful he didn't know her last name or connect her with the newspaper article, assuming he even read a paper.

"Whacha want?"

She had little appetite, but she must eat. Hunger left her shaky. "Surprise me."

He chose a macaroni salad and Coke. Because it was 11:30 the place was deserted. In another half hour State House employees and Suffolk University students and professors would fill the place. She opened a book.

"This is a surprise. Is this place taken?"

She jumped at the voice above her.

Aidan Pelletier stood at her table holding a sandwich wrapped in white paper and a raspberry Snapple.

"I was studying." She looked back at her book.

He didn't go away.

Jess motioned from him to sit. "That sounded ruder than I meant."

The chair squeaked against the floor as he moved it to sit. "You only wanted to be a little rude?" He pushed his hair back from his eyes and once again it fell. It would be rude to ask if he wore his hair collar length to hide his ears. If he did, it wasn't working.

"I'm sorry, I really am. I read your story on Jason. It was good."

"I tried. They edited a bit of the more anti-war stuff out."

"What are you doing here?"

"Covering a hearing." He tilted his head toward the State House. "They broke for lunch early. Can't work too hard, those senators."

"My uncle is one."

His smooth skin was too dark to show if he blushed. "Open mouth insert foot. Who?"

"Connor Flanagan from Newton."

"Here's where I should say he's one of the good ones."

"Only if you believe it."

"There's worse. I'm not sure there are any really good politicians." He picked up her text on marital law. "Dry reading. The butler didn't do it."

Jess agreed. Her studies were dry, but they were the route to her future. She wasn't going to tell him her goal was to open a storefront practice with Amy: Kelly & Kolwaski, Ireland meets Poland in the name of truth, justice and the American way or the mythical American way, which she wanted to make reality for those the least able to live it.

"I semi-fibbed," Aidan said. "I *was* covering a hearing, but I glanced out the window and saw you walking. I rushed out and looked into every restaurant until I found you."

Jess cocked her head.

"I know this isn't a good time, but can we have dinner? I want to get to know you."

"For a story?"

"Only one we would write for ourselves. I know it's tacky to try and date someone I interviewed who is in mourning, but we reporters are supposed to be crass and heartless."

Jess suspected that the reporter was neither.

CHAPTER 18

Candles burned at the tub's edge. Suds came up to Peggy's bust. It was an old tub with claw feet. Bill offered to redo her bathroom with all modern fixtures charging only what they cost him, but Peggy liked her old-fashioned tub.

She'd papered this room with a blue flowered paper, painted the side of the tub blue and stenciled white flowers along the middle.

Jason had tiled the floor for her as he was just beginning to come out of his bad stage. He volunteered almost as an apology. She'd let him. She'd sat on the toilet and told him what a great job he was doing, one of the first positive things she'd been able to say to him in a long time.

When people talked about their houses, they talked about the value, how prices had skyrocketed. Her parents could sell this place for a small fortune, she guessed. Sell it? She couldn't imagine them leaving this house any more than she could picture them walking down Delle Avenue naked. Naked would come first.

When Bill and Katie offered to up their rent from the $125 a month to market rates, both parents had waved their hands in that get-along-with-you gesture. When Bill renovated his flat to improve the market value, Katie explained he didn't want to feel like a leech.

"Leech-smeech," Bridget said. A home was about family not money.

A rap at the door. 'Sorry to disturb you Ma, but someone is on the telephone: a Mrs. Maxwell.'

She didn't know any Mrs. Maxwell. "Take a number."

"She says it's important, and she'll only take a minute."

She reached for her towel. Her hands were water wrinkled. Her body had few sags and little cellulite for a woman soon to be 48. She never joined a gym, lacking the extra money, time and if forced she'd admit no desire. Nervous energy was a better diet tool.

The wall phone next to the fridge was covered with magnets: bananas, the outline of the Commonwealth of Massachusetts, a Red Sox cap, a football with Boston Patriots and a bright red lobster. "Hello."

"Mrs. Doherty, you don't know me. I'm calling from California. I lost my daughter in Iraq."

Peggy leaned against the wall. This woman, a continent away, was a sister from a separate womb. "I know you'll believe me when I say, I understand."

"I won't ask if this is a good time, there isn't a good time these days, but I want to talk to you in depth when you're up to it."

Peggy nodded.

As if the woman heard, she said, "There've been some frauds with family members being called for this or that, so you will want to check me out. My name is Lisa Maxwell. My daughter was Julianna Maxwell."

Peggy felt the pain behind the word was before Mrs. Maxwell added, "She died two days before Thanksgiving in Baghdad. The write-up of her death was in the Thanksgiving issue of the *San Francisco Chronicle*. Have you internet access?"

Peggy wondered who could be so callous to prey on a grieving family, but lately she had felt her world unravel like tearing apart a handmade sweater one row at a time. She didn't know what to do with the yarn. "Excuse me?"

Lisa repeated what she'd said. "I read *The Boston Globe* on line. Your niece is pretty outspoken. Do you agree with her?"

"She came on strong. They didn't use a lot of it. Ya, I agree."

"I feel the same. Do you know I'm more frightened of my

government than I am of terrorists?"

Peggy's head swirled. She'd never thought about it. She pulled one of the kitchen chairs closer to the telephone to not stretch the cord. The wood felt cold through her robe. "Why are you calling?" She hoped she didn't sound nasty.

"Only mothers like us know what it's like. Others try ..."

"I know."

"This stupid war must stop. A lot of groups are springing up founded by people who lost children. It's important we communicate."

"Wouldn't it be better if it were one group?"

"Probably. Strength in numbers and all."

Peggy panicked. "I'm really not a joiner." Hell, she hadn't wanted to join a bank association or a church guild, and now someone was asking about joining an anti-war group.

"I'm not asking. I want to leave my phone number in case you need to talk, even if it's the middle of the night, although my middle of the night is different from yours."

"That's very kind."

"Not really. Reaching out to others keeps my own pain at bay."

The woman is from San Francisco. She keeps her pain in the bay. San Francisco Bay. What a stupid thought. "I'll get a pencil."

After Peggy hung up, she logged onto the internet. The windows grew light the next morning and she was still there, reading about the lead-up to the war. Anger erased her tiredness.

CHAPTER 19

"I know it's tacky having a first date before your cousin is buried," Aidan said to Jess. They were at Mr. Bartley's in Harvard Square. The restaurant, located in the same spot for donkeys' years, specialized in burgers, including veggie burgers for Jess. It was empty except for one waitress, the cashier and the cook.

"If you consider a burger between my classes and my going to the shelter a date."

"The first of many, I hope. I knew from the beginning you were someone different."

Jess knew that she was the only girl in grade school bored by Barbie. She preferred playing archaeologist and digging up Indian relics in the grassy area over the ledge. She had driven the Parker Hill branch librarian nuts trying to find out everything about local tribes. "How so?"

"I bet you don't haunt lipstick counters for the latest color with a silly name like Firehouse Red?"

Jess shook her head.

"See, I knew you were someone I was going to like."

"Okay, Reporter. Let's turn the tables."

Aidan stood and turned the table around.

Jess switched their food plates back. In her rating of a potential boyfriend, humor earned five points, but she still wasn't looking for anyone. If she were … no, she wasn't, but still this man was not like the law school students, with their images of future Mercedes and McMansions, who had asked her out. "Tell me about you."

"My parents were teachers in Reading where I grew up. They died about five years ago in a car crash." He didn't wait for her expressions of sympathy. "I went to Boston University, studying journalism. I worked for a small paper in upper Maine, broke a huge story on corruption in the legislature, and leveraged my way into a job with *The Globe*. Hand me the ketchup." His French fries disappeared in a red sea. "What's your opinion of ..."

They were off on the government, war, Social Security, welfare, education. Each knew the numbers of bills working their way through Congress. They knew the different web sites for conservative and progressive groups and had signed the same petitions, calling for the same congressmen to voice their concerns.

"I've a confession. I sometimes tape C-Span," Aidan said.

"Me too. In fact, they are showing a Senate hearing today that I want to watch after I get home tonight." Jess looked at her watch then pulled her cell out to dial the women's shelter. "I'm running late, but I'll be there as soon as I can catch the T."

"I'll drive you," Aidan said.

Jess started to refuse from habit, but she wanted to talk more to him.

CHAPTER 20

As Peggy entered her dark apartment, she tossed her empty briefcase on the hall chair. Her mood was as dark as the flat. Miners had it worse; factory workers had it worse, but God, being imprisoned in a cubicle shoveling paper, with every movement monitored and no chance to look out a window, was soul-killing.

After a year of unemployment, she should be grateful: she knew that. Maybe her expectations of finding a friendly working environment had been unrealistic in today's marketplace. Maybe it was unreasonable to expect smiles when folders were exchanged. Maybe she was crazy expecting to share lunch with colleagues. Almost everyone ate at their desks as they looked through loan applications. Maybe it was just this bank. There was no maybe about how much her work atmosphere sucked, to use Sean's favorite phrase.

She tripped on his boots before she reached the light switch. It wasn't like him to leave them in the hall. When light flooded the flat, she saw his coat thrown to one side. He was the neat kid. Jason's room was dangerous to walk across.

Sean's bedroom door was closed. She knocked. She never, even when the boys were little, entered their rooms without an invitation. "Sean?"

"Go away."

"I want to talk."

"No."

She knocked again.

"I said go away."

"I heard."

Until now he hadn't reacted to Jason's death, not a tear, and she had been too swallowed up in her own mourning to reach out to make sure he was okay.

The lock clicked. His New England Patriots bedspread was mussed. His eyes were red; his cheeks were red. She hadn't seen him cry since he was beaten up in sixth grade. Jason went after the kids, but Sean had been furious because he wanted to fight his own wars, not rely on his big brother.

When Peggy tried to touch him, he pulled away and rolled over to the edge of the bed. She imagined a crab closing itself in its shell.

"Sean. We need to get through this." When he said nothing, she put her hand on his arm. She felt him trembling.

A three-ring binder lay open on the floor next to the bed. As she glanced down it was full of e-mails. He saw her look at it. One arm shot out to close it.

"What's that?" She usually respected her kids' privacy, but the question fell from her lips before she could stop it.

"Nothing." Then his shoulders started heaving. This time he let her swoop him into her arms, even though his lanky body hovered over hers by five inches. It worked because she stood as he sat on the edge of the bed with his head buried in her stomach, his arms around her. Their tension and pain melded them into one being.

"I'm too big to cry." He still held onto her and she swayed back and forth, a poor substitute of a rocking a baby.

"Not when your brother dies, you aren't. When Aunt Emma died, her son John, you don't remember him because he moved to Arizona when you were four ... well, after her funeral he stood by the casket and cried and cried. He was a truck driver and weighed two hundred pounds." She smoothed his corn-cob silk hair without realizing she was doing it.

Peggy let the silence hang in the air. Words didn't do much. She tried to eye the binder, and he felt her do it.

He drew a deep breath then whispered, "Jason e-mailed me about what it was really like. He said he had to tell somebody. I kept them. Mom, he hated the war so much."

Peggy thought of Jason's cheery messages, how he was doing what a Marine should do. He boasted of winning at card games with his buddies and singing along with someone who played the guitar. At the time she thought this sounded more like summer camp than a war but told herself she was lucky he was given safe assignments and prayed that God would keep him in those safer places. Even at the time, part of her knew she was fooling herself.

Sean wiped his nose on his sleeve as he'd done at five. Only recently had she begun to understand how she would always see her child in the adult. She wondered if Ma saw her in her school uniform and knee socks running back for a forgotten lunch. "I don't understand."

The clock on the nightstand ticked. A car door slammed outside.

Her son slid from her arms. He turned on his side. He drew his knees to his chest.

Should she leave? No, she had to help him as much as she could. "Sean, talk to me."

"He wanted you to be proud of him. After all the shit, er trouble, he gave you." He clasped his hand over his mouth.

"Shit is the right word. Sometimes polite doesn't cut it."

She felt him relax just a bit. "Why would he think I wouldn't be proud of him?" His lowered Venetian blinds caught her attention. Two slats were tangled.

"I don't want to break my promise to him."

"What promise?"

"Not to worry you. You got the sterile version. Jess and I got the truth. That's one of the reasons we kept trying to buy him equipment."

"You sent him goggles."

"And a vest."

'I didn't know about the vest.'

"You weren't supposed to. You'd have worried more."

"I want to read them. It's too late for me to worry."

He pouted. "They'll upset you."

"Do you really think much more could upset me than losing my first-born?"

"Losing your second-born?"

"Not even close to funny. If you dare die before me, I'll kill you."

CHAPTER 21

Peggy opened her bedroom door. The street light shooting in through the bay window illuminated the room. To remove her boots, she slumped on the patchwork quilt she'd made from her mother's scraps of cloth. The squares represented the separate roles in her life: mother, daughter, sister, aunt, television watcher, worker, student, house cleaner and whatever. Some squares touched: others didn't. Her work life and home life had been separate: one paid for the other. God, what a day.

The cold of the floorboards penetrated her stockings: she was almost too tired to look for her slippers. If only she could step into a time machine and redo her life. In lieu of that option she laid down, pulling up the quilt, and slept.

When she opened her eyes, she felt surprised to find herself in bed so early in the evening. So much of her family's lives were imprinted in this room. Here her children were conceived. Here her husband beat her once. She fought so hard, he never touched her again. He died two months later.

Sean and Jason climbed into this bed on snow days when school was cancelled, and they watched Saturday morning cartoons on the miniature black and white TV on top of her dresser while she tried to nap before starting chores. If she didn't drown in the past, she would drown in her own stupidity in encouraging Jason to join up.

For years, Peggy had lived in the immediate future: thinking what she would wear before getting out of bed, plotting her walk to work and deciding whether to eat at her desk or with the girls. Only when she lost her job and Jason left for Iraq did she begin to live in the past. Now she was living in the now, minute by minute.

"Mom, can I come in?"

She sat up. "Yup."

Her son entered, holding the three-ring binder close to his chest. He put it down next to her on the bed. The look he gave her made her want to cry, but she swallowed instead. Without a word he left: she didn't hear the lock click into place.

As a child she loved myths. Her favorite had been about Pandora. She took it as an omen to be careful in what she did. The U Mass insignia was embossed on the binder cover. It wasn't a box. She wasn't a beautiful young girl and no god was about to carry her to the underworld. But as sure as if she were Pandora, she knew that whatever she read would change her life.

CHAPTER 22

From: Jason (jason.doherty20120@hotmail.com)
To: sean.doherty20120@hotmail.com
CC: lawyer.to.be.jess@yahoo.com
Date: April 14, 2004
Subject: I know this is a lot to ask

Hi little Bro (and Jess too…)
Their R things here that R better Mom doesn't know.
I need to share this, because I don't want it to get lst. I
don't know lost from what. When I was a kid, I did what
I felt like. Got me in lots of trouble. Remember all the
times I was groundd? Even U Jess, couldn't plead my
case.

So I wasn't here for the start of Operation Iraqi
Freedom, (thank God I missed it by a year) although
that name seems to have disappeared. Mayeb it was
something TV made up. The way the people R living
without stuff we take 4 granted like water and electricity
doesn't make their freedom seem so great. Wish I was
back at the consulate in Oslo. Now that was good duty.

The guys I hang with most are Ted, Jared, Paul. I met them in Kuwait as we waited to get here. They were all itching to kill "towel heads", and were afraid that it would be over before they could make up for 9/11. U and I know it wasn't the Iraqis that did 9/11. It's like Joe kills Mary, and Mary's husband kills Bob to revenge Mary.

I don't want to kll anyone. Maybe it was Father Zachary who talked about thou shalt not kill so much (along with a lot of other stuff that seemed like crap at the time, but if I live to have a kid, I'll teach them the same stuff. U might ask why I joined the Marines and trained to be a killing machine.

That was pre 9/11. I imagined a nice clean uniform, travel, etc. Basic training killed that idea pretty fast. But Mom was so proud of me 4 the first time. I wanted to prove I could do something right so I stuck with it. what else would I've done? Continue to fuck up my life? The Marines were a way out. The way out of one mess and into another, but I made a commitment. I'll stick to it. God, I sound like Grampy.

Which leads me to u. Stay in school. Continue to get good grades. Go to college. Mom doesn't need another kid to worry about. And thanks 4 the goggles. I won't ask how many grocery orders u rang up to pay for them. Love to u both. Jess I don't have to tell u to stay in school. Someone would have to blast u out.

Jason

P.S. 11 months to go until Mar. 14 and I can rotate out of this hell hole. Pray 4 me.

From: Jason (jason.doherty20120@hotmail.com)
To: sean.doherty20120@hotmail.com
CC: lawyer.to.be.jess@yahoo.com
Date: April 23, 2004
Subject: RE: I know this is a lot to ask

Hi Bro (and Jess)...
Thanks for your reply, and I really, really appreciate U listening er...reading my whatevers.
I've been on patrol. Not to get heavy, but I wonder if I can kill. I know it's to late to think about that, the middle of war and all. What if it is him or me? Him or my buddies?
Once I pull the trigger and a person is dead I can never go back. Thou shalt not kill isn't in the Bible as thou shall not kill except in a war. Yet if someone was to hurt any of my family, Id kill to protect them. What does that make me?
Some of my buddies don't think of Iraqis as people, but I see them on the streets. Yesterday a little girl was crying. I don't know why, but her mother bent down and hugged her just like Mom did us. Sure, some of the men with their beards and heads all wrapped up look funny and dirty. Jared said they didn't wash. I didn't say it, but I thought they don't have much water to wash with and what they do have is filthy.
I shouldn't even be thinking this stuff. Since I can't tell anyone here so U R stuck with me. I'm amazed at how many guys R itching for blood. Some guys brag about killing people. One keeps notches on his belt. Marnes aren't wimps, but I feel like one.

Thanks baby brother.
Jason

P.S. Aunt Katie freaks out if unmarried people have sex. Somehow killing is a hell of lot worse.
P.P.S. This is a nightmare that I can't escape.
P.P.P.S. Jess, keep trying to save the world.
P.P.P.P.S. Ten months and three weeks, to go.

Peggy noticed that the bottom of the page was torn off so she couldn't read what Jess and Sean had written. She thumbed through the rest of the book and there were no replies at all, just Jason's e-mails. For a moment, she thought about asking Sean why but then decided not to. Not now when he was so vulnerable. Maybe never.

From: Jason (jason.doherty20120@hotmail.com)
To: sean.doherty20120@hotmail.com
CC: lawyer.to.be.jess@yahoo.com
Date: May 12, 2004
Subject: RE: I know this is a lot to ask

Dear Sean (and Jess),
God, yesterday I saw so many bodies rotting along the road. The smell. On TV bodies don't stink. I know they R the enemy, and if they had a chance they would shoot me in a second. There was this little girl maybe 3 with curly dark hair. Her big eyes just stared at me until I shut them. Jared mocked me. I just said, "Ya, well, who wants a dead Iraqi brat staring at u," and he left me alone. I sometimes feel as if I'm acting in a movie. I wsh someone would yell, 'cut.'

Peggy shuddered at the typos and misspellings, lowering the binder so that it lay open on her lap. Hadn't he learned anything at sister school after she had scrimped to pay his tuition? She scrunched her eyes shut. My God, she thought, I am thinking of spelling when he is talking about ... about ... murder.

The mother who lost her daughter? Better to think about typos than her son's part ... no, not just his part ... what he was facing while she, she was safe at home. She opened her eyes and picked up the binder. If her son had the strength to go through this horror, she must find the strength to understand it.

> Thanks also for keeping my e-mails from Mom. She doesn't need to know the bad stuff, but someone athome has gotta hear it. Itry and e-mail her every couple of days, but this bad shit builds up inside me and I got to let it out, so its why U guys get hit with it. Probably selfish of me, but Mom always called me a selfish brat.
>
> I wish I hadn't given her all those problems. I know she worried I would become a big time drug dealer, but I only peddled to my friends. She said one day I would wake up and realize what the world was like, but I neverthought it would be this bad.
>
> If reading my shit is too much let me know. I want to get some sleep before we go out again. AND DON'T MESS UP LIKE ME.
>
> And Jess, I know U R looking after Mom. Thanks.
>
> Love Jason
>
> P.S. Two more days and I'll have survived another month. Now if I can just make it the rest of the time.

Peggy shut her eyes to stop the tears, but her eyes burned, and she had to open then.

One of her co-workers used to say guilt is the gift that keeps on giving, teasing Peggy and Myron, their Jewish teller, that Protestants didn't do guilt like Jews and Catholics. "Jason," she said to his photo on the dresser, "if I'd only known, I wouldn't have let you join."

From: Jason (jason.doherty20120@hotmail.com)
To: sean.doherty20120@hotmail.com
CC: lawyer.to.be.jess@yahoo.com
Date: June 6, 2004
Subject: RE: I know this is a lot to ask

This is a definitly don't tell Mom, but Igot hit by a bullet. Just a scratch. Tore my shirt. Hurts tho. When we watch guys getting shot on TV they keep going. That is another lie in a long list of lies we were brought up with.

The medics fixed me up and I'll be back in action. Not even enough of a wound to qualify as a purple heart. Maybe a purple vein? Ha Ha!!!
YELBB (your ever lovin' big brother) and YELC (your ever lovin' cuz)

From: Jason (jason.doherty20120@hotmail.com)
To: sean.doherty20120@hotmail.com
CC: lawyer.to.be.jess@yahoo.com
Date: June 8, 2004
Subject: RE: Are U all right?

Hi there both of U
Yes, Im okay and I didn't mean to freak u out about the bullet. I know u r being good about not telling mom stuff cause she hasn't mentioned it. She couldn't not if she knew.
The difference between the Green Zone and the city is like day and night. Today I spent the day at the pool. At night we went on mission looking for the damned insurgents. Hell if Iraq did to Mission Hill what we did

to them, I'd be an insurgent and want to kill every damned one of them.

Imagine the worse slum inBoston. After the bombings a Baghdad neighborhood is rubble, yet I still see the people going aboutdoing their stuff Daily. I kinda gotta admire them.

Jason

From: Jason (jason.doherty20120@hotmail.com)
To: sean.doherty20120@hotmail.com
Date: July 4, 2004
Subject: I did it and it feels terrible

Hi Bro,
I can't send this to Jess, and please don't tell her. I answered my question. I can kill someone. I killed several someones. We were clearing out this street. They (ever wonder who all the <u>theys</u> are?) said there were terrorists hiding there.

The first house we went into, we got all the two men down on the floor. The looked old like Grampyonly skinnier.

Really scrawny. Paul had his feet on one of there necks. There was a daughter who spoke Englsih. She kept saying they didn't do anything against the Americans. They weren't terrorists. The wife and other daughter looked on. All that training to scare old men and women. Reminded me of another lesson from old Father Zach against bullying. I never thought I listened to that man but I keep seeing his face. It's a moral compass in an immoral world.

We heard a bang from the other room, and I came out shooting.

We shot everyone. I don't know which of my bullets killed them or which were Paul's. I just didn't want my buddies to get killed. I didn't want to die. When it was over we searched the house. We never found a gun. It looked like the woman in the kitchen dropped a metal pan, but I was so damned scared when I heard that bang that I just let my rifle rip.

Later on the day some men shot at us. Paul was driving. I shot
back and saw them fall and we took off. I put a bullet in someone and they stopped breathing. I broke the commandment. I went to confession. The priest said it was all right.
I wonder what their families think?
<u>I feel so fucked up, fucked over, fucked about.</u>

First time I used fuck Mom washed my mouth out with soap, not bar soap but Palmolive. Squirted it in. I kicked and screamed, but she held me down. A word is less harmful than a bullet.

Jason

Peggy remembered. Her mother had done it to her, and the Palmolive cure for dirty mouths seemed the right thing to do: nip bad behavior in the bud, Bridget used to tell her and Katie when their kids misbehaved, although she never criticized them directly.

Ma had a way about her that you knew when you were in the doghouse without her having to say anything. Katie called it Ma's icicle voice. Peggy thought of it as a love control button that would automatically shut off if you displeased her.

She drew the patchwork curtains against the cold night, but she knew more of the cold was inside her.

Once back in bed she picked up the binder. A page was stained. Sean wasn't supposed to eat in his room. If anything happened to him, I would rue the day I yelled at him for eating in his room, she thought, promising herself never to regret again what she did with her remaining child.

From: Jason (jason.doherty20120@hotmail.com)
To: sean.doherty20120@hotmail.com
CC: lawyer.to.be.jess@yahoo.com
Date: October 21, 2004
Subject:

Well Bro, don't worry what u write about. Exams and term papers are unimportant. I like hearing about it. I can pretend life is normal. All I need is Mom screaming to get off my lazy ass and do something. Think u could get her to make a cassette and send it to me? Ha ha.

We shouldn't be here. All the shit about being greeted with flowers was just that – so much shit. Im risking my life to bring democracy to people who want me to get the hell out ofhere and if I don't thy'll help me to go to hell.

Now that I've killed people, I m convinced I m going to hell on my own. We can't win hearts and minds whenwe can't speak the language and sure as hell don't understand their culture.

I met an Iraqui doc the other day. He spoke pretty good English. I'd taken a boy to the Iraqi hosptal. Ted and I were patroling this street, just the two of us. This kid, he couldnt have been more then five, threw a rock. Ted turned around and shot him in the leg. No one else was on the street. Ted and me looked at the kid. His son is about the same age, maybe a little older cause the kids haven't been eating well so they R real scrawny. I heard the government used to give food to everyone but we stopped that.

Ted said we couldn't leave him to bleed to death, so we drove him to the Iraqi hospital. The kid screamed bloody murder when the doctor took him. He studied in the US, Carbondale, Il of all places, the doc that is. He'd been to places in the States I haven't. How weird is that?? We started to leave, but he asked us to wait. We did, even though we shouldn't have been their at all. That bothers me. We r supposed help these people yet we shouldn't take a kid to a hospital? Does that make any sense to u? It doesn't to me.

Anyway, he comes back and tells us the kid is going to be okay. Asks us to have coffee. We do. Wants to know if we can get medicine. We can't. Says over 300,000 kids died during the embargo. I didn't know anything about an embargo.

Anyway, a woman comes up to him, another doc, his wife. She isn't v eiled. Lots of women aren't. Starts yelling at us. Says she didn't like Saddam but at least he controled the different groups. Says she's afraid if the new government is too Muslim she'll lose her job. He tells her to shut up. She didn't. She just switched to Arabic so I didn't understand, but I heard the tone and saw her face. She goes away.

He asks us questions we can't answer. He talks about a factory in his neighborhood that makes cable needed for wiring. Some American company says they can rebuild it for $1 mill. Several neighbors get it up and running using debris, but the Americans won't buy from them, and a tank takes it out. Why, he asks. He asks us why they have no water or electricity. I can'tanswer. My job is to ride up and down streets and kill people who might kill me first.

The Doc was a White Sox fan in the States. I tell him I am Red Sox. Nice guy. He doesn't believe the RedSox won the pennant. What the hell am I doing here?
Love,
Jason

From: Jason (jason.doherty20120@hotmail.com)
To: sean.doherty20120@hotmail.com
CC: lawyer.to.be.jess@yahoo.com
Date: October 23, 2004
Subject:

Hi there...
I got Mom's e-mail about still being outof work. I've asked more of my pay be sent home. What am I going tospend it on in this God forsaken country? God-forsaken, Allah-forsaken.

There's a tent canteen where we eat. There's a PX to buy stuff. This isn't the place to buy clothes. Where in hell would we wear them? We can't date local girls, although there's women soldiers. I don't want a girlfriend who can shoot better than me. I don't want a girlfriend who might get killed any minute.

I was eating one night, and I met a civilian contractor.

Theyre lucky cause every few weeks they get to leave. Says he's here because he's making tons of money. He goes on R&R every few weeks to Europe or Turkey or London or something.
He can quit. We guys have the same risks, r underpaid and can't leave. Some of them r real tough dudes, would sooner shoot u as say good morning. I was out the other day and a car stops an Arab to ask something, and my commanding officer who is with me starts firing. Before we know it everyone is dead. All old people. They didn't have any weapons. We just took them out.

I don't want to write any more about what I see on patrol. One of the guys got an IPod. He was killed. Someone stole the IPod. It wasn't with his things, but no one would dare be seen with it.

Congrats on yr report card.

U ask if I am voting. I sure am. I voted 4 the asshole Kerry over the asshole Bush (absente – if they bother to count it). Kerry voted 4 the war, but at least he knows what war is like. Most soldiers here r Republican, especially the Southern guys. They tell me Bush is a moral man. I ask 'em would a moral man send us here. They don't answer.
Yelbb,yelc

From: Jason (jason.doherty20120@hotmail.com)
To: sean.doherty20120@hotmail.com
CC: lawyer.to.be.jess@yahoo.com
Date: November 1, 2004
Subject: RE: Can I help

Dear Sean and Jess...
Ya Jess, I know U want to help, but u can't just keep being the caped crusader. I didn't mean to not copy u on the last e-mail but, I was tooooo tired to think right and I'm to tired tonight tooo. They shot a missile into our barracks. Jared was killed, Paul's leg was mashed. He'll go home now, but what a hell of way to go there. Both my bunk and Ted's were smithereens. If we hadn't had guard duty, we'd be dead. Ted is born-again and doesn't really like Catholics, except for me, but we both prayed, half to say thanks that it wasn't us dead and half for them.

Jason

From: Jason (jason.doherty20120@hotmail.com)
To: sean.doherty20120@hotmail.com
CC: lawyer.to.be.jess@yahoo.com
Date: December 7, 2004
Subject: I hope I make it

Dear Sean
As soon as my tour is up, I'm outta here. I hope I make it home alive and whole. Whats hard is the constant fear. U never know when someone is going to blow U up.

Another topic, Jess your work at the woman's shelter sounds great. At least one of us is doing something positive. If Iget out I'm going back to school, maybe become a teacher.

I was on patrol the other night when a lieutenant came up behind me. I almost shot him. We got to talking about this and that, what we're doing here. He says we're doing more damage than good. Although I've been thinking that for a long time, I don't want to believe it. He said we're damaging this country, we're damaging our souls.

When Iget out of here, if I get outta here, Ill only do stuff to help people, and even that won't make up for what I've done here.
Here's something to get mad about Jess. Some of the soldiers who'd been promised to have their student loans paid for have had letters saying the military won't cover them despite the guarantees when they signed up. Support our troops. Bull Shit.
Yelbb yelc

Until this point the letters were e-mail printouts. The next was a piece of paper with an envelope bearing German stamps and written with Jason's scrawl. Sister Mary Joseph deplored his hand writing. Peggy ran her hand over the paper, touching what he had touched as if the act would connect them.

Dear Bro,

I am asking one of the mercenaries to mail this. The bastards get paid a bloody fortune and get regular leave. He's heading for Stuttgart to spend some time with his girl friend. I don't know if the brass censors stuff, and if you've gotten everything I've e-mailed, but I don't want to take any chances. I haven't slept for days it seems.

We went on a mission and forced ourselves into a house where Some insurgents were supposed to live. There was a man, who kept babbling in Arabic. None of us understood what he was saying and when he reached into his robe, Steve, that's our sarge, went wild. He hit him with is riffle butt and the guy fell to the floor. Steve kept hitting him and hitting him. Pete kicked him in the balls. His wife started screaming and Pete beat her. She rolled into a ball. I couldn't see when she died because her eyes were shut. I couldn't move. I couldn't stop watching. I couldn't stop it. I was frozen.

"Search the fucking house, you pussy," someone yelled at me. Finally I moved. Just as I went back into the main room, the couple's teenage daughter came in and started screaming. (unreadable) Before I could say anything Steve shot her. Whenever I close my eyes I see death crawling from her eyes. I tell myself, I could have stopped it, but I didn't. I didn't. I will have to live with this the rest of my life. (unreadable) And it doesn't make me feel any better that this time we did find Weapons and something that might be used for bomb making. I have never felt so dirty in my life. I don't know how much more of this I can take. When I shave I see my face looking back, but underneath there is some kind of monster that is killing and maiming. If U ever even think about coming over here, I will kill you myself with my bare hands.

Although there were two more pages, Peggy couldn't read any more. If Bush walked into her bedroom at that instant, she would have been able to kill him with her bare hands. Never in her life did she remember being so angry.

CHAPTER 23

As Peggy walked to her desk, she peeked in the cubbies surrounded by the grey, grey half walls. Everyone's head was bowed over. No one looked up. No one said hello, good morning or you look like hell.

Although personal calls were not allowed, as soon as she sat at her desk, left with its perfectly ordered top, according to regulation, she dialed Halligan's. The funeral home at the bottom of The Hill had served half Mission Hill's Irish for generations. O'Malley's served the other. Both looked like ordinary one-family houses and were across from Mission Hill Church. Family tradition, not service or pricing, dictated who went where. The Flanagan family was waked at Halligan's.

"I'm so sorry," Ed Halligan said. He and Peggy had gone to the Mission Hill Parochial Grade School and were almost always on the same side for kick ball. If one were the captain, they always chose the other. Even after school, especially in the spring, they would play baseball although Peggy always hated that only boys could join Little League. Ed said it was a shame too. When they went to separate high schools, they stopped playing together. Maybe because Peggy outgrew her tomboy ways; maybe it was just the natural evolution of kids drifting apart as they grow up.

Jess had been a great pal to one of Ed's sons who went to Boston Latin with her, but that also was usual on The Hill. Second and third generations repeated the friendships of their parents, grandparents and sometimes their great grandparents.

"Ed, I don't want to hear one word about his giving his life for his country." She tried not to sound rude.

"I understand more than you know."

She doubted it. His kids were alive. Although her back was to the opening of her cubby, she felt someone standing behind her chair and she swung around. Her boss dropped six folders into her in basket. He frowned. She turned her back. He tapped her on the shoulder and twirled his hand as if to say, "wind it up."

"Bill called me earlier. He and I've arranged that I'll be notified when Jason arrives at Logan. You can go with us, and we can have a military salute there if you want …"

"No." She said it so loudly that two cubicles away a woman co-worker stood up to look over the wall. "No," Peggy said more softly. "I just want you to get him. Alone. No military. None. Nada."

"He won't be flying alone. The military sends a Marine with him."

Bill and Jess had already explained the procedures to her. Several images flashed through Peggy's mind: Jason's coffin in the aisle of a plane with a Marine sitting in a chair and the stewardesses handing coffee over the coffin. Then she imagined the Marine sitting next to her son's casket in the hold of the plane. The coffin had no American flag on it.

Peggy's boss tapped her on the shoulder again. Again, she swiveled and noticed he had every hair in place; his trousers were creased to a point that they might cut skin if he were to kneel on them. She wished he would.

Keeping her eye on his scowl she said, "Ed, when my son's body arrives, I don't want any Marine near it. If there is one traveling with him, tell him to go home. Just call me when you have him safe with you." She put the receiver down.

"Jonathan," she said, "I know there's a rule against private calls. There should be a rule against your kids dying and having to arrange their funerals during worktime."

A rose color infused his face as he went back to his office without saying anything.

Peggy picked up a loan folder and forced herself to look at it.

CHAPTER 24

Bill stood on the porch of the triple decker with his keys in hand. Sooty piles of snow still blocked much of the street. Parked cars were jammed in between banks higher than the average adult.

"We'll be late," he called upstairs.

The truck's engine was humming. Bill hoisted himself behind the wheel. Unlike when he waited for Katie in the morning, he didn't drum his fingers on the steering wheel.

Peggy picked her way around the tunnels between snow banks to reach the passenger side. Her straight skirt was too tight to climb in. She pulled it up, revealing more thigh than she liked to show.

As Bill started to pull out, Sean walked up the center of the street. The sidewalks weren't shoveled. Bill stopped and rolled down his window.

"Where ya going?" Sean shifted the Stop&Shop bag from his right to left hand.

"Halligan's." Peggy leaned toward the steering wheel so her son could see her.

"I'm coming."

"There's really no need." She wanted to inoculate him against more pain the same way she made sure he had shots against measles and mumps. She couldn't, any more than she could have kept her other son alive.

"He's my ..." He kicked at a clump of snow. "... was my brother."

"Get in," Bill said.

Peggy opened her mouth then shut it. If Sean wanted to deal with the details, she had no right to deny him.

No empty spaces existed in front of the funeral home along Tremont Street, although the snow piles had been funneled onto trucks to be dumped in Boston Harbor. Bill let Peggy and Sean out and went to park at the Post Office two blocks away. Mother and son waited for him before ringing the bell.

Ed Halligan, the third generation of Halligan's to operate the home, answered. After a hug for Peggy and a handshake for the men, he led them to his office. Dark green velvet drapes covered a window beside an oak bookcase. Instead of books, framed photos of caskets lined the shelves. Four green leather chairs circled a fireplace with wood stacked on a hearth. From the cleanliness of the stone, it looked as if it had never been lit. "Peggy, Bill, Sean, let me say again, I'm so sorry, so very sorry."

Sean sniffed several times. He had no cold. Had he been a girl the tears dripping down his nasal passages would have escaped his eyes. Peggy fought the temptation to touch him, thinking it better to let him hurt without scrutiny until he regained control.

"Tell me what you want," Ed said.

Peggy resisted saying, I want my son alive. "Have you seen him?"

"Yes. With a little work we can offer an open casket."

Her baby was home, almost home, down the street from home, where he should be sitting at the kitchen table complaining about Peggy's cooking. "When can I see him?"

"Now if you want, but I recommend waiting."

Without looking at her, Bill reached for one hand and Sean for the other. No ballet could have been better synchronized.

"I know you didn't want the military around, but he is entitled to the full military ..."

"And that includes ..."

"A flag-draped casket, the Marines there, the flag folding, 'Taps.'"

"I want the flag folded. And 'Taps' played. One bugler."

"You can't. Not after you read ..." Sean started to say.

"We'll do what your mother wants," Bill said.

"But J-Jason ..." Sean said.

"Jason was proud of being a Marine," Bill said.

He clenched his fist. "Moooo-ooom, you read what he wrote."

Peggy knew with every eon of her body that she must have at least the last part of a military funeral, but not for the reason Sean thought. "Trust me." This time she put her hand on Sean's arm but not as comfort as she turned to Ed. "Who do I contact?"

Gone was the easy smile Peggy saw whenever she met him and his wife for coffee after Mass. Ed's lips stayed locked in a serious position. "Peggy, we take care of all those details. It'll take about twenty-four hours to arrange. There's usually a recording for 'Taps.' They sometimes send a bugler, but they're short of them these days. You can have a caisson pulling the casket." He looked at his hands. "Where Jason died because of a military action, we can ask ..."

"I don't believe this!" Sean stood up so fast his chair fell over. He fled the room.

Bill rose to go after him. Peggy stopped him. "I'll take care of it. Later."

Ed hesitated as if making sure the drama was over. "What do you want?"

"I want the flag on the coffin, but only at the burial, not the wake, not the Mass."

Bill frowned the way he did whenever he didn't understand what was happening.

"I just want the flag folded and given to me. No cannons, no guns fired. And I want the Marines only at the cemetery." She squeezed Bill's hand. I should be wearing the Trust-me-I'm-a-mother t-shirt that Sean gave me years ago, she thought.

Bill and Ed looked at each other before Ed continued. "About burial clothes ..."

"No uniform." Could she find something that fit? During basic training, he'd filled out. No suits. He hated suits. Jeans? And the new Irish knit sweater she gave him. He'd left it saying Iraq was hot. He'd always looked good in beige.

105

"I'll bring his clothes down when you decide," Bill said. "Do we need to pick out a coffin?"

"The military provided him with a steel one made by Batesville Casket Company. They're in Indiana."

Peggy didn't give a damn where they were made.

Ed looked at them. "Of course, you can buy one, but I would feel guilty selling you one, when you've a perfectly usable coffin. I know you've been out of work ..."

"We'll take what he came with," she said.

"He would be eligible for Arlington ..." Ed said.

"No!" The force came out like a slap. Peggy refused to have her son spend eternity with a military that had killed him.

"B-but you want a military ceremony," Bill stammered. Her look stopped him.

"I know what I want," she said. "My folks have a plot in Forest Lawn."

"We'll need plot numbers," Ed said.

"I'll bring them with the clothes," Bill said.

"There's a death benefit,' Ed said, 'I suppose the military has ..."

"The military sent me a letter of regret. A fucking letter of regret." She ignored the exchanged glances of the two men. "I won't take their Goddamned blood money." She had also rejected any other help from the Marines.

Bill turned to his sister-in-law.

Ed's posture said he wasn't getting involved in this family discussion.

"I'll pay whatever bills there are, Pegs. It's my last gift to Jason to make up for all the times I yelled at him." He smiled the impish smile she'd known for years, the one Katie claimed was the real reason she'd married him.

"But ..." said Peggy.

"You're good at giving, dear sister-in-law, but you're rotten at taking. Now shut up."

"As soon as we have the clearance on a date with the Marines, I'll call," Ed said. "Will Father Leary do the Mass?"

"Desmond is flying in from Rome," Bill said.

"I haven't seen him for an age. How's he doing? And Connor too?" Ed asked.

"Well. Connor's family is well. My parents are well. Everyone is well except Jason." With each sentence Peggy's voice rose. For a second, she felt she couldn't breathe. She wanted to slam out the same way Sean had. She still had to deal with him. He'd been too small to remember when his father died. This was his first real loss, and it shouldn't be someone of his generation. It shouldn't be his brother. Shouldn'ts sucked as much as the thousands of shoulds. Both sapped her energy.

The manners drilled into her by her parents overcame her outburst. Poor Ed, even if he must be used to people exploding with grief.

"And if the press shows up? It sometimes happens in these high-profile cases." Ed's tone was the same as if he mentioned the weather.

"I want the press there, and my son wasn't a case." Peggy bit each word.

Ed patted her hand before she could pull it away. "I'm sorry I phrased it that way."

As if someone hit her in the stomach, she realized there was something she didn't know and although she didn't really want to ask, the words fell from her mouth before she could stop him. "What killed him?"

"There were lots of wounds, Peg. By the bruising I would guess shrapnel, but I saw bullet holes, too. I don't know which came first. His face is intact."

Peggy removed Bill's arm from her back. "Are they still in my son?"

"That is macabre," Bill's voice carried his shock.

"I want to know it wasn't an American bullet." She'd heard of deaths by friendly fire. She'd read of uranium-depleted bullets from Jess's raging about them. She was afraid her son would glow underground. "I don't suppose you've a radioactivity detector?"

Ed looked at Bill. Bill shrugged.

"I saw that look. I'm not crazy."

"But you're upset," Bill said.

"And that is natural," Ed said. "My suggestion is go home. Get some rest."

"I'm supposed to go to the office but screw them."

CHAPTER 25

The doors to arrivals for Terminal E at Logan Airport opened and closed, opened and closed. A few people trickled out, some hidden by baggage carts laden with luggage. Others slung single bags over their shoulders. Some were greeted by hugs and others by people with signs bearing names: Chin, O'Reilly, Wilson, Gillette, Federated Stores.

There won't be too many more Gillette signs, Bridget thought, since they've been sold and probably would be moved to another city. What would happen to one of her customers who worked there, a woman who talked career, career, career whenever she ordered a suit?

Several planes had landed, not just from Rome, but also from Frankfurt, Paris and Dublin, places that she had never seen or would see. She stood on tiptoe to see over the man in front of her each time the door opened in hopes of glimpsing her son.

Then he was there, with only slightly greyer hair than when she'd hugged him goodbye in this same terminal. He carried one travel bag and gripped his passport in his hand.

She waved frantically.

His eyes crinkled when he spied her. Without upsetting the woman pushing a cart with luggage piled over her head and carrying a mewling cat in a cage in her hand, he rushed to his mother. He dropped his travel bag, picked her up and whirled her around.

"You're looking good," he said after he put her back down, "and still a light weight."

"A girl has to keep her figure. You, on the other hand look tired."

"I worked late last night trying to clear everything up before I caught a seven a.m. flight. You know how early you have to get up to catch a seven a.m. flight?"

"Peggy will appreciate it."

A frown crept into his face. "How's she doing?"

"Better than I would have thought. Your father, Sean, they're suffering more. I don't mean she doesn't care, she just seems to have it under control, although the first few days she was a zombie." Bridget wanted to say more, but she didn't know how to describe her daughter's mood: angry, driven, pained. All and none worked.

Desmond shoved his passport inside his breast jacket pocket. With his free hand he put his arm around Bridget's shoulders. She encircled his waist.

"Once I thought Jason might die from street violence. I didn't expect to do a hero's funeral Mass," he said.

In the parking lot Bridget located the car and opened the door with a key.

"I didn't know you had a car."

"I don't. It's Bill's."

As they drove through the tunnel, Desmond gaped. "Where's the Central Artery?"

"Gone underground."

"They'd started the Big Dig before I left, but it's weird seeing the Artery gone."

As she angled onto Storrow Drive, he pointed to the Hatch Shell. "Remember our Fourth of July picnics? We'd spend the whole day to make sure we got a good spot for the Boston Pops and fireworks."

"And I remember worrying we would go home with only three kids instead of four. And the next day you'd all be sunburned."

"All the cars seem so big. They couldn't get down the old Roman streets."

She wished she didn't have to concentrate on traffic of any size.

Later she could stare at her son, drink in his presence. "Tell me about the Vatican."

"Still there."

"Go on with you. Is the Pope as ill as they say?"

"He can't last much longer. Ma, it's unbelievable working there. My office has a Titian, and the corridor outside has two Raphaëls."

Bridget wasn't sure what they were, but she nodded.

"And yet my office is wi-fied."

Bridget, who only dipped into anything computer based, was startled to think that a church dating back centuries could be so up to date with technology. As for herself, she answered an e-mail from Jason on Peggy's computer. She tapped the words using two fingers, searching for each key. She always started out with "This is your grandmother ..." and ended with "I'm turning you back to your mother."

"Half of it is modern technology, but it's like being in a museum or a time machine sending me back to the Middle Ages. Imagine Ma. Boston was settled almost four hundred years ago, but the Vatican goes back to the Romans."

Bridget couldn't. Again, she regretted that she never traveled. Patrick didn't want to, but she loved watching the travel documentaries and imagining herself standing on the Great Wall of China, sheltering her eyes against the sun while staring at the Pyramids and kissing the Blarney Stone. Now Ireland, that's a place she really wanted to see. Funny how her friends would say they were Irish when they'd been born in the States and had never left the country. Even the Old Goat said he was Irish, despite being so proud of his American nationality. Maybe after Patrick ... no, she didn't want to think about any more death.

CHAPTER 26

When Peggy arrived home, Sean had written a message on the white board in the kitchen saying he was going out. He didn't say where and when he would be back as the house rules dictated. She had to let him handle this his own way. She curled up on the couch and pulled an afghan up to her neck. She would have loved a cup of tea, but making it took too much effort.

She couldn't move, not even to put on the light as the sun set. She trembled, not from cold but from an anger so huge that she felt she might explode, splattering body parts all over the room. The dark night matched the dark in her heart.

When Desmond and her mother switched the light on, Peggy screamed.

"Why are you sitting here in the dark?" Bridget asked.

"Thinking." She kissed Desmond's cheek. He was never one to accept hugs.

"Peggy, I am so ..."

"Don't say it. I've heard sorry enough for several lifetimes."

"Let me pray with you?"

"Always the priest. Prayer isn't what I need." What she needed was to stop the insanity that killed her son. She would try to get it, but prayer was too damned slow.

"It is, if you let it," he said.

"I'll put the kettle on," Bridget said.

"Tea, the Irish-American solution to every problem." His remark broke the tension.

When her brother and mother left, she drifted into the safer past. In seventh grade science she didn't care what rock was what or which weather symbol stood for what condition. It was her only flunking grade. As her father held her report card she flounced out of the room. He followed. She expected a slap. Patrick didn't take kindly to rebellious children. Instead he sat beside her. "A Flanagan never gives up. Never."

When her husband hit her, she hit back. When he died, she returned to school while keeping a job and raising the boys. When Jason cut classes and the school called to tell her, she asked her boss for a break and why. Her boss, who had a troublesome son, agreed. Peggy had searched the streets until she found him and dragged him back to school. When he'd broken windows, she insisted he fess up then work off the debt.

What a battle that was. Battle was what her old life had been. She fought for her degree, fought to put food on the table, even with her parents as a backup. Pride kept her from asking. "Shit!" The word exploded in the empty kitchen. "When have problems ever stopped me?"

CHAPTER 27

When Jess came home from the woman's shelter, she planned to study. No matter that she was exhausted. Her day had begun at 7:00 a.m. when the alarm stuck its tongue out at her and didn't stop till she entered her parents' home at 10:36 p.m.

This was a double shift because two of the workers were home with the flu. The manager had called the night before and begged between statements of sympathy and apologies.

Although Amy was taking notes for the classes Jess would miss because of Jason's death, she wanted to keep catch-up to a minimum. She studied through lunch and on her T ride to and from the shelter.

Unlike some shelter shifts when everything was quiet, there had been no time to study. Four women had shown up with their children. There had not been enough beds: six telephone calls later, she found places for them all.

One of the children staying there had vomited in the hall and the mother had the flu and was too weak to clean up, leaving Jess to do it. Good thing she had a strong stomach. The volunteer doctor was unavailable during the day, but arrived after dinner, some five hours after he'd been called. As much as Jess wanted to yell at him, she knew he was a volunteer, an idealist such as herself who gave up billable hours to serve these women.

She'd helped two women draw up restraining orders and failed to talk a third through a decision not to go home to her abusive husband, resisting the desire to shake her for being so stupid. Okay, she knew that she had to work on empathy. Although, she thought she would know how she would react in the same situation, maybe if she had all the same parameters, she might just react as that woman had, not as Jessica Kelly.

But God, if you keep doing the same thing, you get the same results.

Jess knew she would never make a non-directive counselor. It was a good thing that wasn't her goal.

Her parents looked up as she entered. Her father's L.L. Bean fuzzy-lined slippers were on the hassock next to his feet. Her mother wore her red bathrobe. Kirstie Alley was on television.

"I left some corn chowder," her mother said. "And applesauce."

"Thanks." Jess realized that her mother was examining the circles under her eyes but pretending not to.

"I'll serve it up." Before Katie headed for the kitchen, she added, "Aidan called: said you could catch him at *The Globe*."

Jess wondered if he would call. A lot of guys said they would then didn't, which never bothered her. She'd already lost her virginity while at Boston University to a teaching instructor. He almost had a heart attack when he discovered she was a student where he taught. Probably visions of sexual harassment charges danced in his head. They'd met at a Bob Franke performance at the Harvard Square Unitarian Church coffee house.

To Jess it was a chance to get rid of her hymen, despite Katie drumming into her that marriage came first. Katie didn't know about Jess's soiled status, and Jess had no plans to enlighten her mother.

Jess's reaction to her single experiment into sex was – is that it? She preferred being pals with guys. With her schedule, dating would be another chore, yet something about Aidan nibbled her interest. She wandered into her room to call.

"Aidan Pelletier, how can I help you?"

His voice made her smile. Complication alert! Complication alert! She had no time, but … "Jess Kelly, and don't you sound professional."

"If someone is calling with a tip, I want to sound open. If it's a pretty law student, I want to help her to a nice dinner when we both have a free moment."

"If that's the criteria, maybe December 15th two years from now."

"Smart ass."

"Not just my ass is smart, my knee, nose, eyebrows …"

"I'm off this weekend."

"My cousin's funeral is Friday. Saturday might have some merit."

"Dinner isn't related to this, but I want to come to the funeral."

"Are you using me to get a story?"

"Yes and no. I want the story and dinner."

At least he was honest. "Any place in mind? For dinner?"

"Grendel's Den? Maybe wander in and see whoever is playing at the Regatta afterwards."

Jess never had time to do stuff like that. A knock at the door interrupted. She covered the phone with her hand.

Katie entered with a tray. "Ginger ale okay?"

"Perfect."

"And when you're through, go see your aunt. And oh yes, your Uncle Desmond got in, but I imagine he's asleep by now." Katie closed the door.

"Grendel's Den and the Regatta will be great. And I'll ask my aunt about the funeral."

* * * * *

Peggy's apartment was dark when Jess opened the door. The hall light illuminated the corridor in the center of the apartment. A light sliver crept from under Peggy's bedroom door. She didn't want to knock in case her aunt was asleep so she peeked through the crack.

Peggy sat on the bed, her head resting on her knees that were drawn up to her chin. She looked up to see her niece. "I didn't hear you." She patted the bed.

Jess sat facing her aunt. They often sat like this while Jess confided information she couldn't share with her mother. Peggy, unlike Katie, never expressed shock, no matter what Jess said, including the loss-of-virginity confession.

Peggy was Jess's lightning rod, deflecting problems with Katie as Jess deflected Jason's actions with Peggy. The image of a woven basket flashed through Jess's mind. The Flanagans were interwoven straw, each strengthening the other.

Jess waited for her aunt to speak. When several minutes passed in silence she said, "Aidan, that reporter from *The Globe*, wants to attend Jason's funeral."

Peggy pulled both arms downward with her fists clinched and said, "Yes!" the same way Sean and his friends did. "Ask him what we have to do to get maximum coverage. I want Jason's funeral to make news in every state in the country, and when I am through, I want to end this war. Will you help?"

"What do you think?" Jess wasn't sure what Peggy meant, but it didn't matter. Even after Peggy explained what she wanted, it didn't matter. She was on board.

CHAPTER 28

Peggy's boss tapped his Bulgari pen on the desktop as Peggy entered his office. She already had on her hat and coat. "You're not working this afternoon?"

"I thought I would wake my son instead. Just for a lark." Since she wasn't invited to sit, she stood. Papers and his laptop case covered the spare chair.

He leaned forward in his chair. "It's too bad for you to have to go through this during your probation period. Black marks and all."

Peggy didn't see black, but red. She fought to control her voice. "Black marks?"

"Absenteeism. Now, you've used four of your ten …"

She'd heard it before. "Three and a half after today."

"You'll take the whole day for the funeral?" Dumb question, she thought. "If you pass your probation period, you won't have much time off for another year."

Hell! She was old enough to be this brat's mother. She emptied the chair, placing the papers and case on the floor, and sat. "I had a year off while I was job hunting. I didn't ask an Iraqi to kill my son to avoid working."

"I didn't mean that. I mean, I am sorry, but the … well it isn't the bank's fault."

"It sounded that you think I arranged this just so I could have some time off."

He pressed on. "Two other things I want to discuss. One is the training next week. I wanted to make sure you still plan to attend."

"I am."

He ran his hand through his blond hair. "The other is this loan." He passed her a folder. "You turned him down."

"He wanted an SUV." She flipped through the pages. "I must have checked the wrong box. It was less than forty-eight hours after I learned my son died."

"Probably," he said. "Work can help us forget our personal problems if we throw ourselves into it. Therapy, so to speak."

"So to speak," she said.

"I'll excuse this little lapse considering all you've gone through." He picked up a folder from his in-tray.

Peggy thought about putting his laptop case and papers back on the chair but decided to let him do it. As she walked to the elevators she thought, like hell did I make a mistake with that loan. She suspected her employment with the bank would not endure a long time and although that should worry her, staying in this inhuman place worried her more.

CHAPTER 29

Peggy rushed upstairs to her apartment without taking off her coat. She tossed it on her bed and started rifling through her closet. On the T ride home, she failed to make up her mind what to wear. She had a plain black dress for the funeral tomorrow. She owned a navy-blue suit. What bank officer didn't?

Jason liked gay colors. At 11 he painted one wall of his room fire-engine red. Her red suit would shock the neighbors. "What will the neighbors say?" became the Flanagan's mantra and was as much of a deterrent to bad behavior as the fear of hell.

In the end, she chose the blue suit, blue stockings and blue flats, not to quiet neighborly mouths, but because her red heels pinched her feet. She would be standing too long to opt for even moderate heels. As a young girl, she would have suffered: as a mature woman, comfort won every time.

Her parents were still getting ready. Sean would be home shortly to change. Jamie and Jess were going directly to the funeral home from their schools. Rachel and Connor were coming this evening, because of a fund-raising lunch. She wished Connor could have put her before politics. Rachel had told her they'd fought about it in the apology call.

As she let herself out of the house Bill's truck pulled up with Katie in the passenger seat.

"If you wait until we change, I can give you a ride," Bill called out the window.

"I'd rather walk. I need the air," she said.

Katie glanced at her watch. "You're early."

"I want to see him."

"I'll go with you." Katie opened the door.

"I need a few minutes alone with him before people come."

* * * * *

The smell of flowers battered Peggy as she walked into Halligan's. An easel with a ribbed black velvet board and gold border spelling Jason's name in gold letters pushed into the ribs stood outside one of three visiting rooms. Below the name were two crossed American flags. Peggy started to pull out the flags, but they were anchored too well to respond to her shaking hands.

"Can I help?"

She jumped at Ed's voice. "Get them off." Peggy knew she sounded hysterical, but she couldn't control it. If she were having problems now, she worried how she would be able to get through today and tomorrow, especially tomorrow? She glanced over his shoulder into the room, which was bathed in a half light, and saw the coffin for the first time. The American flag was over the bottom half and an American flag, a Massachusetts flag and the Marine emblem were standing behind the platform where the coffin rested. She began to shake. "Get those flags out of that room."

"The Marine must have ..." Ed said.

Peggy pronounced each syllable separately and distinctly. "I asked for 'Taps' and for the Marines to fold the flag and present it to me. Nothing more. Get those off of him! Now!" She tried not to scream.

Then from the shadows there was a movement and a Marine stood.

"What are you doing here?" Before he could respond she went on, "I do not want to see another uniform until we are at the grave tomorrow."

The blond, blue-eyed Marine could not have been 30. He looked as if he grew up on milk and love. He rotated his hat in his hands. "Ma'am, I want to offer my condo ..."

121

"Get out of here! Now!"

He kept rotating his hat, opened his mouth but said nothing.

"Please." She heard the begging tone of her voice. What she wanted to do was beat on his chest for the sin of being alive. Her more rational mind told her that this had to be awful for him too, but she didn't care. He'd enlisted. He was part of it. Instead, she put her hand on the sleeve of his dress blues: "Please."

Ed started to touch her. His hand dropped when she wrenched away. He used his head to point toward the door. The Marine double-timed out of the room. A blast of cold air came into the hall as the front door opened to the street.

"I'll make the changes," Ed said.

"Thanks. I'll wait in your office until it is done. Then please come get me."

Within five minutes, Ed stuck his head into his office. "We're still redoing the sign, but you can go to Jason now."

"Thanks." On her way past Ed, she put her hand on his arm. "I really mean it. Thanks."

He put her hand in the crux of his arm and led her to the room. "If you need me, I'll be in my office." The double doors of the visiting room made a soft click as Ed shut them, leaving her alone with her first born.

Jason's head was visible in his casket resting on the platform. The hope, no matter how unreasonable that another boy was in the coffin, that the Marines made a mistake, died too.

Flowers surrounded the casket. Three wreaths had white banners with gold letters: From your loving Grandparents, From your Aunts and Uncles and From your Cousins. Neither she nor Sean had ordered flowers. She trembled: the thought of ordering flowers had never entered her mind. Funny she hadn't heard anyone discuss it. She wished she had asked that in lieu of flowers for people to contribute to an anti-war organization or to one of the few U.S. Senators that had the balls to vote against it.

She read the cards. Arrangements came from her old office mates, from Sister Benedict at St. Mary's, Jason's elementary school, from

Jess's friends at Latin and another from those at Suffolk Law. Nothing from her bank.

Twenty chairs were placed auditorium-style in four rows of five on the left. On the right, chairs were in groups for people to sit and talk.

She mounted the two steps to the platform where the casket rested. She grabbed one of the icy metal handles as the room swirled. She'd forgotten to breathe: she inhaled in gulps.

Jason looked older. She would deck the first person who said he looked as if he were sleeping. He looked dead even though the make-up was well done. The Irish knit sweater hid the wounds in his neck and chest. His hands were folded around the rosary that Desmond had sent their mother. Although no one could see it, his jeans were held up by a favorite leather belt that Jess carved for him one Christmas when she was in an artsy phase.

She knelt and took out her rosary. "Hail Mary, full of grace, blessed art thou among women." Mary knew what it was like to lose a son, only hers rose again.

CHAPTER 30

The people came in a blur with the same mutterings over and over. They were non-working neighbors, school teachers and the cousins' classmates. Tonight, would be the people who held nine-to-five jobs. When the last afternoon guest left, Bill pushed Peggy into a chair. He insisted his father-in-law sit with her and not let her get up.

Desmond sat next to his father as Connor and Rachel walked in with Ashley, who limped across the room and threw her arms around Peggy. As she hugged her aunt, she made short glances toward the casket.

"Would you like me to lead a prayer?" Desmond asked.

Peggy nodded. "Ask for strength and courage for what I must do."

Desmond clasped his hands. "Let us pray: in the name of Father, the Son and the Holy Ghost." The family crossed themselves.

As they left the funeral home, Bridget, the Patron Saint of Never Waste a Morsel of Food, said, "I know we've enough food to feed an army, but I don't want to go home. Let's go to Flann's?"

Patrick used his finger to tote up the number going. "We're too many. Especially because there's a Celtics game on later."

"The Penguin?"

The family picked their way over icy patches on Tremont Street. Rachel and Connor flanked Ashley, ready to catch her if she slipped but letting her make her own way. Bill and Jess did the same with

Patrick who eye-balled them as he let his cane absorb the weight of his game leg.

They crossed Huntington. The old Peter Bent Brigham building, now part of Brigham & Women's Hospital, was lit, its pillars bright against its brick surface. Across the street other triple deckers painted in reds, blues and greens glowed under street lamps.

The Penguin was a long restaurant with the bar to the left of the entry. Jess asked for a table where they wouldn't be disturbed.

"No problem," said the waitress. She could have been a poster child for *River Dance,* with her long red wavy hair, green eyes and freckles. They followed her to the back and she pushed several tables together.

"And where would ye be from?" Patrick asked, his own brogue coming out.

"Killarney."

"And so would I, but long before your parents were a gleam in your grandparents' eyes."

"Do you ever get back there?" she asked.

"Not once."

"I'm moving back next week, but tonight I'll give a fellow countryman even better service than usual," the girl said.

"Now why would that be, girl?" Patrick asked.

"The good service?"

"No, moving back?"

"Health insurance and a better salary. I've had fun here though."

"I'd love to see Ireland someday," Bridget said.

"It's a beautiful and friendly place," the waitress said.

"But I remember only the poverty." Patrick mumbled it.

"You wouldn't recognize it today, then. What would you like?"

Patrick ran his finger down the pizza listing. "Pumpkin and leek pizza? What kind of cockamamie place is this?"

"It's good Gramps, but they have more normal stuff." Sean pointed to normal pizzas and pastas.

"Pasta. Stupid word for spaghetti. People should say what they mean instead of fancy-schmancy words," Bridget said.

"You tell 'em," Patrick said.

"Ma, you're getting as crotchety as Da," Katie said.

The talk evolved into who came during the afternoon and who might come tonight.

"I remember when we did funerals at home. Packed the corpse in ice so he or she wouldn't stink too much," Patrick said.

"But ice melts, especially in summer," Jamie said.

"Trust my cousin to come up with details," Jess said.

Jamie stuck her tongue out.

Jess made a face back.

"Enough," Bill said.

Jess's phone rang. She answered then held the phone out to Peggy. "Aidan for you."

The two women went to the alcove near the toilets to talk.

"How are you holding up?" Aidan asked.

"I'll survive," Peggy said. "Is everything arranged for tomorrow?"

"Just like you and Jess asked. I've talked to people at Channels five, four and seven and the Fox rep. Also, at *The Herald*."

"So, the burial will have coverage. Did you stress the burial?"

"I did. But there'll probably be media at the church as well."

When Peggy returned the phone to Jess, she noticed her niece's face. "Ask him to come over and eat with us," she mouthed.

Jess clicked her phone closed and dropped it in her pocket. "He's working. But another time would be great when things calm down."

If they calm down, Peggy thought.

CHAPTER 31

The first limousine held Peggy, her parents, Sean, Desmond and Jess. Katie, Bill, Connor, Rachel, Ashley and Jamie were in the second. Friends, neighbors and the press followed. The cars, their headlights lit, crawled through the cemetery gates.

The snow storms that battered Boston repeatedly hid the gravestones. The cemetery looked like an open white field dotted with rocks, but the rocks were the top of the grave markers. At least today the skies decided to hold their snow, but the rippled grey sky made everything bleak.

"Is everything ready?" Peggy whispered to Jess as the car stopped. Her hands shook until the girl covered them with hers.

"My friends arranged everything." Jess looked closely at Peggy. "Don't chicken out."

Ed got out of the hearse. He tapped on the window, which Patrick lowered. "Wait here until we get the coffin in place, please."

"How'll we know?" Patrick asked. His hand trembled. He was breathing heavily.

"I'll come for you," Ed said.

Patrick pushed the button to raise the window.

"The Mass was beautiful," Bridget said.

"Thank you, Desmond. How much longer can you stay?" Peggy asked.

"I need to be back by Monday."

No one said anything else until Ed reappeared.

Sean held his mother's hand as she led the procession. She, like everyone else, had changed into boots. A wide path to the gravesite had been shoveled. Desmond walked with his mother, while Connor guided his father. Bill and Katie followed.

"Damned ghouls." Bill pointed to the newsmen with their cameras, milling around. They were dressed in jeans except for the anchors. One person combed the hair of a man holding a microphone.

"I'll get rid of them," Connor said.

Peggy grabbed his arm. "I want them here."

"This should be private," Patrick snapped.

"*I said I want them here.*" Peggy spoke through clenched teeth as she saw the casket, now with the flag covering it, resting next to a gaping hole. Ed had told her that special equipment dug through the frozen ground.

Two Marines, a rank higher than Jason, stood at attention at either end of the casket. She looked at their faces and wondered what horrors they'd seen. How like babies they looked. Had they killed someone else's son? Would one day their parents be standing over their coffins? "God give me strength," she prayed silently.

Jess moved her head slightly. Peggy followed her eyes to where a group of Jess's friends stood. The news people faced them. Two cameramen balanced their cameras on their shoulders. Jess stationed herself in such a way that the news people would have to knock her down to leave.

"I smell gas," Sean whispered to his mother.

Peggy's knuckles were white from clutching her handbag. She handed it to Sean to keep her hands free. Out of the corner of her eye, she saw one camera man begin to leave. Jess stopped him.

Her brother finished praying over the casket, but she didn't listen. The final notes of 'Taps' brought her back from the place her mind had hidden to survive. Her heart raced as she watched each of the Marines drop their hands to their sides after their salutes to the casket.

The Marines marched to the casket, one on each end. In perfect synchronization they picked up the corners of the flag and moved four steps to left. The first and second folds of the flag were vertical. Than the Marine holding the stripes end folded the fabric so there was a triangle. He repeated it 11 times until only white stars on the blue field were visible. The Marine, the same one Peggy had thrown out of the funeral home yesterday, who held the star end took a sharp right and walked slowly towards Peggy.

"On behalf of a grateful nation ..." he began.

When she glared into his eyes, he faltered and looked away.

"On behalf of a grateful nation, Mrs. Doherty ..." again the glare stopped him.

"I ... want to present this flag ... in recognition of the sacri ..."

"This isn't your fault," she whispered as she grabbed the flag. The cloth was rough. When it flew, it looked so silky dancing in the air. Once when she looked at it, she felt proud. Now it inspired fear and a sadness that went so deep she couldn't describe it.

She inhaled, filling her lungs. "And I accept this flag from the nation that killed my son for nothing." Oh, how she hoped the news people heard her.

The Marine's face crumpled.

Without saying another word, she turned and marched towards Jess's friends who waited apart from the others. They all held lighted candles. She heard her niece admonish the newsmen, "Don't stop filming."

She wanted to vomit, but if her son could fulfill a commitment that he no longer believed in only because he had made that commitment, she had the courage to do what she could to stop the war.

"Where are you going?" Katie asked as Peggy passed her.

Peggy clutched the flag. Don't let me slip, she prayed.

Jess's friends parted like Moses parted the Red Sea.

"Imagine there's no countries ..." the young voices sang out in the cold.

The last two of Jess's friends moved aside to reveal a tin garbage can, the old-fashioned metal kind. Peggy wondered where they'd found it, but then her mind came back to what she was about to do. Please God, help me.

"It's easy if you try ..." A soprano soared above the others.

"She's throwing the flag away," someone said.

"No one to kill or die for ..." The soprano riffed the word die.

Peggy could barely breathe. She dropped the flag in the can. A young man whom she had never seen before handed her his candle. She dropped it and stepped back as the fire soared. Heat singed her skin.

She turned to face the shocked expressions. The limousine seemed miles away, but she made it step-by-step, the John Lennon song ringing in her ears. The reporters reached her faster than her family, who seemed bolted to the ground. By the time Peggy put her hand on the door of the limousine she was surrounded. "Why did you do it?" a woman shoved a mike in her face.

Peggy saw a camera pointed at her. "Any country that goes to war for fake reasons doesn't deserve a flag." She got into the limousine and slammed the door. Through the darkened windows she saw their astonished faces, but they couldn't see her tears.

CHAPTER 32

The driver opened the window between his seat and the passengers'. "What a commotion out there."

"I noticed." Peggy's stomach felt as if wires were wrapped round and round it then pulled tight.

"Where's the rest of you guys?" the driver asked.

"Coming."

The doors on both sides opened. "No, I didn't know she was going to do it. If I had, I'd have stopped her." Patrick flung himself into the limousine, followed by Jess and Desmond.

Peggy saw the hovering reporters and cameras before Patrick slammed the door. He glared at her. "Everything we have is because of this country, and you just desecrated its greatest symbol." His face was red.

"The country you came to isn't the country we live in today."

"Jason died for this country. You just stamped on everything he believed in."

Desmond told the driver. "Let's get the hell out of here. Don't hit anyone."

Before the driver could move, Bridget's face appeared at the rear window next to where Patrick was sitting. He opened the door.

"You bastard," she screamed. "You left me. You rushed after her and just left me. And you," she turned to Peggy, "what did you think you were doing back there?"

The driver inched the car forward, leaning on the horn. Peggy felt the car pick up speed. Her mother wasn't a screamer. That was her father. Her mother had ways of showing her anger with an icicle voice, or worse her voice got softer and softer until the words were inaudible. Or there was the arm pinch that brought any of her four under control.

"I can't believe you did that, I just can't." She noticed the chauffer glance in the rear-view mirror. "You, you keep your eyes on the road." Bridget pushed the glass between the driver and passengers shut.

"I had my reasons, Ma."

"There's never a reason to disgrace your family. I never thought I would be so ashamed of my daughter." Bridget threw herself back into her seat with her arms folded across her chest.

No one spoke. Despite the warmth of the heated car, the atmosphere was glacial. Jess started to speak, but Bridget shook her head. The traffic must have been minimal, because it took no time at all to park on Delle Avenue but to everyone in the car it took forever. Peggy was the first out of the car.

The second limousine pulled up behind them.

Connor flew out and grabbed Peggy by her shoulders and spun her around as he hollered, "What the hell were you thinking?" Unlike Bridget, none of the men, including Saint Desmond, had a problem raising their voices.

"I made a statement."

"And ruined any chance of my ever being president."

"You never had one. You can't even get out of the State Senate." She stomped up the stairs.

"Leave her alone," Rachel said and disappeared into the house.

When they were upstairs, Bridget looked at them all through squinted eyes and spat out, "We're going to act like none of that happened. At least until everyone leaves."

Cars began to arrive, followed by people clumping up the stairs.

In Katie's kitchen Rachel took out trays of cold cuts prepared before they left for the funeral. Peggy lined baskets with napkins and filled them with rolls, potato chips and nachos. Jamie grabbed mustard and ketchup.

"There's more paper plates." Katie pointed with her chin as she carried a borrowed 64-cup coffee maker to the closest electrical outlet.

Jess and Aidan walked in just as Peggy asked, "Where's Jess and Aidan?"

"Someone mention us?" they said as one.

Connor appeared from nowhere. "Aidan, you here as a reporter or a friend?"

Aidan and Jess exchanged looks. "Friend. Although I'll do a write-up of the funeral."

"And the flag burning?" Connor asked.

"I called the story in on the way over."

"Then please leave. We don't want this event in the papers. This is private."

Jess stepped in between her uncle and the reporter. "He's off duty now. And Aunt Peggy wants it in the papers."

"Is that true?" Bill stepped up to the brother and sister, locked in scowls, and looked at his sister-in-law's ashen face.

"What do you think? I did it as some new pagan ritual?"

"Let's leave her alone." Bill put his hand on Connor's shoulder. For a moment it looked as if Connor would shake it off.

Bridget took that moment to walk in. "People are arriving; go greet them."

Connor looked at Aidan, Peggy, Jess and his wife, shrugged and left the kitchen. They heard him welcoming the first arrivals.

Upstairs Peggy's phone rang. No sooner did it stop than it began again.

"You should think about getting an unlisted number," Jess said.

Guests dropped their coats in the master bedroom and shed muddy boots to pad around in stocking feet. Only about 20 percent of those at the church showed up. Some went back to jobs after the service. Some hadn't gone to the burial: those that had been at the burial and didn't come were probably so shocked they chose to ignore the collation, or so Peggy guessed. What amazed her, no one, not one person, said anything about what she did. People could talk about the tsunami, the war, kids killed, but a symbolic act of resistance called for silence.

"Where's Patrick?" someone asked.

"Exhausted. He's resting," Bridget said.

Peggy knew her father was avoiding her. She would deal with him later. Now she wanted to collapse on her bed and sleep, but it wasn't one of her options until after everyone had left.

* * * * *

The last guest was gone, the paper dishes, cups and napkins were in black trash bags sitting in the front hall to be taken out later for the morning pick up, the leftovers were stored in the fridge. Peggy walked into the kitchen. Bridget was sitting there alone. The older woman glared at her daughter. "I don't understand you."

"Come with me, Ma."

"I can't imagine anything you can tell me that will make me understand why you would do that to your country." The clock ticked. "What would Jason have said?"

"Just come."

Bridget put two hands on the table to raise herself, then shook her head.

Peggy sighed. "Then wait. I'll be back." When she returned, she was carrying the binder with Jason's e-mails. "Read 'em, Ma, then ask me why I did it."

Unlike Peggy, who couldn't force herself to read every one, Bridget read every word as her daughter sat opposite her as if she were a statue. No longer did she imagine her grandson standing between the family and the terrorists. She saw him as the terrorist, albeit unwilling. She read how his commander had ordered him to kill a wounded boy in front of his mother and sisters.

Peggy watched tears stream down her mother's face.

Bridget closed the binder and let out a long sigh. She looked at Peggy. "Are you going to tell the others?"

"I don't want them to see how much he suffered. It's given me nightmares ever since I read them. I see him there. I see ..." Peggy shrugged.

Bridget reached over and put her hand on her daughter's arm. "I've never been so proud of you as I am at this moment."

* * * * *

Aidan and the family, except for Patrick, gathered around Katie's and Bill's television. The men drank beers from cans.

"This is too cool." Jamie sat on the floor, a can of Coke between her legs. "I never thought you had it in you, Aunt Peggy."

"What? In her ... her ..." Connor paused, "stupidity?"

"A rebel spirit. I always thought she was a drone who just worked, worked, worked," Jamie said.

'With two kids to feed, I worked, worked, worked.' Peggy clicked the television news on and decided to ignore her brother.

"At least the phones have stopped ringing," Rachel said.

"I pulled the plug," Connor said.

"You what?" Peggy wanted to pummel him. Bridget punished the boys for hitting the girls, something Katie and Peggy took full advantage of, although the boys found their own avenues of revenge in holding dolls for ransom and missing treasures. "What gives you the right to ..."

Natalie Jacobson filled the screen, interrupting. Natalie had reported news as long as Peggy could remember. She liked that the newscaster hadn't been replaced with eye candy.

"A gunman is holding three employees hostage at an insurance office. We have live coverage. A fire destroys a home in Revere, and Mission Hill says goodbye to a fallen hero. Those stories in a minute." Most of the news involved the hostage situation.

"The gunman was an employee, who hadn't received a raise," said a woman holding a microphone. She was wrapped against the cold in a coat, hat and stripped scarf. In the background were police cars, an ambulance and an office building.

After a commercial for a store where people went crazy running up and down aisles and throwing things into overloaded shopping carts, the Mission Hill Church flashed on the screen and Jason's flag-covered coffin carried by the pallbearers emerged, followed by the family. The screen cut to a Marine handing the flag to Peggy. Then they returned to the hostage story. The sound of bullets being fired from the building echoed – then silence. "That's it? They didn't show it?" Peggy screamed.

"We can be grateful," Connor said. He sat with his sock feet on the hassock.

"Grateful?"

"It was a terrible thing to do." He sipped his beer.

"No, it wasn't. The terrible thing is that Jason is dead," Peggy said.

"And why he's dead. That's what's terrible," Jess added.

"Stop it, all of you," Bridget said in the same tone that had broken up sibling fights since her children were old enough to realize they had siblings. "Change the subject."

"Long live Queen Bridget," Jamie said under her breath. Connor hit her on the head with a rolled-up newspaper.

They watched the other newscasts, but the gunman story dominated them all. None showed Peggy's flag burning.

Aidan looked at the door. "I really should be going. I gotta get back to work." He met Bill's eyes. "I'm writing nothing about what has gone on in this house."

Bill glared at Aidan until Katie nudged him. "Thank you."

"I'll show you out," Jess said. In the hallway as Aidan wrapped his crimson scarf around his neck, Jess closed the living room door. "Will the burning go into the paper?'

"I'll certainly try."

"Good. I kinda feel like a tree fell in the forest with no one to hear."

"I know." His lips brushed hers before the open door let in an icy blast of Boston winter air.

CHAPTER 33

Connor's knuckles were white from gripping the steering wheel. He, Rachel and Jamie were heading home after dropping Ashley at her school following the newscast. "I don't understand why she did it."

"I do." Rachel wondered how she would survive if it were one of her girls who had died.

"She might have had some consideration for my position." He flicked his high beams to low beams as another car barreled down Route 127.

Rachel stared at him. What had happened to the idealist she had fallen in love with, the one who was going to save the world? Jess was so much like her husband had been then, and she wished he still were.

"Have you sent your acceptance to U Mass?" Connor asked Jamie.

"I'm, like, waiting to hear from Brandeis."

Good change of subject, Rachel thought. She would mention it when Jamie wasn't listening. If not arguing in front of them gave the children an unrealistic viewpoint of marriage, so be it.

When she told Connor what she thought, she would cloak it in the form of questions rather than a direct frontal attack, although she imagined his face if she said, "Listen, you asshole, your sister is one brave bitch." The chances of that happening were in the same category as she would walk out of this family. No way, never. Losing one family in a lifetime was enough. If there were moments when she resented that it was on her shoulders if the marriage worked or not, she swallowed them.

"You can only go to Brandeis if you raise the money beyond what U Mass would cost. End of topic," Connor hunched over the wheel trying to see. The street lamps made eerie patterns through the light fog.

Rachel heard her daughter mutter "cheapskate" under her breath. Connor didn't hear or wasn't paying attention. He would never have let it go.

Rachel resisted letting out a long sigh. If she were honest with herself, she would admit how much she hated conflict. However, she married into a family where everyone said what was on their minds. Ever so slowly she was adapting, but like Frank Sinatra she would do it her way. She hummed "My Way" to herself until Connor swung into their driveway and Jamie slammed out of the car and stomped into the house.

CHAPTER 34

When Peggy woke the morning after the funeral, she saw more snow falling outside her window. Last night pulling the curtains would have taken too much energy. She barely had the strength to pull up the covers.

She looked at the clock. Getting out of bed was hell, always had been, always would be, even though she set the clock 10 minutes before she had to get up to gentle herself awake. One advantage about unemployment was she rose at her own speed. She could send out résumés in her pajamas, drink her coffee leisurely and/or shower at will.

Now she must plan what to wear. Although the loan department never met the public, they dressed as if hordes of clients would come marching through, judging whether to do business based on the stodginess of staff suits. There were no casual Fridays. Her blue blouse was ironed. Her pin-striped blue suit was clean. Her blue stockings had run the last time she wore them, but she had a new beige pair. She was living in the future again. Why not savor these last few minutes under the warm covers before getting on with life?

People kept telling her a funeral brought closure. They were right. She accepted that this morning and all her mornings would be Jasonless. He was dead, buried: she prayed for his soul to be at peace.

She'd almost lost her guilt for her happiness when he joined the Marines: almost, but not quite. That would take more time. As she'd waited for his body to arrive, she'd reviewed everything she'd done raising him. Some things she might have done better or differently. Nothing, not one thing, was done for the wrong reason. Parents were flawed. Peggy was a parent; therefore Peggy was flawed. Sister Mary Joseph, who had taught the senior class logic, would be proud of her. The remainder of the guilt she could live with.

Sadness raked through her for his too-short life. He would never feel the joy of holding his own child, or know the Pats won another Super Bowl. A small bit of her wished he'd lived long enough to fulfill the mother's curse: may-you-have-a-child-just-like-you.

Peggy had forgiven the Iraqi, the nameless man, who killed her son. She hadn't forgiven President Bush for starting the war, nor would she.

Who pulled the trigger?

Did he have children? Were they dead?

What was his wife like? Did he have one? Or was he too young to be married?

Had he seen Jason's face?

Did he enjoy watching his life ebb away, knowing he caused it?

Had victim and killer locked eyes?

Somewhere in Iraq faceless women mourned the deaths of the sons whom Jason killed. Maybe they cursed him, not knowing he was dead. Maybe their curse had killed him.

She imagined the mother of the person who killed Jason and the mothers of the men that Jason had killed sitting down and talking with her, but where? Better neutral ground, but where was that? Another Arab country would favor them, the U.S., her. Europe? She'd never been to Europe. She had never been further south than Connecticut nor further north than Kittery, Maine's beaches and factory outlets.

She could, however, imagine a room with a couch, a rusty color, the color of dried blood. What would the walls be like? Stone. White stone, cold white stone. Cold like death.

No tables to create barriers between the mothers. There were enough barriers. She wanted bridges.

Would the mothers speak English, or would they need an interpreter?

Who would start?

Sean tiptoed by her door on his way out. The door clicked shut and his footsteps disappeared into the morning.

Back to her fantasy: the women put their veils aside. Tea was there, a large pot with cups and saucers. Was Arab tea different?

The mothers would show pictures of when their sons were little with their grimy faces squinting into the sun, holding balls. Some wore their Sunday best. Somewhere she'd heard the Muslim's Sunday was Friday: it would be their Friday best. Their hair was slicked down, forced into a state that would last only until the shutter clicked.

She would show Jason's first grade class photo with his two front teeth missing. His face sent the message that his tie was strangling him.

Of course, she had no idea what typical Iraqi women's names were. Maybe they were as strange as the men's that she'd read in the news: Mohammed. Mohammed was the Muslim Jesus. Only Spics named their children Jesus. Spics was one of those PC no-no words, but the political correctness didn't exist in her house. Good manners, yes.

The women would exchange stories about broken arms, good grades and sibling fights. Peggy assumed little boys everywhere were the same, pushing and making vroom-vroom noises as their arms flew through the air while holding small cars, trucks and planes.

Peggy wanted to see the soul of the woman who raised the boy who ended her son's life. Maybe her son was no longer alive either, killed by Jason's mates, with bullets fired fast in revenge. Maybe the women whose sons Jason had killed wanted to peer into her soul to see what kind of woman would raise a killer. The Marines had turned her son into a killer. That she could not forgive and doubted that she ever could. She didn't even know how to start.

A wave of anger hit Peggy so hard she jumped from the bed, making the toilet in time to spew bile into the bowl. Rinsing out her mouth, she glanced at the clock on the shelf above the sink. Damn, she was so late.

Twenty minutes later, Peggy left the triple decker. Snow covered the sidewalk, hiding icy patches. Not everyone shoveled their walks, requiring her to walk in the street, always keeping her eye on cars that might skid into her.

The E-line was, as always, irregular. By the time she entered the office it was 10:00. Other desks were empty, probably loan officers from the suburbs, stuck in traffic. They said the storm was worse west of the city.

She passed her boss's office on the way to her desk. He carried a Styrofoam coffee cup in one hand and a blueberry muffin in the other. "You're late," he said.

"The T ran late."

"Next time try to leave earlier."

For a moment Peggy imagined hitting his coffee cup and the splotch spreading across his pink striped shirt.

"I brought muffins for everyone. They're in the coffee room. Thought it might help on this miserable day."

Well, she thought, he has done at least one human thing.

CHAPTER 35

Jess shook the snow from her blue beret as she walked into the Suffolk Law School building. Her books were stashed in her backpack. Even if her next class wasn't for two hours, she wanted to hole up in a comfortably padded chair in front of a window looking out at the Park Street Church. Every time she saw the red bricks, "My Country 'tis of Thee" played in her mind. She wished she'd never been told that it was first sung there.

She was tired to her bones. Jason's death was her first death from her age group: well not entirely true. Marianne Loomis had died of cancer in sixth grade, but she'd been sick so long Jess had forgotten she was a classmate. Her great grandparents had died, but she'd been little. Their loss meant little to her. During their funerals, she'd been bundled off to school as normal.

Although the Church told of heaven and hell, she wasn't sure she was a believer, but if there were hell, maybe Jason would be there for what he'd done in Iraq. She remembered Dylan's song saying if God were on our side, there would be no more war. She had always found it hard to think of God playing favorites among nations.

Her cell phone rang.

"Hello, beautiful Irish girl," Aidan said. "Meet me for breakfast? Dunkin Donuts. Tremont Street."

Tremont Street had many Dunkin Donuts shops splattered throughout the city. The first store faced the Common and the others

143

ran down to the last one located at the foot of Mission Hill.

"Which one?"

"Across from the Common. I've something to show you."

"Five minutes."

The snow fell faster, hiding the sidewalk bricks and making it impossible to see where there was a safe place to put her feet and which were ready to trip her.

She walked by the gold-domed State House on Beacon Hill, home of the Brahmins who wouldn't hire her ancestors. What would those snobs think of having John Kerry, an Irish Jew, living there? Okay, not where she was walking. He lived in Louisberg Square, around the corner from the Shaw statue of Civil War black soldiers. Blacks had lived on the wrong side of The Hill back then. Although there'd been some leveling of society, it wasn't enough to suit her. Making it happen would be her life work. More than one professor had said that sooner or later she would give up her idealism for the money side.

The Dunkin Donuts' window was steamed up. Aidan waited at the back with a blueberry muffin and a vanilla latte. "You ordered this last time, so I took a chance. I didn't know how much time you'd have."

Her annoyance that he had made her decision for her disappeared in the pleasure that he remembered what she'd ordered. "Not that long. What do you want to show me?"

He handed her *The Globe.* "Couldn't convince my editor to put it on the front page." He opened the paper to the obits. A photo showed Peggy in front of the burning garbage bin.

She scanned the write-up that include her friends singing and handing Peggy the candle, the flames soaring, melting the snow and Peggy saying her son died for nothing.

His writing was tight. "You did it."

"I got it on the wires, called the San Fran Chronicle and the Madison, Wisconsin paper and talked to the editors. I sent it to the websites Common Dreams, Truthout and Buzzflash."

"I can't think what to say."

"Say you'll go to dinner and a movie Saturday night."

"I'm working. Sunday night?"

144

"I'm working. Saturday or Sunday lunch and movie?"

"Saturday." She gathered up her things.

As she walked back, she called her aunt at work and told her about the story.

"I know," Peggy said. "My boss saw it and told me it was good they didn't say where I worked."

CHAPTER 36

"Shut off your computers." The overweight woman, who had led the course, looked like a giant blood spot in her red pantsuit. "We'll send your certificates to your bosses. That'll show them you didn't play hooky."

Peggy slipped the workbook into her empty briefcase. At her old job she brought loan applications home. This bank insisted work be done on the premises. If you didn't finish by five, you stayed like bad boys and girls kept after school. She wondered what a single mom without family support would do. She suspected there were some mothers among her colleagues, but even halfway through her probationary period no one had reached out to her. When she suggested sharing a coffee or a sandwich, the person always put her off, including the woman who asked her to lunch her first day.

Peggy wanted to ask if there was a rule against employee fraternizing, but if no one really talked to her, who would she ask?

The course had been fun, not just because it got her out of the office atmosphere, but the teacher joked. At one point she sang the instructions. Peggy wondered what headquarters would do if they caught the instructor letting people have fun?

Today, Peggy decided to look for other work. Granted, she didn't expect to duplicate the environment of her old branch, but there must be work places where growling didn't replace breathing. Life was too short to work like this.

The other attendees from the bank were from different departments. At lunch they discussed "careers" as if they were animate objects to be purchased in a store, brought home and displayed. All but one was younger than Peggy by at least a decade. Peggy wondered if just listening to them made the grey follicles under her dyed hair push faster, her skin wrinkle and her bones grow brittle.

Outside the late afternoon light carried a hint of more snow. The parking lot had been plowed. Banks of snow separated the lot from the street.

A woman, who had sat two rows behind Peggy in the class, strode towards an SUV, a behemoth that drank the oil that caused the war that killed her son. Peggy could see over the snow banks to Route 128 where the traffic whooshed by. SUV after SUV crossed her range of vision. She wished she had a mini missile to shoot them off the face of the earth.

The woman, whom she knew was a high-placed manager in business development, passed the support-our-troops yellow ribbon plastered on her back bumper.

"Excuse me?" Peggy said.

"Can I help you?"

For a nanosecond, Peggy almost regretted what she was about to do. The woman was probably nice. She probably had a nice husband at home judging by the wedding ring and diamond. When Jason's face flashed in front of her face, the words came. "Exactly how do you support the troops?"

"Er, I ..."

"Do you write Congress to ask for money for more equipment? Have you sent goggles or vests to our servicemen?"

The woman started walking towards her car.

"Are you using less gas? Have you visited any of the wounded in a Vet's hospital? Did you send any money to that veteran who had to hitch his way home after he was released from the hospital after being wounded? Do you help the wounded vets pay for their meals?"

Anger flashed across the woman's face. "Leave me alone." She opened the door.

"My son was killed last month in Iraq, and because you're driving that SUV which helped kill him, you're as much of a murderer ..."

The rest of the sentence was lost as the woman slammed the door, started the engine and peeled out of the parking place.

Maybe I *am* crazy, Peggy thought as she watched the car turn onto the service road leading to the highway. Or maybe I need one of those anger management courses. Or maybe, just maybe, I can do something useful with this anger.

CHAPTER 37

The needle struck a thread, wrinkling the satin. Bridget took her foot off the sewing machine pedal and worked the thread back to its normal tension. This dress was a problem. The emergency wedding was this weekend and the design had to cover the bride's stomach. The shotgun wore white, although this was not that unusual these days.

When her daughters walked down the Mission Hill church aisle they were entitled to white dresses. She suspected it was neither the training from the nuns nor the threats from Patrick, but opportunity. They'd watched their girls like hawks.

Although Bridget hoped Jess had retained her virginity, her realistic side laughed at the idea.

Jamie was too young, although Rachel told Bridget about rushing Jamie to Children's Hospital with stomach pains when the child was 11. The doctor asked Rachel to leave. When she was allowed back in, Jamie said, "They wanted to ask me if I were virgin. They didn't think I would tell the truth if you were here."

"But she's only eleven." Rachel claimed she'd stammered out her question. Her Jewish upbringing was as strict in its way as Bridget's Catholic one.

"We get a lot of pregnant eleven-year olds. Some have sexually transmitted diseases," the doctor said.

Bridget would never shake her head and say, what is this world coming to, but she didn't have to like the changes since her childhood.

There was right.

There was wrong.

But in the scheme of things, how could making love be wrong, when the government told her making war was right? If she voiced these ideas, her daughter Katie, bless her, would faint on the spot. Katie didn't allow nuance. Sometimes she wished her youngest had just a mite more tolerance.

The needle pumped up and down, up and down, securing the seam, binding together two pieces of fabric, a bit like the marriage ceremony. Marriages start with hope, then reality sets in: money problems, job losses, alcohol, abuse, too many children too fast, or no children, other loves. It wasn't easy to make marriage work. Lord knows, she and Patrick had had their problems over the years, but he'd never hit her, and he always brought his money home.

She wished her Old Goat had more interests. She pulled the fabric from the machine and cut the thread. The seam satisfied her. She went to the ironing board to steam it. Good dressmaking was in the details. Skimp once and it looked all right but not spectacular. Skimp many places and the garment looked bad. She never skimped, making sure the seams were pressed, reinforcing buttons, double-sewing seam edges.

Doing things right, she called it: it went beyond dress making. It included letting a clerk know he'd given her too much change, not lying about your age to get into the movies cheaper. If only someone would doubt that she could qualify for the seniors' price. Once she said to the cashier, "You could make an old woman happy if you would ask, 'Are you sure?'"

She went to the movies on her own when looking at one more spool of thread would cause her to scream. She chose matinees on the Fenway while Patrick took his afternoon nap. Patrick said it was stupid going to the movie: the film would be on TV later.

She didn't do it too often, because Patrick sulked when she was away, even if he slept through her absence. Downstairs wasn't away. Outside, even next door with her friends, was away in his book.

Why couldn't retired men entertain themselves? Her friends

complained of the same thing as if a retired husband's syndrome existed. Lord knows, there was a syndrome for everything these days that used to be just considered life. If it were a syndrome, then there would be a high-priced prescription drug to cure it.

As she sat back in her chair, she wondered what she would do if she didn't have the business. She wouldn't be bored, that was for sure. Rather than stuff activities between work projects she could do them at her leisure. She wished she had time to volunteer at church, not to mention the pile of magazines to read.

Her Old Goat pasted himself in his chair by the television hour after hour. Maybe he felt bad because he was so sedentary. Her mother and mother-in-law nagged their husbands – don't do this, do that, take that pill, don't stink up the house with cigars – a thousand and one restrictions. Although she understood their frustrations, their complaints colored the air grey. She vowed she wouldn't do that, but she had become like them and disliked herself for it.

Each week she put his medicines in the compartmentalized box with the days of the week marked on each section of the box and left it where he could see. The pills were almost a meal in themselves. When he forgot, she nagged.

She nagged about his cholesterol: she refused to cook eggs and cheese. When he brought them home, she clucked. A cluck wasn't a nag, although he said it was. She'd worked hard perfecting the cluck.

The bodice of the dress was embroidered satin. The sleeves reminded her of the girls' books about knights and damsels. As she pinned the pieces of fabric together, she was careful not to leave marks.

Marks were good and bad. She left character marks on her children. Giving back was one lesson. It was okay to charge to shovel the walks of the able-bodied, but not for wheelchair-bound Mrs. Manning. Hers was done in the name of Christian charity. Connor had complained more than Desmond, if she remembered right, but in the past few years she sometimes confused the memories of one child with another.

Patrick stood in the doorway. "When's lunch?" Before he added, "what are we having?" he saw her tears. "What's the matter?"

"I just thought of Jason."

He gathered her to his chest.

One of the buttons of his sweater pressed into her cheek, but the feeling of being held felt good, safe.

CHAPTER 38

"Meet me in the fifth-floor ladies at 10:00. Say nothing to anyone and tear up this note. MA."

Peggy found the message from her HR friend in an envelope between her first and second loan folders. She glanced at her watch: 9:10, before shredding it.

At five of 10, she picked up her finished folders and walked through the mouse maze of grey cubicles. No one looked up. She took the elevator to the fifth floor.

After setting the folders on the three-sink counter, she washed her hands, although she hadn't gone to the toilet.

Mary Ann appeared within two minutes. She looked both left and right down the corridor before closing the door. Bending down, she checked under the stall doors. She then took a sign from the folder she was carrying that said OUT OF ORDER and slapped it on the ladies' room door.

"This is like a spy movie. What's up?" Peggy asked.

"There's been a complaint against you by the woman you attacked in the Burlington parking lot."

Peggy grabbed the counter to steady herself. "I didn't attack her."

Mary Ann inhaled deeply then spat out a sentence in blast. "We've been friends for a long time, but I can't protect you when you behave like this to other employees. Can you give me an explanation?" When Peggy stayed silent, Mary Ann grabbed her by the shoulders and stared into her eyes. "Give me something to work with to save your job."

Peggy thought of her budget. She thought of how depressing the office was. She thought of the saying it's easier to get a job when you have a job. Peggy told her what had happened in the parking lot.

Mary Ann nodded. "I would have done the same thing. I doubt if I can help you, but I'll try." She hugged Peggy, opened the door, looked both ways and left, taking the out of order sign with her.

* * * * *

Lunch came and went. Her job had become a parallel universe that had nothing to do with her reality. The only thing real was the paycheck.

At three her boss stood at her desk. "Come with me?"

She followed, thinking of a sheep following the Judas goat.

They walked into the conference room bordering the Human Resources Department, a small room with a circular table, four chairs and a side table where a coffee pot, Styrofoam cups, a bottle of powdered creamer and a box of sugar cubes were arranged on a black plastic tray. The room was the same dull grey as the rest of the bank. An oversized color photograph of the bank's New York headquarters decorated one wall. Photos of President Bush and Cheney were on the opposite wall.

Mary Ann was seated with the SUV woman. They had half-drained cups of coffee. The faces were locked into frowns. Peggy did not repeat her mother's maxim about faces freezing in unpleasant expressions.

Mary Ann invited Peggy and her boss to sit. "I think we all know why we're here."

Peggy expected to be dismissed on the spot. Relief that she wouldn't have to be imprisoned any longer flooded through her.

The woman leaned forward. "Mary Ann explained to me about the loss of your son and the stress you've been under. I'm willing to overlook it ... *if* I can have an apology."

Apology, Peggy thought. I can have a paycheck for an apology.

Would the woman agree to drive a more fuel-efficient car if I apologize?

"Peggy," her boss said. "That's most generous of Pam."

So – the woman's name was Pam.

"This bank isn't heartless. We'll give you another chance considering your recent grief," her boss said.

"We know that you'll be a good addition to the loan department." Mary Ann's eyes met her friend's, begging her to go along with the deal she had brokered.

Peggy wanted to let loose with her hatred of SUVs, the war and the bank. She wanted to throw the coffee pot at the portraits of the president and vice president. The fingernail of her little finger on her right hand had a rough spot. She ran her left thumb over it. Years of her parents and her teachers telling her to be a good girl battled her desire to tell them all to go to hell. "I'm sorry."

Pam didn't smile. "Accepted." She stood. "I need to get back."

"Me too." Peggy's boss followed Pam out of the room.

Mary Ann threw herself back in her chair and let out a long sigh. "I never thought I'd pull it off." She stared at Peggy. "I used every chit to do it. Don't let me down. Please."

Peggy knew she should thank her buddy. What she felt like was a total coward.

CHAPTER 39

"I don't need him in my life," Jess said to Amy Kowalski and Amy's mother.

They were in the kitchen area of the loft where Amy lived with her mother, an artist who had bought the building in South Boston when it was worth nothing. Now the area was developed, but she had stayed.

Her loft was still that of an artist without any of the chichi details of the converted neighboring condos. It smelled of turpentine and dust.

Had Amy and Jess been children, they could have roller-bladed around the empty space only if they didn't bump into the giant canvases stacked for Trinka Kowalski's next show or the screens that hid the sleeping areas.

Jess loved the free-flow environment, so unlike her own home with matched everything. In one fantasy she dreamed of giving her mother a transfusion of Trinka's blood. Katherine Marie Flanagan Kelly would not only become less prudish, she would become earthy. Reality told her that most likely the transfusion would kill her mother.

Trinka Kowalski sat with the two law students. Her mid-back length wavy hair was like Amy's except the black was streaked with grey. All three were dressed in jeans and Suffolk University sweatshirts, but Trinka's clothes were a pallet of oil paints. Trinka saw no reason not to wipe her hands or brushes on her clothes. Her breasts, never contained by a bra, jiggled freely when she moved.

A casserole dish, filled with the remains of an egg-kielbasa, potato and cream dish crusted around the edge, sat in the middle of the table along with half-empty bottles of beer. "Need isn't the word." She waved her fork in the air.

Ever since Jess met Amy's mother during the girls' freshman year at Suffolk, she had watched the woman talk with her whole body. The more emotional Trinka became, the more in danger nearby objects were. "Want is the word. Do you *want* him? Hormonally too." Trinka's accent revealed her Warsaw origins.

When Jess said nothing, Trinka leaned forward staring into her eyes. "Aha. I see it in your eyes." She threw herself back in her chair so hard the front legs came off the wide-planked floor. "So, have you slept with him? You're blushing. Look Amy, she's blushing."

For a second Jess tried to imagine her mother asking the same question. Tears and talks of damnation would follow.

"If you haven't, you should." Trinka nodded several times as if the force of the words weren't enough. "I know, I know. Your mother would have a heart attack, but ..." As the rest of the sentence hung in the air, she put her hands on the table and leaned gorilla-style over the havoc of the meal. "You know the song, Cher's 'Sloop Sloop Song'... it's in his kiss. Screw his kiss. It's in his prick and how he uses it."

Jess looked at Amy for help, who was too used to her mother to be shocked. "You're on your own, friend. "'Sloop Sloop' song,' Mom? Do you mean 'Shoop Shoop'?"

"Shoop Shoop Sloop Sloop! If he loves you so, it's in his prick, that's where it is," she sang off key.

"It doesn't rhyme," Amy said.

"So, what's your problem? You afraid of sex?" Trinka asked.

"No, it's just that I have too much I want to do to be tied down just yet."

"And he's stopping you?"

Jess knew they hadn't talked about the future. Their conversations were more about politics. Much of her fear was based on what she suspected Aidan wanted. "A lot of my friends when they say I do then have to say I don't because of their husbands."

Trinka motioned for Amy to start clearing the table. Part of the wall of the kitchen area was brick-and-board shelves holding pots, pans, glasses and dishes abutting an old-fashioned soapstone sink from the days when the loft had been part of a factory. On the other side was a counter, a wide plank of wood balanced on sawhorses. "Take him as your lover: he doesn't have to be permanent."

When Trinka went back to her easel, the girls settled in the corner of the loft behind the screen that gave Amy a private area. Their text and notes were spread out on Amy's mattress that was on the floor. "I sometimes wonder," Jess said, "if our mothers are of the same species."

"Probably not," Amy said. "Seriously, Jess, if you want Aidan, go for it. It won't change our plans to do storefront law."

CHAPTER 40

Peggy dragged herself home. She wanted to broil under a hot shower, to drink tea and to climb into bed. The telephone rang as she walked through the door. Her boots left wet marks as she walked across the floor.

"You don't know me," a woman said. "I'm part of Military Families Speak Out. I would like to have you help us."

Peggy sighed. What could she do when even burning the flag had brought scant attention?

"March 19th and 20th there's a major demonstration in Fayetteville, North Carolina."

When Peggy didn't respond, the voice added, "The home of Fort Bragg. Some of us New Englanders will leave really early Friday. We hoped you'd come. We saw your photo in *The Globe*, and ..."

"May I ask your name?"

"I'm sorry. I should have introduced myself. Judy DelSandro. My son was killed in Afghanistan last July."

"I'm so sorry."

There was silence before the voice continued. "It's funny. People say they know what I'm going through, but they haven't a clue. You know and don't say it."

Peggy pictured spending hours in a car with other people who'd lost sons and daughters, husbands or wives. She pictured herself at a demonstration. She liked the view. Then she saw her empty office desk, another black mark during her probation period. She saw Mary Ann being criticized for her absence. "I just started a new job and my bosses didn't like all the time I've taken off for the funeral and all."

"Don't decide now. Take my number and get back to me."

As always, no paper or pencil were anywhere in sight. Cradling the phone between her neck and shoulder, Peggy walked to her computer, booted it and clicked to Word. "Shoot," then shuddered. They'd both lost children to shooting.

Judy rattled off her phone number.

"Have you a deadline?"

"The last day. If we get enough, we'll rent a bus, split the cost. Otherwise we'll convoy, but the idea of burning all that gas to protest a war about gas ..."

"... doesn't make much sense."

"Nothing does anymore. Please think about it. I'll call in a couple of days."

"Please do," Peggy said.

T.G.I.F. At least she would have two days of rest. She put the whistling tea kettle on and turned up the gas. As she reached for a mug she thought: all the way to Carolina. In a car. With strangers. At a protest. That was something other people did. Not her. But why not her?

CHAPTER 41

Rachel stepped off the Greenline at Brookline Village. She had given up driving places, if she had a choice, in Jason's memory. No car, no oil burned, less excuse for war, not that one person could make much difference.

Connor had mocked her, but Jamie had defended her much to Rachel's surprise. Most of the time Jamie was anti both parents. Lately Jamie had become a raving environmentalist and was talking about majoring in environmental science. Connor had muttered about needing higher math grades which led to slammed doors. Another normal breakfast among the Newton branch of the Flanagans, Rachel thought.

The Commission for Women's Clothing Drive, her destination, was being held in the police station's community room. She participated in many more things than she wanted to in the name of her husband's career. However, this group which collected professional clothing for poor women entering the workforce, was something she supported – better than serving tea at some State House function.

What would it be like to work again, to stand in front of a class and talk about Wordsworth and Hawthorne? To teach she would have to get her master's degree, and with Ashley's and now Jamie's tuition, the money just wasn't there. By the time Ashley finished school, she would be in her fifties, too late to start a career. Once she thought a Catholic school would accept her Boston University degree without a masters and let her teach. A Jewess turned Unitarian teaching in a Catholic high school was about as ecumenical as it was possible to get unless she practiced a bit of Buddhism on the side and worshiped pagan goddesses. Not wanting to face rejection, she hadn't applied.

The puppet theatre across from the T stop had a new display. Two marionettes dressed in Indian costumes stood in front of a Taj Mahal type cut-out building. When her girls were smaller, they never missed a production. Once, when they were at *Aladdin*, her brother Samuel had come in with his wife and two little boys. Rachel had never met the wife, nor did she know the children's names. He spied Rachel and ushered his family out. The boys had screamed in anger at not being able to see the performance.

Funny how much she was thinking of her former family. Former. Interesting term because she still carried their genes. Maybe, with Ashley away during the week, she had more time to think. Or more likely it was because Connor was getting stuffier and stuffier. She missed the man she married.

She turned the corner. Perhaps she should pick up Mexican food to take home to avoid cooking. As the red brick library came into sight, for a second she thought she was looking at her mother.

It was her sister. My God, she must have packed on at least 30 pounds since the last time she'd seen her.

Her sister didn't notice Rachel until she blocked her path.

"Don't you think it's time to forget the past, Sharon?" Rachel asked.

Her sister brought up her glasses from where they hung on a chain against her chest. Her eyes grew bigger. She brushed by Rachel.

Rachel watched the woman, whom she had loaned blouses to years ago, run away. At least no one was on the sidewalk to see. Rachel realized that at one time she would have cried. Damn them all. She turned and marched toward the police station.

As her mother said, she had made her bed, now she lay in it, but even with Connor's stuffiness and Ashley's CP it was better than being married to Saul Cohen, her parents' choice.

CHAPTER 42

Peggy padded down the stairs in her oversized fuzzy slippers and the blue sweat suit that she slept in on cold nights. Her *Sunday Globe* waited on the table at the entrance.

Katie's and Bill's door was open. Katie sat on the sofa, reading the women's pages in her own *Globe*. Her feet propped on the coffee table. Bill marking a page with a yellow highlighter. Peggy didn't need to look closer to know it was the real estate section.

"Coffee?" Katie asked.

Peggy wanted to be upstairs when Sean woke. He'd come in late last night. She suspected he'd been drunk by the bumping and muffled "shits." Granted, that was normal for college kids, but having had an alcoholic husband she froze when her Sean drank too much.

She hated being around anyone drunk. One party does not a drunk make, she told herself. Challenging him took more energy than she had these days.

"What time is Ma serving lunch?" Katie tossed the newspaper on the read pile.

"As usual, 12:30. Stay there, I'll get my own coffee." She went to the kitchen, poured a cup, came back and started reading her own paper.

Sun streamed in the window warming the living room.

Jess wandered in with a coffee cup in her hand. She picked up the editorial section of the paper.

"Can you come upstairs?" Peggy asked.

"Secrets between my daughter and sister?" Katie pulled her legs up underneath her and turned to face Peggy, who at this point was on the edge of the couch ready to escape the same way birds perch ready to flee an approaching cat. Since they'd been girls, Katie would say tell me everything about the dance, tell me everything whoseitmacallit said, tell me everything about this or that. Sometimes Peggy made up stories to satisfy her sister's imagination.

Peggy carried her paper with one hand and the coffee mug with the other. "Nope."

* * * * *

Upstairs Peggy told Jess about the demonstration. "What do you think?"

"I think you should go."

Peggy then told her about her apology at work.

Jess hugged her aunt. "That must have hurt."

Peggy wondered how her niece could be so smart so young. "And if I take time off, I'm not sure I'll have my job."

"And the worse case scenario?"

"I don't think I'll be eligible for unemployment."

"Temp. It can't be worse than what you're going through now."

* * * * *

Peggy rinsed the dishes in her mother's kitchen as Jess put them in the dishwasher. If the Olympics had a dishwasher-stacking event, her niece would take the gold. She made putting them away easier: spoons, knives and forks together in their own baskets; same-sized plates marched large in back to small in front; glasses arranged by size.

Peggy wanted to live to be an old woman to see what Jess would be like at 40, 50 even 60. Watch out world. And now it seemed that Jamie might take after her if their discussion about ecology and saving the world was any indication. The next generation seemed hell bent on doing right. If they were Peggy, they would go to Fort Bragg.

Bridget stuck her head in the kitchen. She wore her apron over her sweater and tweed slacks. Only a few years ago, she gave up dresses or skirts. Peggy tried to picture her mother in jeans and failed.

"How's Grampy?" Jess asked.

"My Old Goat complained he wasn't tired but fell asleep before his head hit the pillow." She closed the door behind her without any click.

When Bridget's footsteps disappeared, Jess said. "The more I think about it, the more I think you should go to Fayetteville. What's more important, your country or a job?"

Peggy laughed. "Well, just like the Church won't support kids when rhythm fails, the country won't support me.

"Especially this government. Go! They'll be military families, people who lost people. You can't be accused of being unpatriotic if you've sacrificed a family member." She took her aunt by the shoulders and looked into her eyes: she had to scooch a little to do it. "Ex-soldiers who know what it's really like will be there. How can you not go?"

Peggy let the water drain from the sink and dried her hands on a towel hanging on the knob. "Tell me about Aidan."

"Changing the subject?"

"Yes."

"Aidan? I'm in like."

"In like?"

"Too early to be in love – but he's bright, politically where I am, and ..." Jess paused to emphasize the point, "he understands why I've so little time." Her face lit up as it had when she brought home an all-A report card, won the declamation prize at Boston Latin and got a full scholarship at Boston University.

"Let's not forget cute, despite his big ears."

Jess giggled.

Since she wasn't a giggler, Peggy decided Aidan most likely would be around for a while. Once she'd worried Jess's force would keep her from finding a man willing to put up with her. She needed someone special. Maybe Aidan was it. Her confidence that Jess wouldn't do anything stupid was unlimited, and if something bad happened out of her control, Peggy knew Jess could pull out of it.

Her imagination meandered to Aidan's and Jess's wedding with someone asking her how the bride and groom had met. "He was a reporter covering my son's murder," she would say. Murder was the only word that she felt was right to describe his death. She didn't blame the Iraqi who pulled the trigger.

She blamed Rumsfeld.

She blamed Cheney.

She blamed Bush.

"Aunt Peggy?"

Jess's voice pulled Peggy back into the kitchen.

CHAPTER 43

Patrick awoke on his left side. The first thing he saw was the Blessed Mother's statue. If he were on his right side, he would see the black shutters of the triple decker next door and Bridget's dresser, two comforting views in their familiarity. Not much these days felt familiar. The world had gone mad.

Life was once simple. A man supported his family. That's why his father left Ireland to support Patrick and his brothers and sister. Work made a man a man.

Bridget worked. Had they not wanted to send their kids to parochial school, she wouldn't have had to, although he hated to think of what she would be like if she didn't have enough to do. She'd probably wash the ceilings at five in the morning.

His medicines lined up on the night stand, white-hatted orange soldiers, marching to a silent melody. Stupid adult-proof tops. Why must adults without any kids around battle with those dumb-ass tops? The price of those pills would have paid a year's tuition for one kid at St. Mary's. Jesus, Mary and Joseph he hated it all.

When his kids were little, at the end of the month, there was money left over; not much, but enough for a bit of savings and maybe a day trip somewhere.

The good old days. A codger's expression if he ever heard one. His father never used it. For his father, the good old days were the new days after he left Ireland. Patrick had read in *The Globe* yet another article that the Irish were moving back to Ireland in record numbers. That's where the opportunities were. "Who'd have thunk it," as his mother used to say.

His parents were on his mind a lot these days, especially his mother's crinkly eyes and her laugh. He could imagine her voice, "get out of here" or "go on with you," pushing them out the door. If he'd a penny for every time she'd said that, he wouldn't worry about paying for medicine.

His life had been good. His parents made him finish school. He survived Korea. He had a good wife, good kids and good grandkids. Thank God, he wasn't facing the world that his grandkids had to. Talk about not wanting to be in someone else's shoes. This was the price of living too damned long.

The voices from the television room told him the herd hadn't gone home. He reached for the cane, which he always left next to his bed before his nap, a doddering old man who couldn't keep his eyes open. He struggled to his feet, grabbed the dresser to steady himself and made his way the living room. Everyone was there except Sean, who had left for work.

On the television President Jeb Bartlett was having trouble putting his pants on. Patrick watched him struggle. "What's the matter? He drunk?"

"MS, Grampy," Jess said. "I love this series. Would that we had a president like that."

Patrick wanted to slap her. It was my country, right or wrong. You vote. You live with the results even if you voted the other way. Voting was his father's biggest thrill after he became a citizen.

"Bush is still your president." Patrick said, despite believing the war was a total disaster based on lies. "Respect the office even if the occupant makes it difficult."

"Bush killed your grandson," Peggy hissed.

He couldn't let the rebellion continue. This wasn't about politics: this was about respect, respect for the president, respect for him as patriarch. "You're out of order, young lady."

"I'm neither young nor a lady. I'm one mad woman, and I'm going to do something about it."

Jess pushed the pause button on the remote. "Does that mean you're going to Fayetteville?"

"You better believe it." Peggy stood and put her hands on her hips.

"What's Fayetteville?" Connor asked. He took the remote and lowered the volume.

"A major demonstration against the war," Jess said.

"Good God, you'll get yourself arrested and for nothing. The papers will pick it up and who knows what will happen to me next election."

Peggy swung around and hovered over her brother. "Shut up, Connor. You're just like the yellow-bellied Washington pols. I can't imagine what you'd be like if you were from a red state."

"You'll lose your job, if you take more time off," Katie said.

"Job is the least of it. She'll be marked as a traitor," Patrick said. Good God, what was happening to his family?

Peggy turned her back on her brother and sister as she pulled her chair up in front of her father's. When she reached for his hand, he didn't pull away. "Be proud of me, Da. I'm fighting for what I believe."

His girls could always turn him into melted ice cream with a look. "I've always been proud of you, even when I've disagreed, but this is different. This is attacking your country in a time of war."

Jess started to say something, but Peggy shook her head. "The war was our choice."

"They attacked us," Patrick mumbled. He read enough to know the girls were right, but he wouldn't want to admit it, even to himself.

"Saudis, not Iraqis," Jess said.

Jeb Bartlett had his pants on. Patrick felt like he no longer wore his. It was hell getting old and useless.

CHAPTER 44

Peggy's bed was littered with pajamas, a bathrobe, several sweaters, three sweatshirts, slacks, jeans, six pairs of underpants, three bras, tampons, which the change probably made unnecessary but better safe than sorry, make-up, and several socks, some with mates. Boots, sneakers and loafers were on the floor.

Two suitcases, a medium and a small one, lay open on the bed. A backpack that had belonged to Jason hung on the bottom bedpost.

She knew the proper clothes for work: Emily Post never ruled on the etiquette of demonstration clothing. She'd seen marches on television, especially the gay pride marches, but none of those outlandish costumes would work.

What would the weather be?

When the genes for loving travel were being handed out, she was in the liver line, she told people. Her idea of a wonderful holiday was to spend it at home free from work pressures, maybe a day trip to eat lobster and to browse the shops on Bearskin Neck, and even more rarely to spend a few days in a New Hampshire or Cape Cod cottage rented by her sister's family. She could almost be poetical about sleeping in her own bed, pulling her home-made quilt up to her neck or reading a romance until dawn. She loved listening to the house's morning sounds: Patrick stomping above her head, the flush of the toilet at the same time each morning, Bill calling to Katie to hurry up. Routines gave her structure.

I'm testing myself, she said to her reflection in the mirror. In my own territory, I'm strong.

Katie kept trying to talk Peggy out of going, over and over, warning of exhaustion and uselessness. "If you're unemployed, don't say I didn't warn you."

Besides being totally confused on what to pack, she felt emotionally deserted by most of her family.

She looked up to see Jess in the doorway. "And you're planning to be gone a month, a year?"

"I don't know what to take." Peggy held a hangar in her hand.

Jess grabbed three pairs of underpants, a pair of jeans, a T-shirt, sweatshirt. "This will do it. Add your tooth and hairbrush."

"That's all?"

"Yes." She hugged her aunt. "This is your first demonstration, but I bet it won't be your last. Think of it as a First Communion."

"If your grandmother heard that ..."

"... she'd cross herself." Jess stuffed underwear in the backpack. "Wear the jeans, T-shirt and sweater. It'll be warmer there. I checked the CNN weather. Layer."

Peggy watched her niece. "Maybe I shouldn't do this."

Jess sat on the bed in front of her aunt. "Maybe this is one of the most important things you've ever done."

* * * * *

Peggy waited on the porch. Her backpack was beside her. It wasn't too late to back out. She could say that she had a stomach upset. How could she be that far away from everything and everyone she knew? What if she got lost? How would she ever get back?

A station wagon parked in front of the Flanagan triple decker. The street was dark, and she could only tell it was some dark color, black or maybe blue. It didn't matter.

The driver, a woman near her own age, hopped out and ran up the stairs. "I'm Judy. We talked on the phone."

Peggy swallowed her fear, retrieved her backpack and hurried down the stairs. Judy opened the rear of the station wagon. Peggy threw her things on top of the other backpacks.

Once in the car, Judy said, "We'll be crowded as sardines. I'll let everyone else introduce themselves and why they're here."

One by one, the people in the car spoke.

"Gina. My husband is over there."

"Paul. I served in Iraq."

"Jack. My kid brother is there."

"Lisa. My big brother is there."

"Maureen. My husband is there."

"I was there. I'm Jennifer. Jen. There'll be a quiz on our names when we hit the Mass Pike."

"I'm in trouble, except for Jack and Paul." They were easy to tell apart: Jack was heavy and bald. Paul was drop dead handsome.

All the women, except for Judy, were probably in their early 30s, had short brown hair and were overweight as if there were a let's-go-to-the-demonstration mold. Jen was the least overweight, but she'd been a soldier.

"Here's the plan," Judy said, "we'll take turns driving, share expenses, stop for regular pee breaks. We'll drive through. After the march, we'll come right back. You will be late for work on Monday if you have the energy to go at all."

"We've jobs, except for Jen," Gina said.

"I lost mine when my unit was called up, even though I shouldn't have," Jen said.

"Tell them about your car," Paul said.

"Ya, my car was repossessed. I couldn't get the bank to believe there's a law against the repossession of property of a fighting soldier."

"I bet the banker had a support-our-troops ribbon on his car," Lisa said.

Aha, Peggy thought. I'm not the only one annoyed by those fucking stickers. She could almost taste the Palmolive at the use of the F-word.

"I never saw his car, but probably."

"What bank?"

When Jennifer named Peggy's, she said nothing about working there.

Peggy listened. When she was in a new situation, she tended to be quiet, unlike when she was with her family.

Jack turned around from his position in the front seat. "Who do you have over there?"

"My son was killed not long ago."

"Oh God, I should've been more careful," Jack said. "Gotta change the subject. Pretend we are on a school trip. We can sing songs."

"Like 'Little Bunny Fu Fu,'" Judy said. "Only I want to sklonk Bush on the head instead of that stupid rabbit." She drove through the Mass Pike toll without paying. For a moment Peggy was confused then realized Judy had that thingamajig on her windshield that automatically charges a credit card.

What an innocent she was, limiting herself to Boston's borders.

The late hour and moving car had the same effect as a sleeping pill although she battled to listen to the different conversations. Bits of different speeches drifted in and out of her consciousness.

"What really hit me when I was first there was the poverty. When I left, it was worse. No electricity, no clean water. What keeps me awake nights is that I feel I added to their problems," Jen said.

"The news says ..." Judy said

"They don't cover the story," Paul said. "In my unit, bullets were rationed."

Peggy thought, my God, her son might not have had enough bullets to protect himself.

"We weren't properly equipped either," Paul said. "Some stuff was Vietnam era."

Peggy's head jerked, and she mumbled, "My other son sent night goggles to Jason."

She lost her fight to stay awake in Connecticut. She woke in Maryland.

The miles melded into broken naps, conversations, toilets and roadside stops. They didn't just drive south: they drove into spring. Trees began budding; a few were in full leaf. The passengers of the Demonstration Express, as they called themselves, shed coats somewhere after D.C.

They listened to the radio, but as they drove deeper into the south it was difficult to find anything but country and western or religious.

Paul took the wheel. They crossed a bridge not like the pretty Boston bridges but one with long metal bars that ran parallel to the road. The sky was grey, the river dirty brown.

"We're almost there," Jack said. "I remember from last year."

"Look." Maureen pointed to a sign that read Fort Bragg, Home of The Airborne and Special Operations Forces. White letters were written on a big chocolate-colored board.

Paul said, "I was stationed there. Sure am happy to be a civilian again."

"Last year we had about 1,000 people, but it's going to be bigger this year," Jack said. "Turn left at the little square gas station."

"Will they try and stop us?" Peggy asked. She'd seen newscasts of protestors being dragged by police. What would it feel like being dragged along a sidewalk? If she were jailed, who would bail her out? She swallowed her panic: I can do this, I can do this.

"Not really. They've the necessary permits," Judy said. "Jack, help us find our motel?"

Peggy swallowed. She hadn't thought about a motel. What an idiot she was.

"We're sharing a room," Gina or Maureen said. Their voices sounded alike, and since they were side-by-side in the front seat she wasn't sure which head the voice originated from.

Maureen turned into a motel. "Okay guys, let's get what we need and get to our rooms. We need to nap for a couple of hours. We're in for a couple of really long days."

* * * * *

Three hours later the group sat in a diner booth where the smells of coffee and fried onions were woven into the faded curtains. A waitress in a pink uniform and white apron. Her badge read: Hi, I'm Andrea, kept glancing at Paul. When she asked, "What are y'all having," she directed the question at him.

"I recommend a big breakfast, because we aren't sure where or when we'll eat again," Jack said.

"Y'all here for the demonstration 'cause y'all sound like Yankees."

"We are. What do you think of it?" Judy asked.

"Well I voted for W, because he's a godly man." She continued to look at Paul. "Someone has to protect us from terrorists."

Paul winked at her. "But the terrorists were from Saudi not Iraq. I'll have two eggs over easy, sausage and some grits."

Peggy had only heard of grits. The words "the same" seemed to fall from her mouth. What would she do if she didn't like grits? Leave them on the plate, her inner self chided. It's no big deal. It is a big deal, another voice drowned out the first. She resisted the desire to run but only because she couldn't run all the way back to Mission Hill. I was crazy to come she thought. I am going schizoid if I'm having arguments with myself. As she looked around, her new friends' faces were smiling.

Andrea filled their thick white mugs with coffee, starting with Paul, but forgetting Peggy's. "I might not agree with y'all, but we got free speech."

"You got that right," Jack said. "You from around here?"

"All my life." She still looked only at Paul.

"I think I took an invisible pill." Peggy held up her empty cup. She wished she were in her own kitchen where she could get coffee whenever she wanted and wasn't held hostage by a drawling redneck. She glanced at her watch. Forty-eight hours and she would be home. However, when she got home, she would know she'd done this for Jason. She forced herself to ignore her discomfort.

"Sorry." The waitress separated her eyes from Paul long enough to pour coffee into the cup.

The taste was slightly weaker than brown-dyed water.

When they were alone, Judy distributed maps. "After we eat, we head over to the Cumberland Health Center."

"There's a rally at eleven. The march starts at noon," Judy said. "Then we need to move our butts to Rowan Park. They've got speakers there until four this afternoon."

"If we get lost?" Peggy asked. Her sense of disorientation was increasing by the moment.

"We meet back here at four-thirty."

Jack looked at Peggy. "You're going to like the coming-together feeling. If it's anything like last year, you'll feel real close to these people, even without learning names."

* * * * *

The haunting, sad notes of bagpipes played by a grey-haired woman in a red sweater whined as Peggy and Jennifer walked toward Rowan Park. Too many people to begin to count milled around as the notes floated over pallbearers carrying flag-draped coffins. No matter that the coffins were cardboard boxes were empty and easy to tote, they were symbolic.

Willpower alone kept Peggy from sinking to the ground when she saw them. Peggy wondered if she fainted would she be trampled to death.

"*Bush lied, soldiers died.*" A chant mingled with the bagpipes.

At first, she thought the hole in her stomach was the memory of the single coffin holding her son. This was the flag she once revered. The bagpipes played the 'Star Spangled Banner' and the lyrics she had sung at countless baseball and football games ran through her consciousness.

"Oh, say can you see by the dawn's early light

What so proudly we hailed at the twilight's last gleaming?"

"*Bush lied, soldiers died.*"

"Whose broad stripes and bright stars thru the perilous fight,

O'er the ramparts we watched were so gallantly streaming."

"*Bush lied, soldiers died.*"

"And the rocket's red glare, the bombs bursting in air,

Gave proof through the night that our flag was still there."

The bagpipes kept whining.

"*Bush lied, soldiers died.*"

Peggy fought to keep her mind on the lyrics. It was the first time she thought of their meaning. Singing it was something that you just did, like pledging allegiance to the flag and saying the Lord's Prayer every morning in school. But the war that inspired the anthem was to preserve the country. What type of country thinks more of the celebration of war than the celebration of peace? The flags on the fake coffins in front of her, the flag on her son's real coffin, they represented an attack on another country that had done nothing to the U.S. What about 'God Bless America'? That talked about the prairies, the mountains, the productive stuff. My God, my God, my God.

The bagpipes kept whining.

"*Bush lied, soldiers died.*"

Peggy walked on, her arms linked to two other women. One patted her hand.

The bagpipes kept whining.

"*Bush lied, soldiers died.*"

Was she free? Was she living in the home of the brave? She thought of all the congressmen and women who bleated yes to the president's threats.

The flag on the coffin directly in front of her slipped and was adjusted by one of the bearers. That was now a flag of aggression. When she looked at it, instead of pride drilled into her by her father, she felt shame and pain.

The bagpipes kept whining.

"*Bush lied, soldiers died.*"

"My God, my God, my God."

She must have said it aloud because the woman who patted her hand, who might have been in her 60s and was waving a sign with tears of blood coming from the Statue of Liberty's eyes, asked. "My God what?" She put her free arm around Peggy's shoulders. "Is it the coffins?"

Peggy swallowed several times. Taking a deep breath, she choked out, "The flags. I never thought I'd be scared when I saw my country's flag."

The older woman whispered, "I know," and disappeared into the crowd. Peggy wondered what her story was. Each person here had a reason for coming. For the first time she felt proud not scared of having gone beyond her limits for Jason and for herself.

The marchers moved out. Peggy wished she had a sign. Next time.

The bagpipes whined.

"*Bush lied, soldiers died.*"

Stores had boarded up their windows, but the crowds marched by. Outside a McDonald's, police with clear plastic shields and visored helmets defended hamburgers. As she walked by, Peggy stared into their faces and saw scared boys.

The bagpipes whined.

Peggy chanted with them. "*Bush lied, soldiers died.*" By the end of the march, neither the lead chanter nor Peggy could speak above a whisper. She wondered what was going on at home where life was normal, and police didn't stand behind shields.

Instead she walked to the place where Cindy Sheehan was going to speak about her son Casey, killed in Iraq.

Like Jason.

CHAPTER 45

B ill and Katie sat at the kitchen bar savoring the last minute of calm before leaving for work. The smells of toast mixed with freshly brewed coffee.

Neither spoke as they ruffled through the morning paper, but the silence was neither resented nor planned. It just was, until one wanted to share something. Bill shifted in his seat. Katie, without putting down her section of *The Globe*, refilled his cup.

Bill turned a page in *The Globe* sports section and reached for another piece of toast. He buttered it with a small slab. When Katie said nothing about cholesterol, he added more and a dollop of strawberry jam. "BC is doing well in hockey."

"Bia Bistro has an Irish chef. Maybe for our anniversary ..." Katie said.

"Hmm. Bausher has been optioned by the Sox," Bill said. "Uh oh."

"Uh oh, what?"

"A Red Sox plane was used by the CIA. Better not let Jess see."

At the mention of her name, the young woman appeared dressed in her cat burglar outfit, jeans and a dark blue turtleneck sweater. "Jess see what?" She touched the toast. "It's cold."

"Nothing," her father said.

She reached for *The Globe*. "Oh my God, I don't believe this ... the country kills over 500,000 people in Iraq, supports the death penalty, but has had a special session of Congress to spare the life of Terri

Shiavo, who has been a vegetable for years. Bush, who couldn't leave his ranch for the tsunami, comes back to sign this law ... are we nuts or what?"

Bill put down his paper. "We should have her DNA tested."

"You think I was unfaithful?" Katie asked.

"Not a chance. Maybe the hospital switched babies. She's so political I swear she knows when Bush goes to the toilet. Jess, you need to be more laid back."

"And if more people were like me, this country wouldn't be in the mess it's in."

"Watch your tongue. This is the greatest country in the world," Bill said.

"Then why are we thirty-fifth in health care?"

"We've the best health care system in the world. Your mother works for it."

"Sure, Harvard covers her, but all the uninsured ... oh what's the use?" She put three sugars in her coffee.

"Did Peggy get back last night?" Katie asked.

"I didn't hear her come in," Bill said.

"She'd better be careful. If she misses too much work, she won't get by her probation period." Katie looked at her watch. "We better go. Everyone here for dinner tonight?"

"I'm going to see *Diary of a Mad Black Woman* with Aidan."

Katie dropped a kiss on Jess's head. Bill followed her out of the room.

He stopped in the doorway and looked back at his daughter, who had her pen out and was circling something on the front page of the newspaper.

"Have a good day, oh freedom fighter of mine," he said.

CHAPTER 46

The Park Street Church clock showed 11:30 as Peggy emerged from the T-station. She rushed by the usual carts selling sweatshirts emblazoned with Harvard, Boston College, Red Sox, Patriots, Celtics and the usual, "My parents went to Boston and all I got was this stupid sweatshirt."

Although she wanted to pop into Finagle A Bagel, she was much too late. She needed coffee. Having slept all night in a moving car and arriving back only at 9:20 a.m. made her feel as if she were walking through water. Nothing seemed real to her, neither the weekend nor her return.

She inhaled great gulps of air as she almost ran, narrowly missing an older woman toting four Filene shopping bags. At this point, how late she was made little difference. If arriving at 9:01 was worth a frown and 9:05 a reprimand, 11:45 was heresy. Of course, they never complained when anyone worked after five, but even those who worked till seven or eight at night were expected back at their desks at nine.

As she walked by the fountain flowing down the black marble wall the receptionist looked up from her keyboard. "They want to see you in Human Resources."

For once Peggy was alone in the lift. A few minutes later, she sat on the blue-tufted chair outside Mary Ann's office as the departmental secretary glared at her. When her friend emerged, her face told Peggy what Mary Ann would confirm.

"I'm fired. This is becoming a tradition with us," Peggy said. Although Mary Ann was hunched forward, her hands folded on her desk, Peggy relaxed back into the guest chair. She imagined her sister trying not to say, I told you so.

A new job hunt, lack of money: none of that seemed important. No more imaginary bars at the entrance of her cubby. She imagined stacks of paper to check yes, giving people money for things they didn't need in the first place, burning. The image made her smile.

"I'm so sorry. This last absence did it. I tried ..."

"I am sure you did," Peggy said. She patted Mary Ann's hand.

"It's not fair. your son ..."

"It's not fair my son was killed, it's not fair that I'm not given time off to grieve, it's this bank with its rotten policies that isn't fair."

Mary Ann reached for a box of tissues. Peggy was nowhere near tears. "They said your loan approvals seemed to reflect a personal agenda. And to top it off they called you at home. You didn't answer."

Peggy wanted to dance and sing, no matter that she could barely carry a tune. The thought that she hadn't worked long enough to qualify for unemployment flashed through her mind. Tomorrow she would think about that, she and Scarlett O'Hara Butler. "This must be hard for you, Mary Ann."

"It is. I've always liked you and although I shouldn't say it ..."

"You don't much like this job."

"I love HR, I don't like this bank."

"Then quit."

"I need the salary."

CHAPTER 47

On Saturday morning Bridget listened to CNN as she hemmed Tiffany Murphy's bridal gown. CNN repeated the same things over and over: the Pope was dying. Bridget didn't often work in front of the television, but she wanted to be there when the news of his death broke. She sewed a prayer with each stitch. An American tourist visiting the Vatican talked about how she was feeling part of an historic occasion.

Patrick dozed in his chair.

"More historic for the Pope," she harrumphed. Patrick didn't wake. She hated the media's feeding frenzy. Jesus, Mary and Joseph, she was becoming a COW, Cranky Old Woman.

The newscaster talked about the Pope being the third longest-surviving Pope and how many people in the world didn't know any other one. Now didn't that make her an old lady? She'd lived through six Popes, starting with Pius XI.

She wondered what Desmond was doing in the Vatican at this second. Two friends had called to ask if he'd contacted her. She'd told them that he was much too busy without letting on how annoyed she was that he hadn't.

Later she would go to church to pray for the Pope. She saw him when he'd come to Boston: was it '78? No, maybe '79? She tried to remember by how old her children were at the time, but she had long ago forgotten those details. Was it Katie or Peggy who had measles?

She knew both boys had. Connor had had chicken pox. He bore a tiny scar at the tip of his eyebrow where he'd scratched the scab.

Even though she considered herself as devout as anyone, she didn't like the Pope's stance on birth control. Too many people lived in the world. Glancing at Patrick, she thought of all the times they didn't dare make love. Four babies were enough. There were times he pleasured her almost to insanity and left her there because it was the wrong time. Her mother had told her to suffer "the *thing* men must do" in silence.

She'd enjoyed *that* part of marriage ... no, she wouldn't think of it now. It was over although she and Patrick had exchanged glances during Viagra ads. With his medical cocktail, another chemical was unwise.

All those stupid pill ads were the same: "Are you suffering from too light pink nails? Maybe you have too-light-pink-nail syndrome and blah blah is right for you. Ask your doctor. Should not be taken by men and women between 0-100 and side effects can include loss of fingers, toes and premature heart arrest." She chastised herself for not appreciating what might be keeping her husband alive.

Patrick stirred and jumped awake. "What's for lunch?"

"Chicken noodle soup?"

"I want a BLT."

The word cholesterol popped into her mind. Her husband looked grey. What if he were like the Pope who was beyond eating whatever was his favorite food. Kielbasa? Pasta? Popes have kitchens that prepare whatever they want. Was food one of his earthly pleasures? She knew she had lettuce and tomato.

"I'll ask Peggy if she has any bacon."

Patrick sat straight up. "What? You sick, woman?"

"A BLT sounds good with lots of mayonnaise."

"Why are you occupying my wife's body, stranger?"

"Go away, you Old Goat. If you give me any more lip, it's soup."

Patrick pretended to zip his lip.

CHAPTER 48

If Katherine Marie Flanagan Kelly and William Xavier Kelly had gone to the same high school, they would have been voted class couple. However, he'd attended Boston College High. Katie, like her sister, went to Elizabeth Seaton.

From the time their mothers plunked them into the same playpen while they enjoyed a cup of tea and chitchat, they'd been inseparable. Bill boasted that his buddy Katie pitched better than a boy, not underhanded, but a real pitch, scaring any batter facing her. As a result, she was allowed into all his playground games, traded baseball cards, knew every Sox batting average and impressed the hell out of Bill's chums.

He was an only child. His mother was never quite right after she lost yet another baby when Bill was five. Not quite right was one of those phrases traded between women, which Bill and Katie never understood. His mother died when he was 10.

His father worked the night shift, sometimes double shifts at the Sealtest ice cream plant in Framingham, sometimes not coming home at all. Things like laundry, cleaning and meals became non-existent. Bridget added Bill to her table and his clothes to the laundry as easily as her needle went through the cloth of the hundreds of dresses she made.

Only once did Katie date another boy. A classmate's cousin invited her to his junior prom. The day of the dance Bill told Katie,

"I forbid you to go."

"And what right do you have to do that William Xavier Kelly?" she'd asked.

"You're my girl," he said to his baseball-throwing-bigger-bubble-gum-blowing-laugh-helping-history chum. "I'm going to marry you."

"Not until after tonight's dance." She wanted to wear the plum-colored gown her mother had made and didn't want to stand up her friend's cousin, whom she met once, pronounced cute, but too bookish. He talked too much about computers, which Katie knew nothing about and cared less.

When they decided to marry a week after graduation, Patrick and Bridget talked and talked and sent them to Father James who talked and talked. They talked about money, children, responsibility. Then later talked about a lasting bond that couldn't be broken and the importance of purity before marriage as well as limiting carnal pleasures afterwards. The money part made sense, but they never accepted the carnal pleasure limitations.

When the adults couldn't dissuade the young couple, Bridget and Katie went to wholesale cloth warehouses on Kneeland Street in Chinatown to look at the floor-to-ceiling bolts of cloth. Katie chose off-white silk. Bridget sewed Katie's dream dress, because despite being a tomboy, the girl still pictured her wedding as the day she would be a princess giving herself to her prince to live happily ever after in a state of holy matrimony blessed by God. That she now had an approved outlet for the cravings that attacked her between the legs was no small thing either.

The Kellys moved into the ground floor apartment vacated the month before their wedding when Bridget's 94-year old mother toddled up Mission Hill from Calumet Market where she had bought three apples, sat down with a cup of fresh tea brewed to cup-dissolving strength, closed her eyes and never reopened them.

Katie was pleased to discover that her wedding day wasn't the happiest day of her life, for she planned to follow her maternal and paternal grandmothers' path of living into their 90s and the idea that the best was behind her at 18 just wasn't her cup of tea in a family where tea was central to daily life. No serious conversation, nor for that matter a happy one, could be held without the kettle going on. Although coffee too was drunk, tea was for important things, while coffee was merely a beverage.

Katie's grandmother had left the first-floor apartment furnished in dark Victorian furniture. Hand-made doilies covered the backs of velvet chairs. Each room had its own religious statue hidden against dark floral pre-war wallpapers. No one was sure which one, Korean or WWII. Just walking in could create a depression.

Bill worked as an apprentice plumber before starting his own company. One month after moving in found them stripping wallpaper and sanding walls. When they could afford paint, painting them. By the time Jess was born after numerous miscarriages, the apartment would be welcomed in an *Architectural Digest*. Unlike Peggy, they didn't refinish old furniture but saved up until they could walk into a store and write a check.

They had gone from watching pennies to watching nickels, working up through dimes, quarters and dollars. Unlike 99 percent of Americans, Bill didn't believe in credit cards, but believed in savings. He wouldn't play the stock market, saying he would prefer a small interest rather than losing what he had.

"My husband sleeps like a log," Katie would say. Part of his log-like sleep was his knowing that if the business had a bad month, he could make payroll. He could buy the equipment he needed when he needed it. He used things up before replacing them. New for new sake wasn't how he spent his money. Thus, tossing and turning was unnecessary.

Shopping wasn't a pastime that either enjoyed. Need and value determined what separated them from their money. They looked for quality, for what would last.

When Jess was young, the convenience of never worrying about babysitters or having an egg in borrowing distance made up for lack of privacy. Katie traced Bill's pressure to move from after Jess's high school graduation. The first conversation came as they waited for their daughter to return the purple robe and mortar board. He began dragging her to open houses in Brookline, Newton, Chestnut Hill, and Jamaica Plain.

Since Jason's funeral, they hadn't visited one house. Katie didn't think that her husband had changed his mind, but business had been unusually heavy.

Weekends were spent collapsed on the couch watching TV and running whatever errands couldn't be ignored, hoping that there would be no customer emergencies during the weekends when he was on call. Bill felt he couldn't ask his employees to do things he wasn't willing to do himself.

Since she met Aidan, Jess was home even less often. Always busy between school and her work at the women's shelter, her little free time, when she wasn't locked in her room with her books, was spent with him.

Nice boy, Katie thought. Despite her daughter being in her 20s, she was always relieved when she heard the door click shut late at night. It meant that Jess had not spent the night in Aidan's bed. Sex was for marriage.

The Saturday of their 29th wedding anniversary the couple drove to the restaurant in their car, a six-year-old Ford Escort with less than 7,000 miles on it. "Why buy a beautiful car in a high-theft area?" was part of their economic philosophy.

Eating out was for special occasions, although they didn't really consider pizza at Penguin's or pub grub at Flann O'Brien's eating out. Eating-in gave pleasure. Bill liked to cook, although in the early days of their marriage before Katie went to work she did it all. Bill started when Katie was laid up with the flu. Everyone called his spaghetti sauce the best ever. Since both cooked, neither felt overburdened.

Thus, meals in good restaurants were for birthdays, anniversaries or celebrations. Restaurant reviews were researched, co-workers' opinions solicited and past dining experiences examined for a possible rerun. Some places that they had loved like Veronique's and Dini's had disappeared: others had changed. They had lived through many incarnations of the revolving restaurant at the top of the Hyatt in Cambridge.

"I want lobster." Bill's breath hovered in front of him as the heater cranked into action.

"Let's go to the Union Oyster House," Katie said.

"We'll never get in."

"Let's try."

Extreme cold and snow might be bad for the restaurant's number of covers, but it was good for the Kellys. The hostess, her smile frozen, promised that a table would be theirs in 10 minutes in this, the oldest restaurant in the country. She directed them into the long dark bar only half filled by men and women who created a low but constant hum. Bill nudged his way to the bar and returned with two flutes.

"Champagne?" Katie asked.

"Nothing's too good for my girl on our anniversary."

"Kelly?" A voice, as if from a deity speaking to his flock, called them to a table on the second floor reachable through rabbit-warren rooms with the original dark plank flooring. They passed an aquarium with lobsters stacked double and triple in the water as bubbles burst to the surface.

"One of you, prepare to die," Bill said in the direction of the crustaceans.

"It makes it so personal," Katie said as they followed the black-skirted waitress weaving around tables.

"But he'll nourish my body and soul."

"I remember when I first came here," Katie said. "It was Desmond's graduation. We had to order the cheapest thing on the menu except for Desmond, because it was his party."

Before he could respond, a waitress with spiked hair appeared. Bill ordered for both, including a clam chowder.

When she left, Bill reached into his sports jacket pocket and pulled out an envelope.

Katie didn't notice. "I wonder what poor Peggy will do now."

He played with the envelope, turning it back and forth in his hand. "She really was dumb to go to that stupid demonstration. Your father and brother called it right on this one."

Katie spied the envelope. "What's that?"

"Your anniversary present."

She reached for it. In the early days of their marriage they gave things for their functions – snow tires, an iron, plumbing tools. Even as their finances improved their gifts were practical.

As much as she might have wished for Bill to surprise her with clothing or jewelry that he chose himself, that wasn't one of his characteristics. She accepted it the same way she accepted that he stood 5-9 and was a Red Sox fan. At one point, Katie overheard Jess offer to take him shopping to choose a dress for Katie. He'd said no without explanation and even Jess's wheedling, which she'd mastered to bend her father to her will, fell into an abyss. As husband faults went, it was merely a blip.

The envelope had Kelly Plumbing embossed on the outside. "I've a plumbing certificate?"

"Just trying to keep the surprise for the very last minute."

She put the envelope down on the white linen table cloth and poked it, watching him watch her. Never, ever could he hide anything. She could read his body, the direction of his eyebrows, the twitch in a cheek muscle. Most times she could narrow down the subject: all he had to do was fill in the details.

She used the dinner knife to slit the seal and pulled out two airline tickets to Fort Myers. Their vacations had never been more adventuresome then cottage rentals on the Cape or in Maine, so Peggy and her kids or her parents could join them. A couple of times they went to a B&B in Vermont for a long weekend, hiding out from their regular responsibilities. She'd never flown. "Florida for two weeks?"

He studied her. "I want to look at houses there."

Oh God, she thought, it was bad enough when he wanted to move to another town. Another state?

The waitress interrupted by bringing clam chowder with oyster crackers which gave Katie time to think. She opened the plastic package and dropped the little beige circles into the creamy liquid so thick it could almost be cut. She blew on it and watched the steam scatter, wishing it would spell out a prediction. Clam chowder makes a bad Ouija board.

Bill didn't move as Katie repeated the process until her chowder was half gone. Finally, he leaned forward so he was well into her space. "Well?"

"You need to tell me more," she said.

"Snow."

"Snow?"

"I've had it. I want to sell the business, not work for at least six months, then start again in Florida."

CHAPTER 49

The window was open for the first time in months, letting fresh air waft the scent from the lilacs that choked the tiny side yard belonging to the house next door. An unknown species of bird must have thought he was recording a music video considering his enthusiasm.

Peggy swiveled around to her computer. She expected her computer chair would assume the imprint from her bottom on its blue wool from all the time she spent there. Her discovery of online English-language newspapers from India, Pakistan, Israel, Lebanon, Syria and Czech served her in the same way as soap operas and reality shows entertained others. It took up almost all her non-working, non-sleeping time.

Although most of what she looked at was war-related, she got caught up in school-dinner problems in England and the French EU constitution vote. As a woman who four years ago thought a trip was visiting her brother and sister-in-law in Newton, she felt as if she'd invited the world into her dining room. Blair, Brown, Chirac, Howard, Al Hasid, Sharon hung around her as did anti-war writers who made their way onto the net.

When the net didn't give her the information she wanted, she either walked or took the T to the Boston Public Library. Her reading had gone from *Ladies Home Journal* to Zinn, Clarke, Wolfowitz, Pearl, Stewart – any book that Buzzflash.com, Truthout.

org, Alternet.org, MoveOn.org or Commondreams.org mentioned.

Her research brought back memories of writing papers at Northeastern. She wasn't after an A now. She wanted to cure her anger, but what she read enflamed it. Somewhere in the sea of words where she swam, there was a boat and on that boat was her solution.

Her flag burning and going to the demonstration had accomplished nothing besides making her brother and father angry.

Nothing!

They took her behavior as a temporary aberration. Her family was good at pretending problems they didn't want to exist didn't.

Connor had had the nerve to say, "I told you so," when she had lost her job while her father told her not to worry about the rent and her mother made enough food that leftovers made their way into her kitchen. "The Old Goat doesn't eat as much these days," she would say as she plunked a piece of ham, a casserole or soup in Peggy's fridge.

Most days Peggy couldn't sit at the keyboard. One of the three temp agencies she was registered with sent her on assignments: she'd done bookkeeping for a doctor, filed orders for a meat wholesaler as she watched men dressed like moon-walkers come out of the freezer and designed PowerPoint presentations in Harvard's fund-raising department. None engaged her mind, but she found friendly people in most places, making her think the bank experience was merely a blip.

Yesterday she finished a week as a secretary for a law firm. She congratulated herself that she didn't break the photo of her supervisor with President Bush. The jobs kept her electricity on to keep her computer going, or so she convinced herself.

Two of her temporary bosses asked if she wanted to stay. The concept of a steady paycheck made the word yes seem right. As if she were having an out-of-body experience, she watched herself say she needed more flexibility for personal reasons than fixed jobs offered.

Except for Jess, who said, "follow your instincts," she kept their offers a secret. Her family would say she was crazy.

Today, she had no assignments. She yawned as she planned her day's research. At 2:30 a.m. she had shut down the computer and went to bed only because her fingers hurt. She was back at the keyboard at 7:30, a cup of coffee near her right hand.

A photo of a blood-covered naked Iraqi girl came on the screen. Although no age was reported, her breasts, just nubs, would never feel a man's hands or a baby's lips. Blood oozed from her slashed throat.

The accompanying article didn't say if the mother was alive. Peggy hoped not. No mother should see her child murdered like that.

A child dying of leukemia or a car accident was terrible, but to have a child's body desecrated, how does a woman survive that? Peggy wanted to take the mother in her arms to sponge up the pain and say I'm sorry, I'm sorry, I'm sorry.

Peggy counted each of the child's ribs. She stared at the face that would never smile again as she touched the wounds with her finger. Then she turned the photo into her computer's wallpaper as a reminder whenever she booted it up of the horror of the war and what she was fighting to stop for both countries.

The computer clock read 9:13 when the phone rang. Peggy ruffled under a paper pile to locate it. As she answered the phone she clicked onto her e-mail with her free hand. The hotmail screen replaced the dead child. "Hello?"

"Oh Peggy, I'm glad I found you home."

Peggy tried to place the voice.

"This is Laurie from Women Power."

Peggy pictured the woman in her mid-30s who'd sent her to a Big Eight accounting firm. They "hoteled" their accountants, which meant that those who spent most of their time at their clients' had no fixed offices at headquarters. They were assigned free space when they were in, reducing the need for office space. The secretaries spent more time trying to locate their bosses than doing anything else. Popping in and out of different work places convinced Peggy that stupidity and mismanagement were chronic and reduced even more her desire to take on a full-time job

"Could you possibly go out for us today? They need a receptionist at the State Department of Higher Education. Theirs didn't come in at the last minute, but I don't know why. Nice people. Opposite the State House. I know it's last minute ..."

"How much?" Peggy blessed her luck that she had done a research project on temp agency pricing policies for a course at Northeastern.

"Nine?"

"How long?"

"I really don't know, because they don't know, but at least a week."

Peggy did the math: $360 minus tax and Social Security. A last-minute call meant that every second was a loss of money for Women Power. If they couldn't produce, the client would look for another supplier. In her earlier life she would never have bargained, but as a good Catholic girl accepted whatever was offered. Accepting the authority of your parents, teachers, priest, husband and boss was as normal as washing dirty dishes. "I can be there in an hour. But I want $13."

There was a breath-suck on the other side. "I can only go to $12."

What the hell, Peggy thought. Laurie needs her commission. She would make $120 more than if she'd said nothing. "I'm on my way."

"Really? Dress code is casual. The regular hours are nine-to-five. Nice people. Low pressure."

At the Huntington T stop, the blue sky contrasted with the beige wall of Harvard's Countway Library of Medicine. Cars trickled by. Only two other people waited for the T. Peggy took out her phone. First, she called Laurie to report that she was at the T stop. If she were to avoid full-time work and bargain for jobs, she needed to show she had something to offer beyond basic skills such as a sense of responsibility. Laurie thanked her.

Three Greenline cars snaked down the tracks from Brigham Circle. Peggy dialed Jess, who checked her phone between classes. Instead of getting a recording her niece answered. "Are you free for lunch? I'm working across the street from Suffolk."

"Cool. I'm meeting Aidan but join us. At the Fill-a-Buster. You'll walk by it from the T. See you at noon."

* * * * *

The state office building entrance had a guard. No one asked her where she was going, but the guard with a goofy grin wished her a nice day as she picked up her bag after it had rolled through the conveyor X-ray. From his red hair and freckles, Peggy bet he was Irish. He pointed her to the bank of elevators to take her to the 19th floor.

The woman behind the shoulder-high reception desk was about 40 with short blond hair. "I so hope you're from Women Power."

Peggy nodded.

"Glory hallelujah! Our-receptionist-went-into-early-labor-on-her-way-to-work-there's-so-many-meetings-today-some-of-our-people-are-out-at-the-colleges-and-the-rest-are-bogged-down-in-reports-so-covering-the-switchboard-is-a-nightmare-for-anyone-let-me-show-you-how-the-phone-system-works." All this was said without her taking a breath. "Oh-and-I'm-Karen."

During the morning, people drifted by to introduce themselves and to ask if she needed anything. The phone rang only four times until 11:30 when the husband of the missing receptionist called to report that Jared had entered the world at 9-pounds-6 ounces. Peggy passed the call to Karen.

At noon Karen appeared to relieve Peggy. "Can-you-possibly-get-back-in-a-half-an-hour-if-not-it's-okay-we-are-just-so-glad-to-have-found-someone-so-quickly-we-hope-you-can-stay-with-us-until-Julie-gets-off-maternity-leave-but-we-can-talk-with-your-agency."

"I can stay for a while," Peggy wondered if Karen ever inhaled between words. "I was meeting someone for lunch, but I'll be back as fast as possible."

"Great-can't-ask-for-more."

As Peggy headed toward Fill-a-Buster, she heard her name.

Connor hustled to catch up with his sister. "What are you doing here?"

"I'm working."

"Maybe you can hang onto this job for a while, not like the other."

"The other job sucked."

Connor took her by the elbow. "I don't know what is wrong with you these days. You used to be responsible."

"Let me go." Peggy pushed the words through her teeth. "I've had enough of your big brother act." There were more things that she wanted to say, but he dropped his hand and walked away from her. As she watched him go, she found herself classifying him more as a politician than as a brother.

* * * * *

Aidan put his napkin on his dirty plate. Jess swallowed the last of her tea.

Peggy looked at her watch. "I've five more minutes. Aidan, I'm frustrated."

"Why?"

"I read the anti-war sites, I send letters to Congress and newspapers, but it's so useless." The thought that if she couldn't even convince her brother to stand up against the war, how could she convince any other politician, jumped into her head.

Aidan tore his napkin into pieces. "The problem is that you don't reach those who aren't reading and seeing the same things."

"I can't force people to listen," Peggy said.

Aidan grabbed the check. "Don't say anything. I'm the only one with a decently paying job, and I like taking care of my women." When Jess opened her mouth, he added, "And you take care of me in other ways so don't go women's lib on me."

Peggy took in Jess' raised eyebrow and smile. Interesting, she thought. "Do you have a color printer?"

Aidan nodded.

"If I send you some photos could you print me out maybe twenty, twenty-five copies? I've an idea on how to reach others."

"I'll make it a hundred."

CHAPTER 50

Katie felt as if the world had been bleached. The walls and bedspread of the hotel room were white. The sliding glass doors looked down to a white sandy beach with pale, pale waves too lazy to break into froth. The beige tiles provided the most color.

When Bill and Katie fell into bed last night after their late arrival, they left the patio doors open, using the screen door to keep out bugs and four-legged creatures. To prove the point, a lizard ran across the white tiled terrace, which was surrounded by a foot-high white picket fence. Planters full of white flowers sent a sweet smell into their room. The 70-degree temperature made it pleasant, especially after the weeks of bitter cold and snow.

Bill stood in his shorts and T-shirt, watching the water amble to the shore. Once the lizard had disappeared, he said, "You gotta see this, girl."

Katie rolled over. For the first time in months she wore a flimsy nightie not a flannel one. She stretched. "I prefer ordering breakfast in bed. Then we can plan our day."

Gone was the tension of a late take-off. Instead of getting in at supper time it had been midnight when they locked their motel door behind them. Something in that click defused Bill's anger at delayed flights and incompetent car rental clerks.

The brochures Katie picked up while Bill registered covered the small glass top of the faux-wood white nightstand. She shuffled through them. "I vote for the Ringling Brothers Museum." She shoved the car museum leaflet under the Kleenex box.

"I was thinking we could take a swim, grab some grub, then go meet the real estate agent I contacted."

"William Kelly, I'm not spending my entire vacation looking at houses." When he said nothing, she added. "I'm not."

* * * * *

The white-haired woman wore white creased slacks and a blue top under her Century 21 jacket. She opened the door to a glassed-in patio overlooking a man-made lake with an island. Four flamingos rose as one and landed on the dock at the end of the property. The reason for their flight became apparent as an alligator meandered over to where the birds had been.

"That thing is huge," Katie said. If she could use telepathy, Bill would have heard, "You have to be nuts to think I want an alligator in my backyard."

"Nothing to worry about," the agent said. "In fact, they're quite a status symbol."

"Not one I'd ever choose." Katie watched the alligator slither into the water and float as if pretending he were an old log. The flamingos strutted around the grass. She wondered if they might shit pink, but she doubted it would be any different from Boston pigeon shit that was white no matter the color of the bird. Wherever you are, you have to deal with shit, garbage, dust and dirty dishes. She just preferred it to be on Mission Hill.

The agent ushered them back into the living room, enthusing over each feature.

Everything was Day-Glo yellow with green accents. Katie had the sensation of being bombed by the sun. Did the yellow glow at night? She remembered singing 'Climb Up Sunshine Mountain' when she was at a church camp. This was the 10th property she'd seen since their arrival two days ago, the third mobile home, not trailer as she wanted to call them, to the horror of the agent. They'd looked at a real house not a mobile home in Port Charlotte, which had been badly hit by a hurricane. Storm damage had been cleared away, but the owners had left a photo that the agent had forgotten to hide.

"Blizzards, hurricanes, we'll never find a weather-free place." Bill eyes begged her to be open-minded.

He turned the water taps on in the kitchen and stretched out on the floor to peer under the sink. "Plumbers, are they easy to get?"

'No different than anywhere else,' the agent said. Plumbing questions didn't interest their agent. She stepped over his prone body and threw open two slatted doors at the end of the kitchen, revealing a combination pantry and laundry room.

When Katie was first married, she used the back porch to dry her clothes. By the time Jess was born, she had a dryer. She'd forgotten how she once buried her nose in the air-dried sheets. However, she loved the softness of towels fresh from the dryer.

Katie tried imagining herself putting clothes in the washer and taking the car keys and driving their Escort from under the shelter where the current owners had banks of plants. That was the problem: she would have to drive everywhere. There was no public transportation to the movies or downtown. There was no downtown.

Her life would be spent in miles and miles of traffic hurtling past shopping center after shopping center, which all had the same stores and restaurants as if some giant cookie cutter plunked them down: Bealls, Targets, Walmarts and Olive Gardens over and over.

"Let's go to the clubhouse," the estate agent cut into Katie's thoughts.

Although it was a three-minute walk from the house, they drove. The first thing Katie noticed was the number of parked cars, all huge. IF they bought it and IF Jess were to visit, which she surely would do, she would rant about the environment throughout her stay.

For a second, she worried if Jess let Aidan stay overnight while they were away. What if Jess stayed at Aidan's? She hadn't reminded her to stay pure until her wedding before they left. Maybe the many discussions until this point would have been enough.

Although Jess never openly disagreed with her mother when the topic of sex before marriage came up, she always smiled. Katie didn't want Jess to accuse her of being out of date, as if obeying God's laws could come and go with fads. Perhaps if Jess had lived in a dorm or had her own place, Katie wouldn't know what she and Aidan were doing or not doing. She forced her attention back to the estate agent who opened the clubhouse door.

When they entered the clubhouse, people from aged 60 and up sat at tables eating donuts and drinking coffee. Some had walkers. A few canes rested on the back of chairs. Almost everyone, men and women alike, was dressed in pastel shorts with matching shirts in a variety of patterns. At one end of the room a stage held a lectern and four easels with signs for a funeral home, a car dealer, a life insurance company and a restaurant.

The agent looked at Bill and Katie and then at the group. Katie guessed the agent realized that many of these people could be their parents. She frowned as she pushed them through the clubhouse to where there was a pool with overweight women in swim caps exercising to the instructions of a man that any Hollywood agent would snap up as the next Brad Pitt. The slap of tennis balls could be heard, but the courts were out of sight.

The agent pointed to a bulletin board with May's activities listed. "Everything you could possibly want to do," she said.

Katie read about bridge, a dance, a barbecue, a trip to a nearby theatre to see Paul Anka, before the agent's voice broke in.

"There's a few park rules. No kids under sixteen can live here, no recreation vehicles or campers can be visible, and I can get you a list of acceptable plants, colors, etc."

Katie looked out at the sea of white faces and felt as if she were drowning in homogenized milk. She saw her husband frown.

"Children *can't* visit at all?" he asked.

"Of course, but only for two weeks." She thumbed through the folder she'd created for them. "It says your daughter is grown."

"Maybe we'll be grandparents someday," Katie said. "Do you handle rentals?"

"I don't. The office does. I thought you said you were interested in living here."

Katie resisted saying he is I'm not. "I thought maybe we might rent it winters."

Bill cocked his head in a way that showed he considered her comments optimistic.

When the agent dropped them at the hotel, Katie took her bathing suit off the white plastic chair on the terrace. "Sit, William," she said.

He did.

"From now on we will spend mornings looking at Florida, have a nice lunch, and if you insist, I will look at one and I mean only one house in the afternoon."

CHAPTER 51

No one would know it was May unless the poets had created a new poem about May showers bringing June flowers. Jess' Saturday plans were to study. Her next shift at the women's center was Sunday evening. Aidan was working that day, too, but she'd invited him for Sunday lunch.

She hoped her parents were enjoying themselves in Florida and wondered how vacation vs. house-hunting was playing out. Her father house-hunted like some men played golf. If he did buy something, he would need a new hobby.

Like him, she'd thought about getting her own place, but it was so expensive. Here she came and went as she wanted, only obeying the house rule of telling where she was going, when she would be back and calling if she were late. Her parents did the same.

She threw a load of her clothes in the washer. While the machine chugged away, she went upstairs. "Anyone home?" she called.

'I'm in the dining room. I'm surfing new sources on the web.'

Jess looked over her aunt's shoulder at the headlines in *The Guardian*.

"Taking your anger pill?" Jess drew a chair next to Peggy's.

"Just reading about the guy that ran against Blair because his son was killed in Iraq. Reg Keys. Came in right behind the major parties."

"You're not thinking about running for Congress?"

"I would if it would help. Running against Kennedy is stupid. He votes like me." She turned towards her niece. 'That's assuming I could raise the money to run. Now if I ran against someone like that idiot Joe Lieberman, who is more Republican than Democrat ...

"But you would have to move to Connecticut and be part of the party and ..."

"More and more I'm discovering the system doesn't work because of people like me."

Jess frowned. "I don't understand."

"I didn't pay attention to what was going on. I trusted. Trusting is dangerous. Another topic. Did you read about George Galloway's testimony in front of the senators?"

"Loved it. Told it like it was. The war wasn't necessary. And did you see Senator Coleman's face? He's too used to everyone being mealy mouthed."

The two women were silent, the type of silence where minds flow in the same direction and words are unnecessary.

"I only wish those words had been said by our senators." Jess ruffled through the papers on Peggy's desk. Her aunt found incredible photos, sickening photos of body parts. One showed an Iraqi family outside their destroyed home. Another was of an American soldier, his rifle butt ready to come down on a child's head. She refused to think about the copyright violations. Justice and legal were two different things. Given a choice, she would opt for justice. "How is your flyer distribution working?"

Peggy gave a smile, bigger than Jess had remembered her having for a long time. "I've run out. The people I rode to Fort Bragg with are all putting this stuff on windshields, telephone poles, everywhere.'

"Aidan will print more when you need them."

"The problem is we're too far away to blanket cars and poles in red states. It's frustrating as hell."

Jess gave her aunt a conciliatory shoulder pat. Then an idea struck. The totals of people who voted Bush in the red states were not overwhelming majorities. In the blue states they weren't overwhelming for Kerry either. Peggy had to reach beyond her local borders. "Aren't you e-mailing other Gold Star mothers from all over?"

"Except Alabama." When Jess frowned, Peggy added, "The mom there couldn't bear to think her son died for nothing. Still thinks if he hadn't died, she'd have to learn Arabic and wear the veil." She let out a long sigh. "The waste is the hardest part." Any trace of the earlier smile had disappeared.

Jess picked up one of the photos. It was of two Iraqi children reading in a small shed without a roof.

"You can reach the red states?"

"I don't have the time or money to go there."

"E-mail the posters you've made to the people on the list. Have them print them out and put them on cars, like you're doing. Network."

Peggy turned to her laptop. Jess looked over her shoulder and could see that she was accessing her e-mail list.

CHAPTER 52

Patrick woke to the buzzing of Bridget's sewing machine and no other noise. When he was awake, she played the radio, but never if he were asleep.

The curtain rippled against the open window. He stretched, remembering his dream: the kids were little. They were at McDonald's. His tray was filled with double cheeseburgers and fries. No one cried or fussed. When the kids were growing, they ate at McDonald's twice a year, but never in a month when tuition was due.

He padded to the bathroom. His urine hit the water – nothing like the first pee of the day. It was impossible to pee quietly. In Ireland, they hadn't had a toilet. He peed into a pot which made a different noise from pee hitting water. Once he and his brothers all peed into it at the same time to see how loud they could be.

At least prostate problems didn't bother him. Heart, cholesterol, blood pressure, arthritis, a bum leg, and diabetes were enough. He felt he was trying on every disease in the book, one by one, the way women tried on clothes. Good thing his family lived within walking distance of five major hospitals and Harvard Med School.

He stuck his penis back in his pajamas. For years he'd slept in shorts and T-shirts. In the last few years though, he woke-up feeling cold and began wearing pajamas with long-sleeved jerseys and elastic cuffs that didn't ride up in the night leaving his legs cold.

He wasn't as cold as Bridget's feet. Those could be used on a fish trawler to preserve the catch.

After splashing water on his face, he went to the living room. He knew better than to kiss her while the machine chugged. If the fabric slipped, she would let him have it. Pow!

She let up on the pedal. "Morning."

She was dressed in slacks and a blouse. Still slim, not like many women who went to fat, still a looker. Too bad he hadn't been able to do anything but cuddle her for years.

"Morning."

"Ready for breakfast?"

"Eggs and bacon." That would get her goat. Stupid phrase. Still he loved watching her eyes flash when he baited her.

"I don't think so. Toast and coffee." They went into the kitchen.

He sank into the chair with its back to the window. He felt the breeze on his neck and shivered. She saw and lowered the window.

After popping two slices of raisin bread into the toaster, she took down his white plastic box divided into 28 compartments, four rows time seven. The seven days of the week were printed on top. The side rows were marked for breakfast, lunch, dinner and bedtime. She emptied a compartment of six tablets.

He wondered if he really needed everything there. Sometimes he suspected that it was a plot, but he wasn't sure who was behind it, the pharmaceutical companies? The government? The HMOs?

Damn it, he used to be able to walk into his doctor and talk to him, get a word of advice, maybe a prescription even. Now those fancy-shmancy HMOs took his money and wouldn't let his doctor talk more than seven minutes which were used mainly to list hundreds of tests that never showed anything new anyway.

Old Dr. O'Brien's office used to be in his home. Patrick's HMO was in a brick building that could house a major corporation. It had hundreds of offices and colored stripes rolling down corridors to help you figure out where the God-damned department you needed was. You had to be an MIT graduate to figure it all out.

"How'd you sleep?" Bridget asked.

He had been so lost in thought, mentally railing against HMOs, he didn't hear her.

She repeated it. "How'd you sleep?"

"I dreamed we ate at McDonald's. Tasted damn good. No one said the word cholesterol."

Bridget stopped with his coffee still in her hands. She drank a large swallow.

"Hey, that's mine." Maybe she was going dotty on him. "Let's go to McDonald's for lunch." Usually that led to a mini-battle, which kept her with him and away from the damned sewing machine.

As she handed him the coffee, she wondered how many times they'd have this argument. She was sick and tired of it, well not really sick just tired, the same old, same old. She looked at her husband and saw through the thin white hair and the droopy jaw to the boy who had asked her to dance and who burst into her hospital room after their Connor was born, weeping at being a father. She imagined him as a boy, a young man, a middle-aged man, stripping off the face masks of different ages like computer-generated graphics.

Her mother had nagged her father; her friends nagged their husbands, do this, don't do that, eat this, don't eat that. That was what she was sick and tired of – Bridget the nag, Bridget the scold, Bridget sometimes giving in with a BLT, doling out treats like a mother. Well no more. "I should finish that dress about ..." she pursed her lips as she thought, "about 11:30. Then I think we should go to the Fenway Mickey Dees for a Big Mac and giant fries."

"Have you lost your mind, woman?"

"I think I found it. I won't spend the rest of our lives together bickering."

* * * * *

Three college boys in Northeastern sweatshirts and a girl, toting a backpack and holding her shoulders as if under a great weight, stood in line waiting at the one open cash register. The air smelled of fat and cooking meat.

Patrick leaned on his cane as Bridget ordered a salad. Jesus, Mary, Joseph, that was like ordering Chinese food in a steak house and vice versa. He selected a Big Mac, the biggest fries he could get and a large Coke. He wasn't sure when this windfall of cholesterol would fade into the fog of nagging.

Bridget carried the red plastic tray to a plastic table. As she'd done with the kids, she started to open his box. After glancing at his face, she asked, "What?"

"Any man, who supported a family, can open a box." He did. It was like Christmas morning. As he tore open the ketchup packet, he watched her watch him. Any second now she was going to blow.

She didn't.

What was happening? He stretched his bad leg. He'd forgotten how hard the seats were. Hell, he hadn't been in one since kids started calling it Mickey Dees.

"How do you think Peggy is doing?" Bridget broke into his thoughts.

He picked up his burger. A bit of ketchup oozed out onto his tray as he took a bite, such a treat. "I still don't understand why she burned that flag." When his daughter had dropped the candle into that metal garbage bin, it was as if he'd been sucker-punched. He had crawled in foreign mud to defend that flag.

He understood their girl less and less.

Now she spent all her time working on that stupid computer. She'd offered to teach him, had shown him an Irish newspaper, pictures of his old home town. He hadn't recognized much. Only the church seemed the same. A horse and buggy carried tourists. In his day buggies carried locals. If she had been born in Ireland, she would be sharing a small cottage, a farmer's wife, a much harder life than she had, although of all his kids hers was the hardest.

"I do," Bridget said. "She thinks the country let Jason down, let us all down."

"She let her country down."

He didn't want to think of Peggy any more.

A woman with three children too small to be in school carried a tray to a table. She plunked the tiniest in a highchair and dealt out burgers like a poker player dealt cards. The larger boy stole a French fry. The girl screamed. The mother grabbed one of the boy's French fries and handed it to the girl, who stuck out her tongue at her brother.

Patrick wondered what they would do if he reached over and took a fry. "I'm still hungry. I'm getting another burger." All the way to the head of the line he expected Bridget to come after him. Where was the woman who would throw her body across a gram of fat to protect his arteries?

* * * * *

Back home Patrick headed for a nap. His stomach felt as though he had swallowed a pillow. Ordering that second Big Mac was just plain stupid.

"Don't go to bed just yet," Bridget called from the kitchen.

"What are you yammering about, woman?" He hobbled toward the kitchen.

"I need to show you something."

He joined her as she was lining up his orange bottles. She had the weekly tablet counter box open. "You can take over your meds. I'll show you how I do it." She picked up one bottle. "This says morning and evening." She handed him the bottle.

"What do you want me to do with it?"

"Put one pill in the breakfast and bedtime slot for each day. If it says take with meals, make sure you put it in a meal slot. Otherwise evening is fine."

"I'll just leave them in the bottles." That would show her.

"Okay, tell me what you take next."

He picked up several bottles, putting aside the one that said three times a day with meals. He picked up the next bottle. It read take one at bedtime. That was clear. He dropped the pill in the proper slot.

"I'll leave it to you, then."

All in all, he preferred the nagging Bridget to this new Bridget.

211

CHAPTER 53

Sean wore his backpack and a grin that Peggy could read as only joy that he wasn't working this Saturday night. "Don't worry about drunk driving. I'm staying on the Cape."

Peggy looked up from her computer at her second-born, half her total kid production, a 50 percent success rate if she could compare kid-raising to business. He stood by the front door, his lanky body producing a wave of immeasurable love that poured through her.

"If you get lonely, you can go downstairs." Sean hovered in the doorway.

She didn't think so. Bill and Katie were in Florida, and she relished the silent time for what she thought of as *her work*. And she had tomorrow's meeting to prepare.

A horn sounded outside. "That's my ride."

"Go. I'll be okay."

"But ..."

"But nothing. You aren't normally here Saturday nights anyway."

When he opened his mouth, she wadded a piece of paper and threw it. "Go."

He blew a kiss, which she caught in the air, and heard his steps running down the stairs, then back up.

"What?"

"I'll be back in time for your birthday party tomorrow."

"Go." No need to speak of her relief that he would stay over. She wondered where on the Cape he would be. Over the years she had logged more than enough hours worrying about her boys when they were out. Whenever they were late, she knew, just knew, that they were dead. She planned funerals and set up scholarships with non-existent money. When they walked through the door the strength would ebb from her legs. Although she knew she was foolish, she still screamed at them. When Sean was a parent, he would realize that the yell was of relief.

Maybe.

Jason would never know.

What happened to Jason was never on her worry list. Her kids were born after Vietnam. The Wall had come down. The Gulf War had been a blink. Someday maybe she would stop beating herself up that she hadn't connected the Marines with war but thought of them as a disciplined force to shape up her problem child.

Sean had written his host's phone number on the slate hanging in the kitchen. The message board was started so long ago that she couldn't remember when. It had held thousands of messages: the time someone would be home, phone numbers, dentist appointments, reminders of chores. What she would give to see Jason's scrawl on it.

The clock read 12:30. The dining room table was covered with boxes of paper and posters. There were folders color-coded by topic, all related to the war or anti-war activities. She wanted her dining room back.

She paused at the door to Jason's room. The dirty clothes smell was gone. When he lived at home the floor was hidden by dropped clothes. Now except for a dust bunny or two it was clear. A sun-faded Celtics poster over his bed had lost its upper right thumb tack and the corner hung down hiding one player's face.

Peggy began putting his clothes into bags. She worked fast to keep herself from thinking of nuns from her school erasing the kitchen blackboard. Words, numbers, connections ... disappearing into nothingness. Jason's presence into the house was disappearing into nothingness.

She found porn magazines hidden in the closet under his shoes.

Maybe Jason hadn't seen them when he cleaned his room before leaving. Little of the personal was left: his Little League baseball bat, a high school blazer too worn to give to Sean, a few letters from a girl who Peggy didn't know. She read the first, begging Jason to spend less time with his "horrible friends" and more with her. The postage cancellation was six years old when Jason was at his worst. The return address was in Brighton. Peggy debated returning them then threw them in the black trash bag.

By seven Jason's room was gone, replaced by her new office. In an earlier life, she would have repainted it, made curtains and refinished the furniture. Now she just needed a place to do her work.

The telephone rang.

Peggy's hair stuck to her scalp from sweating as she tugged and shoved the furniture and put things for Goodwill into black plastic garbage bags. The Celtics poster and a broken chair had been carried to the trash cans. The bed, mattress and night table were in the basement. The chest of drawers was filled with Peggy's papers. Although it wasn't the best filing cabinet, it meant she didn't have to buy one.

Her muscles ached as she picked up the telephone.

"All set for the meeting tomorrow?" Judy DelSandro asked.

"Is everyone coming?" The group that had gone to the Fort Bragg demonstration was invited to come and watch the Sunday talk shows. When Peggy called and told them her idea, all of them wanted to help design posters to send to their anti-war contacts around the country. Sunday morning was the one time everyone was free.

"Yup. I'll be there before nine to make coffee," Judy said.

Peggy shut the dining room door, sank onto her couch. Her bones, her muscles, even her eyelashes felt tired. Perhaps it was psychological from cleaning out Jason's stuff, stuff of a little boy who would never have his own little boys. Or maybe because she wanted to do so much more to end this war and couldn't. She didn't hear her niece come into the room and jumped when she looked up.

Jess was dressed in a blue dress. Her hair was swept up and held with a butterfly clip. She carried a book. Without her aunt saying anything, she said, "It's about debt relief in Africa. Did you know that Britain sells $1 billion in arms to them?"

Peggy couldn't remember the last time she had seen her niece in a dress. "Where are you going?"

"Bia Bistro with Aidan, a romantic meal for our anniversary. We still celebrate month anniversaries. Once we celebrated an hour anniversary."

"Hour?"

"It was the first time we ..." Jess blushed.

"Don't give me the details." Peggy was pleased that her niece felt free enough to share things with her that she would never tell her mother. Poor Katie. Peggy knew that Jess' virginity mattered to Katie. Somehow with so many people dying needlessly, sex didn't seem an important morality issue.

"And you're taking a book on Africa?"

"We were discussing microfinance as the only solution to world poverty, and I found this at the library."

Peggy imagined them holding hands, champagne glasses half full, candlelight flickering and saying, "Read this on page one forty-seven." It didn't matter who said it, the other would flick to the spot.

"You look like you've been through a mine. What's up?" Jess asked.

Peggy realized that her hands were dirty. She glanced at the mirror over the mantle and saw a dirty smudge on her cheek. "Come look."

Jess followed her aunt toward Jason's old room.

Jess froze at the doorway and her eyes glistened. "Oh, Aunt Peggy! I'd have helped."

"If you start crying, you'll ruin your makeup." Peggy pulled a tissue from her jeans pocket. Her niece blew into it. "Besides, I needed to do this on my own."

CHAPTER 54

Rain fell too heavily for the birds to sing as they huddled in trees. In the entrance at 40 Delle Avenue a baby cried in her portable car seat. The baby was Maureen-from-the-march's daughter. The father had been killed since Fort Bragg, having never seen her. She apologized for bringing the child as she stashed her next to the couch. The women said she had nothing to apologize for. The men said nothing as they padded around sock-footed. Their drenched shoes were on newspapers in the hallway.

Peggy scooped up the baby and swayed with it balanced on her hip. The motion soothed the baby and she lowered her back into her portable seat. A pacifier was attached by a cord and pin. Peggy tickled the baby's lips, and the child took it and shut her eyes.

She hustled to the kitchen for coffee. Someone, she hadn't seen whom, had brought bagels in a soggy pink and white Dunkin' Donuts box.

Most everyone who had gone to Fort Bragg was there: Maureen, Judy, who had lost her son. Gina, whose husband had died from an IED soon after Bragg. Lisa's brother was still alive but on his third tour. Jack's kid brother was due to return in a month. Paul and Jennifer, both of whom who had served in Iraq, had brought laptops that they set up around the food.

Paul was better looking than ever. Too bad Jess wasn't there. She hadn't come home the night before, undoubtedly taking advantage of her parents' absence to spend the night with Aidan. Good on her, she thought.

However, she wished she had mentioned the meeting to Aidan and Jess because they could have contributed ideas.

Jen uploaded her Iraq photos. They were using Peggy's dining room table because everyone could stand behind the laptop. "Let's see if we can use any of these."

A soldier cried over another soldier whose blood seeped into the sand. Another showed a bullet-ridden ambulance, its back door open showing a human outline under a sheet-draped gurney. A soldier smoked a cigarette as a second leaned against the side of the vehicle. It was obvious there was no need to hurry.

"This is my wounded soldier series," Jen said. "I've another, and we may want to discuss whether we want to take that route. I call it our soldiers doing bad things." That series showed an American soldier, the butt of his gun about to smash the head of an old, veiled woman. Another showed two women in chains. A soldier stood over the bullet-riddled body of a child. "We aren't always the good guys." Jen's shoulders slumped. "We're not only killing Iraqis, we're asking our soldiers to kill their own souls."

Peggy thought of the stories she had heard from her father about how great the American Army had been taking Europe back from the Nazis. The Russians had raped and pillaged, but the Americans brought candy and chocolate and peanut butter to starving children.

Now she wondered if the stories were true. She had never thought that any American might do any raping and pillaging themselves. Maybe she had been naïve.

Maureen said, "I'm not sure about these photos for the posters."

Paul had his arms crossed. "I think we should. We can call it, 'Why Iraqis Want Us to Leave.'"

"People at home have no idea what real war is like." Jen spat her words.

The camaraderie of the ride was melting as if it had been left in the downpour outside as the we shoulds and we shouldn'ts were argued.

Judy tapped a coffee mug with her spoon. The room quieted. "Do you notice how this is breaking down?"

"How?" Jen asked.

"Those who've been there want to show photos. Those who haven't, don't."

Everyone let out a collective hmm. Then everyone talked at once, but certain sentences floated above the rest without anyone being sure who said what.

"We shouldn't fight among ourselves."

"Maybe we should listen to those who were there."

"Let's try a few."

"Wounded soldiers are okay. American soldiers committing atrocities okay," Paul said.

They worked fast to stick the posters on the woodwork and windows until the dining room looked like an anti-recruitment center. As they worked, they kept checking statistics on how many had died, how much money had been spent and how much money went unaccounted.

"What the hell is going on?"

Peggy, who had her back to the entrance and was putting up a poster with a grizzly pile of bodies, hadn't noticed that her father had come into the room. He walked from poster to poster, frowning.

"I asked what the hell is going on. I'm standing here in my own house and listening to all this anti-Americanism."

No one moved.

"Da, this is not an anti-American, this is anti-war."

"I don't care. I don't care." The second I don't care was screamed. "All of you get out of my house." Patrick raised his cane. The baby woke and started crying.

Paul caught the cane in his right hand. "If Peggy wants us to leave, we'll go."

All eyes turned to Peggy.

Connor entered, dripping water onto the floor. "What's going on?"

"This group of traitors is in my house."

"We're trying to get an anti-war message out," Peggy said.

"Jesus, Peggy, how stupid can you be?" Connor asked.

"Stupid enough to believe I have a right to speak out against ..."

"Not in my house, you don't." Patrick held one end of his cane and Paul the other.

Maureen scooped up her crying baby. "Please, Sir. You're scaring my daughter."

Patrick looked at the child as if he were seeing it for the first time. He lowered his voice. "I am giving you twenty seconds to clear out. One, two, three ..."

"Peggy?" Paul asked.

She looked around at her friends. Nothing more could be done today.

" ... four, five, six ..."

When she was little her father counted after issuing an order. "You better go guys. I'll e-mail you."

The group scuttled out, picking up umbrellas on the way.

CHAPTER 55

"Have you gone senile?" Bridget's hands were on her hips as she watched her husband splutter about their daughter's disloyalty to *his* country as if it were his alone and not hers. He paced between the kitchen table and sink.

Connor stood leaning against the doorway. He still wore his raincoat. His eyes flickered first to one of his parents and then back to the other with obvious regret that he had come upstairs.

Patrick put his head in his hands. "What will the neighbors think?"

"Nothing, since they have no idea who these people are and if they did, they would care less." Bridget said. At one time gossip would have bothered her, but that was when she knew everyone's business and they knew hers. There were some advantages to having all those overworked yuppies living nearby.

"It's not funny. We've a reputation."

"Bull, you Old Goat."

Patrick stood up very straight. His words were like machine gun bullets. "I never realized that I was married to a woman who was a traitor to her country." He limped to the front door and picked up the cane, which he'd left on the door knob. "I'm going to the Legion where people are decent and patriotic. I should have known she lost her mind when she burned our flag. We should have kept it to hang out front."

"Be careful you don't slip on the wet sidewalks," she called to his back. She turned to Connor. "At least if he falls, I will know I warned him."

Connor followed his mother and watched her bustle around the kitchen. She put water in the kettle but didn't turn on the gas. "And what do you think?"

"I wish she would drop the whole thing." He took off his coat and started to drape it over his arm, but it was too wet. Instead he put it over a kitchen chair and brushed water droplets from his navy turtleneck sweater. "It could hurt my career sometime in the future."

Although Bridget wasn't surprised at her son's statement, she wanted to hit him over the head with the frying pan. Does mothering never end? "What do you suppose she is thinking of?"

Connor shrugged. "Not her family, certainly."

"Her family has been cut in half." Darn, that was too confrontational. Connor always fought back. He had to be maneuvered.

"And how would you feel if something, God forbid, caused Ashley's death and the school was responsible."

"Jason died in a war. Wars happen."

Bridget heard Patrick slam the front door downstairs. She wasn't going to get anywhere with either man. "Where's Rachel?"

"Talking to Jess and Aidan."

"Why don't you join them?"

As soon as he was gone, she picked up the phone to call her daughter, who sighed when she heard her mother's good morning, although it struck Bridget that it wasn't a good morning at all. "Please tell whoever was there that not all your family is crazy."

"No one could prove it by Da."

"If you and your friends would like to come up for coffee, you'll all be welcome," Bridget said.

"They've already left, but I appreciate the offer Ma."

"Don't forget your birthday supper tonight. We'll talk later. Don't worry about your father."

* * * * *

221

Two hours later while Bridget swirled chocolate frosting from a can over a Betty Crocker marble cake, Patrick limped in smelling of wet wool, beer and smoke. She didn't look up.

Patrick stood over her. "I refuse to have that traitor in my apartment. I don't care if it is her birthday."

Bridget scooped more frosting onto the knife and ran it along the side.

"Did you hear me, woman?"

"I heard you."

"No party."

"No party here." They could hold the party downstairs just as well.

"I won't speak to her. Not until she apologizes. For the flag, too."

"Have it your own way. Leave me alone." A drop of spit flew out of her mouth along with the words.

Patrick stamped into his bedroom and slammed the door.

"Our daughter is right on this one. The world has changed," Bridget screamed at the wooden barrier. And Lord knows, we must change with it, but I am not sure how to do it. Like everything in her life, she knew the answer would come when she needed it to. It better hurry.

CHAPTER 56

When Sean came back from the Cape, he waved limply without speaking to his mother, who was curled up on the couch. He slumped through the dining room and into his room without saying a word. His skin was more than winter white and his eyes were red and puffy.

Too many times Peggy had seen her husband and older son lurch through this same room stoned, drunk or hung-over. She never watched the same movie twice or reread a book. She didn't rewind a DVD to re-watch a scene. She didn't need a repeat of others' drunkenness.

Sean was her baby, the hard working one, not the one that drank. Her sensible self told her that he was a college student who worked almost every Saturday and Sunday until midnight standing behind a cash register, a kid who brought home almost all A's with one B in Western Civilization. He took out the garbage without being asked. He wouldn't turn into a drunk because of one party on a rare night of freedom.

Every parent had their own demons when it came to their children. Her sister worried about sex: she worried about booze.

Now she was the delinquent, according to her father and brother. Sean would have to be briefed before the party. Before she could get up Sean was back and swept his hand around the dining room. "What happened? Here and in Jason's room?"

"I had a cleaning fit."

"I wish you'd waited for me." He sank into the blue easy chair between the side window and the radiator as if his legs didn't want to support his body any longer.

"It was an impulse."

"No, I mean I really wish I could have done it with you." He started to cry.

She wasn't sure how to comfort him, but then got the hassock by the couch and carried it to the chair, sat and took his hands in hers. His sweat and the alcohol seeping through his pores brought back more bad memories. How tired she was of bad memories.

"I guess I wanted his room to stay there, 'cause I could pretend he was coming back."

Then Peggy understood. He didn't want to say goodbye at all. "Someone once told me, that as long as someone was remembered by a loved one, they aren't really gone."

"That's silly. We'll remember Jason, but it doesn't mean he'll walk out of the grave."

Her son wiped his eyes with the back of his hands as he'd done when he was little. When a kid was as big as Sean, it was hard to realize that inside there was a lot of little boy struggling to be grown up. "I've something else to tell you before your grandfather does." And she laid out the scene, the expressions on people's faces as they struggled back into boots and rain gear, packing up the baby, coffee left undrunk and bagels and donuts half eaten.

"Grampy will never change." Then he giggled. "I can just picture it, especially him swinging the cane." He opened his eyes wide. "Sorry Mom, happy birthday." He stood up. "I really want to sleep before your party."

* * * * *

When Peggy walked into her sister's apartment, Happy Birthday was spelled in multi-colored letters across the wide archway between the living and dining rooms. Rachel, Connor and Jamie were seated.

224

Rachel stood up and gave Peggy a more than normal sisterly-in-law hug. Connor ignored her.

Ashley loped in from the kitchen carrying a bowl of chips carefully. Long ago, at Rachel's decree the family accepted spills as better than denying her participation. The bowl reached the coffee table without incident.

The door bell rang. A wet Aidan followed by an equally drenched Jess stomped into the outer hallway. They carried disintegrating paper bags with Coke and beer. He dropped his jacket on the newel post where it wouldn't wet the coats on the rack and removed his shoes before joining the others. Two raindrops hung like earrings from his ear lobes. Jess disappeared into her room and came back without her coat and two beige fluffy towels, one of which she threw at Aidan and one which she used to rub her own hair.

"So? Is Grampy coming or not?" Jamie asked. "I mean, like, just because he and Aunt Peggy had a row about the people who are 'destroying our country,' it shouldn't ruin a party, you know. What's the fuss about anyway?"

Peggy's reprieve was over. The babble broke into bits and pieces of who said what to whom. Peggy felt like a formaldehyde frog in a biology class instead of a birthday girl as her family dissected the morning's scene. Glancing at Connor she saw him staring into space.

"I agree with Da," Connor said. "What you did was ..."

Rachel poked him as Bridget entered the room with the birthday cake. "Upstairs, Sean. Now. For the pokey pot. It's pot roast. Lord knows with the fight this morning how I ever got it done."

She herded the rest into the dining room where each place setting had a birthday hat. At the head of the table there was a Burger King crown and presents. Streamers in purples and pinks coiled across the tablecloth. Everything matched: paper plates, cups, forks, spoons.

"Walgreens had a sale," Jamie said. "Since Aunt Peggy's morning was, like, so shitty, I thought she should have a decent finish."

"Maybe she should learn to behave," Connor muttered under his breath.

"Enough." Bridget pounded the table. "This is out of hand. First,

225

each of us should follow our own conscience. If Peggy feels she needs to fight this war, I support her." She turned to Connor. "We aren't asking you to go to any demonstrations. We aren't asking you to issue any statements to the press. You need to do what you need to do, although I think it would be nice if you gave your sister a little emotional support."

"But, Ma ..."

"Don't but-Ma me. Peggy lost more than any of us. She has every right to be as mad as hell." She turned to her daughter. "If you want me to go to any demonstrations or help you send out stuff, I'm ready."

For the next few minutes she served thick pieces of meat, potatoes and carrots slathered with gravy as each of her children and grandchildren handed her their plates. She gave Jess just vegetables. "This is Peggy's birthday and we're going to make it as happy as we can for her." She drew herself up in a way that made her look far taller than she was. "Understood?"

They all nodded.

Bridget smiled the smile that they all knew meant I still have it in me to rule the roost. "We'll eat, Peggy'll open her gifts, and then we can have coffee and cake."

Jamie's gift was a signed portrait of Jason that she had done herself. It wasn't a straight portrait, but a collage of the Celtics, a photo of his bike, a sketch of his Red Sox baseball cap and his G.E.D. certificate. Jason himself was in profile, looking off into the distance. Peggy reached for her Happy Birthday napkin and blew her nose.

"Don't go getting like all weepy on me," Jamie said. "I put a lot of that stuff in to cover up I'm not a very good portrait painter."

Peggy hugged her niece. "I think you're wonderful."

"We've gone in together on our gift," Jess said. "Aidan and me." Inside a box decorated with tiny birthday cakes on a blue background were two other packages wrapped in the same paper and several envelopes.

"With your anti-war work, you need your own website," Aidan said.

"I don't know anything about website design," Peggy said.

226

"You will now," Aidan said.

The package contained software to make designing web pages easy. The next was a *For Dummies* book showing her how to use the software. The envelopes contained the information for an online website course, a second course in design and a print-out showing that a website had been registered in her name under getthewordout. com and with a one-year paid-up fee to a web host. Peggy was unable to speak. When she could, all that came out was "But ... but ..."

"But nothing," Aidan said. "This is Jess's and my contribution to your effort."

Connor opened his mouth, but Bridget pinched his arm just above the elbow before he could say anything.

* * * * *

Upstairs Patrick sat side-saddle on a kitchen chair, his cane hanging over its back. His fingers beat a steady sound on the wood-design Formica. Bridget had made a baloney sandwich and a few chips for lunch, not enough to feed a hungry man. All the good stuff she'd spirited downstairs saying if he didn't want to eat with the rest of them, he could make do with damned sandwiches, only she had said danged. Damned was implied.

He didn't know what had gotten into his wife lately. He was losing control – that was for sure. Nothing, not one damned thing was like it used to be. His son-in-law wanted to move to Florida. His grandson was dead. His daughter was a traitor.

Even if the war was wrong, you did what your country asked. He remembered those dumb-ass doctors in the pub back in January, who wouldn't put their bodies where their mouths were. Talk, no action. Well he couldn't fault Peggy for lack of action, but her actions crossed everything he stood for. The whole day had given him a king-sized headache, one of the worse he had ever known.

Then his wife wanted him to fend for himself. Where was his daily entertainment if she didn't nag about his medicine? Medicine, that reminded him. He'd forgotten his pills. The container was next to the toaster. He didn't need his cane to walk that far. He filled a glass from the tap. No sissy bottled water for him. Boston water was good enough and a hell of a lot cheaper too. Damn and more damn. Some water sloshed on the floor. Well, it would dry.

He had the box in one hand and the glass in another but when he stepped on the wet floor, his left foot skidded. Although he stopped himself from falling by grabbing the back of the chair, the pill box fell and the pills scattered all over. He lowered himself down to the floor and one by one put the different pills back to where he thought they might belong. He was glad everyone was downstairs, so they couldn't see him crying.

CHAPTER 57

Katie's even strokes took her 20 yards into the Gulf of Mexico. She treaded water as she scanned the shore to see white Floridian sand, the hotel and the palm trees. The distance that she could swim without feeling breathless had increased each day. The smell of salt, the feeling of lightness, the blue of the sky left her contented and relaxed.

Katie admitted she was out of condition. Unlike many of her co-workers she didn't rush to the gym daily. Once she went with Tiffany on a guest pass but felt like a total idiot prancing around the floor.

She'd glanced at the gym pool thinking it would be nice to swim regularly, then put the idea aside. When would she go? After work she had to get home for supper so that was out. No way did she want to get up earlier especially for exercise.

At lunch she savored her break. Lunch was her time of day not to do anything for anyone, not her family, not her boss. Although she had a great boss, the woman still needed this record or that report finished, reasonable demands, but demands nevertheless.

Thus, Katie's pleasure in swimming was confined to her two-week holiday in Maine or on the Cape. Cape water was cold: Maine's was even colder. Florida water must recreate what a fetus felt like when it floated in the womb.

Looking inland, she saw Bill sitting under a garish green umbrella.

He sheltered the sun from his eyes as he scanned the water in her direction. When Jess was little and they were at the beach, he never relaxed. Even when Jess could out-swim a fish, he kept a lookout.

As parents they divided the worrying. He worried about Jess' physical safety in the water, when she was out with friends and her school grades, which was a total waste. Jess never brought home anything lower than a B+. He was relieved that she didn't want to drive.

Katie reserved her worry to Jess' emotional, spiritual and mental conditions. She would relax once she was safely married. Bridget's voice saying, once you have children you are never free again, rang in her ears. When Jess married, Katie wouldn't know if she came home late or not, and if she were late had there been an accident or was she in bed with ... no she didn't want to go there at all. As she treaded water, she realized that her mother never had that freedom because she and her sister lived in the same house. What would her mother do if she and Peggy weren't there?

On the other hand, she liked knowing how her parents were. If they were to move this far away, she would be cut off from everyone she cared about. What would it be like to not check upstairs to see what dress Ma was working on? Listen to her nag Da? Hear Sean clomp downstairs? She couldn't imagine herself in one of those development clubhouses. Outside the family, she never really had developed friends. Could she now?

A bird glided overhead. A school of some kind of fish swam near her, the sun and water making them iridescent. She watched them thinking they didn't worry about their children having sex. Fish made her think of the movie *Jaws*.

Katie swam back. When she reached Bill, she deliberately twisted her hair. Water dropped on his back.

"You're a wicked woman." He pulled her on the blanket next to him and kissed her, reminding her of beach parties the last month of their senior year.

"I am. The only thing to make me less wicked is to go again to the restaurant where we ate red snapper."

He brushed the sand from his arms and legs. "I've an idea that's even more wicked."

"I don't see why it has to be an either or."

* * * * *

Katie let the lukewarm shower wash salt and sand from her bronzed skin. That she looked tanned had more to do with the fact she wasn't wearing her glasses. With glasses, she could see the color was the result of an increased number of freckles.

She heard the bathroom door open. Through the frosted door she saw Bill sit on the toilet, but his pants were up.

"So, which property should we make an offer on?"

Vacations were one thing: living here was another.

"I'm not sure I'm ready to buy." Shampoo ran over her closed eyelids.

"We could make the decision and then we'll have the rest of the time here to play," he said. "Don't think of it as a move, think of it as an investment."

Investment. That's what others made: hoity-toity people, yuppies, not women like herself, not the daughter of an Irish immigrant, not the wife of a plumber, not a secretary. She had savings, money in the credit union that she could call on anytime. Still there was enough to pay cash for a place while leaving a healthy sum for the rainy day that Ma and Da always preached was just around the corner.

Then an idea flashed into her head like a light bulb appearing over a cartoon character. If they finally owned a place, never again would she have to spend a weekend house-hunting. "How about the second one we saw in Englewood?"

Bill opened the shower door. Water droplets hit his clothes leaving hundreds of little spots. "You mean it?"

"Yes."

He got into the shower and hugged her. The water soaked his shirt and pants and plastered his hair to his forehead.

"Idiot. Get out of here."

When Bill left, she thought maybe coming down here for a month each year might not be so bad. Maybe her parents would like to come too, Jess and even Aidan. Even if there were only two bedrooms, a couch could double as a bed. There were worse things than having a second home, although she always thought if they did it would be in New Hampshire or Maine where they could escape for long winter weekends: a cabin in a pine grove with a wood burning stove to set a cast iron kettle of stew simmering all day as they hiked snowy trails. Her husband thought snow was the type of four-letter word that when children used it their parents would reach for the Palmolive.

When she left the shower, she heard him talking on the phone. He certainly wasted no time calling the real estate agent.

The towels at the motel were large enough to sleep under, she thought, as she wrapped herself up. Her husband sat on the bed with his back to her. Something was wrong, she could tell by his hunched shoulders.

"I'll call back to tell you when we'll be arriving," He hung up.

She saw that he was trying not to cry. "What is it?"

He guided her to the bed.

"What is it? What's wrong?"

"Your father. He died about an hour ago."

CHAPTER 58

Bridget stared at Patrick's chair. The red cracked-leather was molded to his shape from countless hours of watching television, the remote in his right hand as he tried to find the best sporting event. Although there was standing room only at the mandatory after-funeral feed, no one sat in his spot.

Instead, her family, Patrick's buddies from the American Legion and the neighbors they'd known since the Flanagan kids crawled on knee-stained coveralls stood crowded together with their white paper plates piled with tuna fish and chicken salad sandwiches, fruit-filled molded Jell-O and chips. The women drank tea, the men beer.

Their voices were a babble, lighter than a couple of hours ago, now that they'd placed Patrick Xavier Flanagan in his grave with all the respect due a man who had lived his life, served his country, raised three good citizens and one priest. He'd been faithful to his wife, to the Democratic Party and to his adopted country.

Connor watched from the sidelines. Then he walked over to sit in the chair. Everyone stared. The king is dead, long live the king, Bridget thought.

From the moment they found Patrick sprawled on the floor surrounded by his medicines, to the rush to the hospital, and during the long wait until the doctor arrived with a facial expression that needed no words, she felt as if she were in an elevator going up and down without its doors opening. Desmond arrived while she slept.

She had no idea who called him and when. Katie and Bill came back, white under their tans.

Although she had taken no sedatives, her mind felt fuzzy. She was a lamb being shepherded from place to place, following without thought.

"What are you doing? That's Grampy's chair." Jamie's voice cut through the babble and Bridget's fog.

"Sitting down." Bridget wondered if she had yelled when everyone turned to look at her. She walked over to the chair and patted her son's shoulder. "Life goes on."

"Thanks, Ma," he said.

The neighbors melted away, two or three at a time. Rachel and Connor left to drive Ashley back to school. Jess, Jamie and Aidan decided to go to Flann O'Brien's for a memorial beer. Even if Jamie were underage, she could drink a Coke. Desmond was downstairs with Bill and Katie.

The kitchen was magazine clean. Peggy had washed every counter top, swept and washed the floor and was now wiping down the outside of the refrigerator. She saw her mother standing there.

The folded flag that had been presented to Bridget was on the empty chair. Patrick would have loved all the vets standing at attention next to his coffin.

Bridget had quieted Connor's worries that Peggy would "attack" her father's flag. The flag covering her Patrick's coffin represented something different than the one on Jason's, she told her son.

Peggy would take no stand, because that would spit on her father's beliefs. Her daughter's actions at Jason's funeral, although perhaps foolhardy, had been brave and made a statement that Jason couldn't. She knew her children well enough to know how each would act. But Lord knows, sometimes she got tired of still dealing with their quarrels.

Despite a great emptiness, she did not regret her husband's passing. He had lived longer than he should have, not for health reasons, although that was part of it, but because he could not cope with the current world. He found little pleasure in each day. When she reached that stage, she hoped someone would put her out of her misery. She also hoped that day was a long way off.

But never say never – or in this case – never think never. And with that never she let her mind turn to her daughter, who was in pain over her father's death. Peggy hadn't said anything, but Bridget knew losing people with unresolved issues was the hardest thing, although anyone who said "unresolved issues" would have led to her flinging the term "psycho-babble" at them. So many times, she wondered how good common sense had been drowned out by jargon and excuses.

"A cup of tea, Ma?"

Tea was the last thing Bridget wanted. "That would be nice."

Peggy filled the whistling tea kettle and turned the knob. The gas flame popped as the smell of sulphur wafted out then disappeared.

Bridget watched her daughter as she started to wash the cabinet over the sink for a second time. She knew the answer but asked anyway. "You all right?"

"I should ask you. You're the widow."

"You're the daughter."

Bridget looked up to see a spider web attached to the ceiling. Peggy's eyes followed her mother's. She started to climb on a chair, although she had nothing to bat the web with. Even with the chair, she couldn't have reached the ceiling corner 12 feet above the floor.

The kettle whistled. "Let's have tea, first," Bridget said. "We'll need a pot." She found the one with violets in the second cabinet to the left of the blue Tupperware flour and sugar canisters. "We'll do loose tea this time."

"You always want loose tea when it's important."

Bridget tried smiling away her tiredness but settled for hoping the smile masked how her arms seemed too heavy to lift. Overriding her tiredness was the need to help her daughter whose unhappiness seeped from her pores. "Stop looking at that web."

"The spider is still weaving." Peggy's elbow caught the tea canister, spilling some of the loose leaves onto the countertop. "Darn."

Bridget ran hot tap water into the pot. Patrick set the temperature too high, telling her repeatedly how his mother poured boiling water over their dishes. Bridget planned to ask Bill to lower whatever it was to reduce the temperature. In the future when she turned on the faucet, she wouldn't be in danger of scalding herself. "She's making her home. We all need homes, even spiders."

Peggy took out two violet mugs that matched the teapot and folded white paper napkins in half. "I'm tired of Styrofoam cups."

"They save lots of washing after funerals." Bridget emptied the pot and spooned in tea.

Peggy started to place the milk bottle on the table. She looked at it for a second then reached for the sugar bowl and creamer to match the cups.

"Like your tea parties, when you were little. Remember?"

Peggy shook her head. "It's another case of you remembering things of our childhood that we don't and vice versa. The same with Sean and Jas ..." Her whole body paused, the creamer hovering over the table as if a film editor had deliberately frozen the scene. Then Peggy put the creamer down and sank onto a kitchen chair.

For several minutes the two women sat with the teapot between them, each lost in their own worlds. Twice Bridget stirred the brew, the spoon clicking against the porcelain, before pouring the liquid into their cups. Every now and then one of them would turn to watch the spider weave another filament.

"She doesn't know disaster will strike after we finish our tea," Peggy said. "Disaster doesn't come with a warning: today there'll be a disaster, wear black."

Bridget needed to adjust her progressive lenses to see the spider closely. In her mind she gave each filament a name: Bridget, Connor ... until she got to Ashley, the last of her grandchildren. There were no Patrick and Jason threads. The web was whole. "Leave it there. Keep her home intact."

Peggy stared at her mother. "You want a cobweb in the kitchen?"

"She'll be company."

"Wouldn't you rather have a puppy? We'll get you a puppy."

The argument about pets had gone on for years. Patrick said four children were all the pets he needed. Although Bridget admitted a dog would be nice, she left the decision to Patrick. "That would be fun, but walking it? Well I'm not sure I'm up to it."

"A kitten then."

Bridget thought of all the little fluff balls she'd picked up in her life. She imagined herself untangling her threads after a kitten had found her workroom a feline paradise of toys.

They drained their first cups. Peggy poured seconds. Bridget debated telling her how wrong she'd been to stop nagging Patrick. Her plan to make their lives more tranquil had backfired. He needed to be cared for.

The doctors said a cerebral accident as they called it. Nothing could have been done, they said. She looked up at the spider. Was that the kind of spider that ate her mate after making love?

The sound of sobbing broke into her thoughts. Her daughter's head was on the table and her shoulders heaved.

When Peggy was under control, Bridget wet a face cloth with cold water. It had lost much of its nap after years of use. She wiped Peggy's face in the same way she'd done when her daughter cried over a scraped knee or some childhood catastrophe.

"I never got a chance to apologize."

"Your father should have apologized to you. Don't look at me that way. He lived to the point that he no longer felt useful. And it doesn't matter if it was in his imagination or not, it was real to him."

"Poor Da."

"Poor you. Your father loved you. In time it would have been okay."

After Peggy went downstairs, Bridget stayed at the table. She removed the teapot's top. The sodden leaves took up a third more of the pot than when she spooned them in. She hoped she'd helped Peggy, but once someone was dead, they were dead. Apologies didn't reach heaven. If they did, she would issue one of her own. "I'm sorry. I thought it would be better if I stopped nagging."

Over her head, the spider had stopped spinning. Bridget imagined that it was waiting for the next step in its life as she awaited hers.

CHAPTER 59

Peggy was hoarse the last Monday in June after watching the Sunday shows and screaming questions at Donald Rumsfeld. She was surprised Tim Russert hadn't heard her in the NBC studios. As it was Bill ran upstairs and Bridget down to make sure she was okay.

She had tomorrow off. The building where she was temping was being fumigated because of a dangerous mold. No one could enter for 72 hours. They'd sprayed late Friday after everyone had left for the weekend. She was happy not to work, although it was the loss of a day's pay. It gave her time for her real work, her anti-war work, and to do her last web course lesson.

Since her birthday, her days started before the birds sang and ended only when she could no longer hold her eyes open. More than once she woke to find herself asleep on her keyboard with ridges on her skin from where her cheek had rested on the keyboard.

Some days she felt she accomplished a great deal. On others all she looked at was what remained to be done. The first item was to end the war, not that it could be ticked off in the same way items like pick up milk or leave dry cleaning could.

The fan on the dresser hummed, turning left-right, right-left, left-right. Sweat ran between her unbound breasts. The back of her white T-shirt where she rested against her chair was drenched. Although she never wore shorts outside the house, she had on a white pair, ages old that should have been thrown out a decade ago. That she could get into them at all was a comment on how much weight she had lost since Jason's death.

She had gone from thin to skinny. Once cellulite bothered her. How could anyone worry about it when so many people were dying?

On the door to Jason's room, for Peggy still had trouble thinking of it as her office, was a sign Frenzy, Inc., a fiery red background with yellow fuzzy letters outlined in black. Sean made it for her. He said it was to help her keep things in perspective.

She had overdosed on perspective and reality. In another time and another place, she might be thought crazy, but the crazies were running the madhouse that used to be her country. It still was her country although it didn't feel like it.

Since Patrick died, Peggy had begun a blog that was attracting mothers who lost a child in the war or had one still serving in Iraq. As fast as she could, she was working on her website ... www. getthewordout.com.

Jess triggered the idea that her campaigning in a blue state wasn't enough. The red states needed information to be shaken up.

As her network grew, so did her sources. Daily she received photos of dead and wounded Iraqis and Americans, stomach-turning pictures that when you looked at them you could almost smell coppery blood. Pictures where a leg lay separated from a child that was breathing her last, pictures where a soldier's parts were strewn in several places. Pictures the media would never print.

These photos she made into flyers with statistics and the slogan, "Stop the Carnage. Call Your Congressman." The flyers were dispatched to her network who printed them out to distribute to wherever the volunteer felt it would create a 'click' moment.

Some days only a few hundred were distributed. She waited for the last of yesterday's figures, but the total would hit 350,000 by the weekend. All her activities flew under the national media radar, although a few other progressive blogs and websites had posted them.

Her website would have all the photos, along with as many stats as she could gather. She had pages with contradictory statements issued by everyone from Bush to the generals.

Her e-mail came up, which she sorted by topic. Then she copied the e-mails and the addresses which she kept on a memory stick in her sock drawer. Although she had heard about electronic surveillance, and she was sure the e-mails were on some server somewhere, she didn't really think the government would bother her. At some level, she wondered if she were growing paranoid, but every time she read about someone being arrested for an anti-Bush sign, she wondered ... but her wonderings weren't coherent.

The first was from Maryanne in Kansas. Maryanne's son died as the ambulance plane that was transporting him from Baghdad landed on the Air Force strip in Germany. He'd been shot in the back. The bullet was American.

> Hi Peggy ...
> Got any new flyers? I printed up over 1000 of the body of the child and put them on every car in the biggest shopping center.
> Love Maryanne

Cut.
Copy.
Paste.

The second was from Emma who had no one in Iraq but was against anything Bush did.

> Reporting in, Peggy ...
> I've 10 more names of people who will distribute information.
> Add them to your master list.
> Emma

Cut.
Copy.
Paste.

The next was titled 'You Bitch' but it came from Karl in Oneonta, NY.

> Take my wife off your list. She is destroying everything
> my son died for. It's people like you who are destroying
> this country.

Cut.
Copy.
Paste.
Peggy had no objectivity left. She couldn't see how others couldn't see what she saw.

Sean snuck up and set an iced coffee next to her computer. The glass beaded with moisture and the red plastic straw stood in the middle between misshapen ice cubes. "I'm off to work."

"You're a sweetie." She knew full well he wanted to tell her not to work so hard. If she got sick, there wasn't any health insurance. A week ago, he'd said, "I'm going to put the take-care-of-yourself lecture on tape and press the button daily."

Role reversal, Peggy thought.

She held the cold glass to her forehead. She couldn't let the heat get to her today because she had her temp assignment the rest of the week and wouldn't have time to work on what had become her major reason for getting up each morning. If she could just keep at this for the next 16 hours that would take a tiny nibble out of her to-do list.

Jess appeared wearing frayed cut-off jeans. Her hair was swept up off her neck and held with a barrette. Escaping tendrils stuck to her cheeks and neck. "Can you take a break?"

Peggy's hair was matted to her forehead. Her deodorant had failed hours before. "What time is it?"

"Three thirty or thereabout."

A wasp whisked by Peggy's ear. "There must be a nest somewhere; this is the third today.' With any bit of luck there would only be a hole in one of the screens.

She grabbed a faded yellow terry cloth towel thrown on top of a stack of papers. The wasp flew out of her reach, but she stalked it as seriously as any big game hunter, until it lit on the printer. She threw the towel over it and grasped the tiny bulge. "I can feel it vibrate through the towel."

Jess put her finger against the lump that Peggy shoved forward. "Amazing. I hope its stinger won't go through the cloth."

"All buzz, no bite."

Wasps were like politicians: awful. She walked through her kitchen to the back porch overlooking the yard. Rose bushes, that Patrick had cared for, almost buried a white picket fence which needed painting. The thorns had discouraged any attempts to get close enough to wield a brush. The flowers were his living memorial, she thought.

Despite what her mother had said, she wished her last words to her father had not been angry ones. Another frustration in a long list of frustrations of having to accept what she hated accepting.

She flapped the towel over the railing. The freed insect flew toward the roses. "Don't come back; tell your friends to stay away."

Back inside, the e-mail beeped. Peggy brought up a message from John Kerry. Peggy had written to so many senators and congressmen that she regularly received their propaganda. "Holy shit. The bastard!"

Jess stood behind her aunt as she read the message.

"Here is my chance to send a Fourth of July message to a serviceman. Kerry'll see it gets through."

With shaking hands Peggy typed in senate.gov, went to the senator list and brought up the Massachusetts contact information.

"Are you sending an e-mail?"

"Calling, then e-mailing. Or I may go shoot the bastard."

She rummaged through her papers, scattered throughout the room.

"What are you looking for, Aunt Peggy?" When her aunt didn't answer, she asked a second time, only louder.

"The stupid telephone. I can't find it."

Jess pulled her cell from her back pocket and punched in her aunt's number. A ring sounded from the bathroom.

In seconds Peggy was back with the telephone.

Jess frowned at her aunt. "Did you forget you left it in there?"

"Don't go getting all worried that I am losing it. Sean lives here. He must have taken it into the bathroom this morning."

Jess raised her hands. "I can't help it if I'm worried about you. It comes with the territory of being loved."

"You're using my own words against me. Now listen to this."

Jess put her head next to her aunt's. Peggy held the phone at an angle.

"John Kerry's office." The woman's voice was laced with a Boston accent, although Peggy dialed the D.C. number.

"I want to register a statement."

"Of course. May I take some details?"

"Zip code 02120, name Peggy Flanagan, that's F-L-A-N-A-G-A-N?"

"Thank you, now what do you wish to say?"

Peggy wanted to ask how many hours this woman had spent in oily-voice training. "It is about sending telegrams to troops in Iraq."

"We've a form ..."

"I got the form by e-mail. I would love to send a message to my son in Iraq, except he died there."

There was a pause on the phone. "I know ..."

"You know nothing. My message to Senator Kerry is that he shouldn't have voted for the war. He should have been anti-war during the election, and this ... this ... this cheap trick of sending a telegram to our soldiers is disgusting."

"I'll pass the message along."

"And add that the only thing the troops need is to be brought home."

"I'll tell him."

Peggy disconnected the phone and threw herself back in the chair.

Jess put her arms around her aunt. "Wow. A year ago, I would never have imagined you doing that."

Peggy still couldn't imagine herself doing it now. She just did it. "Someone has to let these bastards know we aren't fooled."

"Kerry is a good guy."

"Not good enough."

Jess reached over her aunt's shoulder to the computer keyboard, saved everything and shut it down. "That's it. Go take a shower. Aidan and I are taking you out for a late lunch. Now!"

Peggy's back ached, although she hadn't been aware of it until she was interrupted. "Let me just show you the website."

"Later. Do I have to throw you into the shower?"

"You and what army?

"I'll get Aidan. I'm not joking."

* * * * *

Flann O'Brien's was cool and dark. As Peggy, Jess and Aidan entered, the one man at the bar dropped a 10 on the counter and left. The odor of beer made the pub smell like a pub should.

After greeting Janie, the waitress, Aidan ordered three fish and French fry plates, three Cokes and sides of coleslaw. Peggy noticed that Jess agreed to eat fish without a word about animal rights. Well, it still wasn't meat. They were left alone when Janie disappeared into the kitchen area. The giant TV screen was tuned to CNN, but there was no sound.

"I've good news for you." Aidan pulled out a chair for Peggy as Jess slid onto the bench between the blocked window and the dark wooden table. "Bush's disapproval rating hit fifty-three percent."

"That's not good news. Why isn't it zero after all he's done?" Peggy asked.

Aidan patted her hand. 'Your aunt won't be happy until he's impeached.'

"You're wrong. I'll only be happy when he's tried as a war criminal." She hit the table with her fist.

"The problem with your family, Jess, is that they are too wishy-washy in their opinions."

Janie, on her first of three trips to deliver the meals, said, "Wishy-washy is the last words I'd use for this family. A waitress should know. For instance, Patrick ..." She stopped. "I'm sorry, Peggy, about your dad."

Peggy waved her hand. Janie had been at the funeral but hadn't gone back to the house because she had to work during the noonday rush. "It's fine, Janie."

Peggy's bones ached from too much knowledge. Half of her wanted to be as innocent as she'd been two years ago, thinking of only her job and family, not of Humvees, nor governments going to war. Maybe if she had thought of them earlier and acted on them earlier, she wouldn't have to think of them today. No, that was stupid. One person couldn't have stopped the war. "What do you hear from your parents?"

Jess stabbed a French fry with her fork and dipped it in ketchup. "They made an offer on a house to a widow who said yes and then she died. The daughter wants to keep the house as a winter rental. They're still looking."

"I never thought Katie would buy anything, much less in Florida." Her sister's trips to Florida would also have been on Peggy's unthinkable list last year.

Jess shrugged. "Life changes. I think she's doing it to get Dad off her back."

"Think they'll move there full time?" Aidan asked.

"Mom says vacations only. Dad's master plan is to get her down there for a few weeks here and there. Then he'll sell her on staying longer each time."

Aidan looked at his watch.

"We still have time to get to the beach," Jess said.

Peggy said nothing about how the two understood each other without words. Her niece had found a good one.

"Revere beach is closer," Jess stood up.

"But Crane's is so nice," Aidan said.

"Okay," Jess said.

Peggy wondered how Aidan made Jess so pliable. They were so full of hope, while she was, she was ... a tsunami of overwhelming sadness, something she couldn't afford if she wanted to accomplish even a part of her to-do list.

Before going back to work Peggy popped into her mother's. Bridget sat on the floor turning up a hem on a beige linen skirt draped on a mannequin. Any guilt at ignoring Bridget melted in the heat when her mother said she was going out to dinner at the neighbor's.

Downstairs an e-mail from Mary-Lou-in-Bluefield-West-Virginia's husband said that his wife had been arrested for putting anti-war literature under a windshield in a shopping mall.

Peggy consulted her list of lawyers in West Virginia volunteering their services pro bono and e-mailed to Mary-Lou's husband. For a second, she felt good about what she had accomplished before it disappeared into disappointment about what she hadn't. Pendulums and Peggy's moods were on the same back and forth motion, but pendulums didn't get as tired because it was their job to swing. Peggy fell victim to exhaustion some days. She dug into her project and lost track of time for the rest of the afternoon.

Bridget entered looking smart in slacks with her hair neatly tucked into its chignon.

"Dressed up, Ma?"

"I know its only Angela's for dinner, but I felt like looking snazzy. Good for my soul."

The neighbor, another recent widow, and Bridget had shared meals and television programs since Patrick died. They'd taken up bingo, now that their husbands weren't there to sulk at being left alone. Last week Bridget won $200 and Angela $50. The two women even talked about going on a cruise, although Rome had been mentioned as well. Good for Ma.

She heard her mother's steps fade away. The bone heaviness that attacked her at Flann's grew worse as the room darkened as if liquid had been injected into her bones. She hadn't accomplished even a small part of what she wanted.

Was she doing any good at all or was she just fooling herself?

Nothing would bring Jason back. She flipped on the yellow lamp on her desk. It provided a small halo in the June evening heat.

The fan clicked, clacked and stopped. Its blades were frosted brown-grey with dust. Peggy switched it off and on. Nothing. She checked the plug. Burnt-wire smell filtered through the air.

Tomorrow she would buy another. At one time she would have gone to Walmart for the best price. Now she supported small stores.

She could have had her mother make her clothes, but the last thing her mother needed was more work. Her parents already did much too much for her.

Maybe she would try the Salvation Army store. That was Jess's idea. "Well, what do you think happens to the things you give them?" her niece once asked. "You help twice. Every dollar you spend is a political decision. Not to mention the environment." Crusader Jess. Crusader Peggy.

With the sun set the heat was almost, but not quite, bearable. No more wasps visited, but a mosquito buzzed. Stupid things must have microphones in their bodies.

The doorbell rang. Who would stop by at 9:30 at night?

"I'm coming." She slipped on her sandals.

This was one of the rare times she was alone in the triple decker. Bridget hadn't returned. Jess was still with Aidan. Sean was at work.

Remembering stories about the Boston Strangler, she slipped the door chain on, not that it would do any good. Anyone could break the oval glass pane etched with frosted swans.

Two men stood outlined in the porch light. Murderers don't usually work in pairs. One was probably in his 30s and the other in his 40s. They were well groomed and in good physical shape. She opened the door as far as the chain allowed.

The younger man held up a badge that she couldn't see because the porch light was behind it. Even if she could, she had never seen a real FBI badge. "FBI. Are you Margaret Flanagan Doherty?"

"Yes, and you can't come in." She slammed the door and ran upstairs.

CHAPTER 60

A ngela Durgin's backyard was the same size as Bridget's, but it looked different. Angela's had a high wooden stockade fence enclosing and creating a small refuge which made people forget they were in a major city. Flower beds with marigolds, petunias, begonias, geraniums and zinnias created a cacophony of color right up to the stockade fence. An oak tree, in the right-hand corner, lent shade during the long, hot summer days.

Angela and Bridget sat on pink-cushioned deck chairs, drinking beer. Dirty plates and a half-empty clear salad bowl sat on the redwood round table. Ashes glowed their last in the barbecue that resembled R2D2. Light filtered down from the back porch.

"Did you hear about the O'Reillys?" Angela's grey hair was permed into an Irish Afro. She wore shorts and a T-shirt washed until the original purple mellowed into violet. Because she wore hose under her shorts compacting her cellulite, her legs looked smooth as they had when she and Bridget were in high school.

"Since they moved to Jamaica Plain, it has become a Christmas-card friendship," Bridget said about their former neighbors.

"They moved back to Ireland, every last one of them."

Bridget wondered what made people decide to move. She understood why Connor chose Newton; good schools and a place that needed a state rep. Maybe he and Rachel didn't want his family breathing down their necks. Maybe that was why Bill wanted to move, although she and Patrick didn't interfere, well not too much. When would she stop thinking of Patrick in the present? He was gone. She was going to make the most of her remaining time on this planet. No regrets of his death. No regrets for his life, for that matter.

Angela put her hand on her arm, bringing her back to the now. "Are you okay?"

"Yes." And she was. "It's funny, I always thought Patrick and I made decisions together, but in reality, it was me. I had the ideas and convinced him. And if I want anything from my children I go to my daughters or daughter-in-law. It's almost as if the men were shadows."

Angela put her head back and laughed. "Are you just now discovering the secret of family life? I knew that for decades." She leaned towards Bridget. "Whose idea was it that your kids would go to Catholic school."

"Mine."

"And who found the house you bought?"

Bridget pointed to herself.

"And who started a business to supplement your income?"

Bridget nodded. "But I always talked things over with Patrick."

"Until he did what you wanted. The same with my Liam. Nothing wrong with it, and you know it." Angela stood and picked up the dishes and silverware.

"Let me help clean up."

"Pish posh."

Angela held the plastic tray with a nicked corner in her hands. "You know I still have a great body for an old Irish broad. And you aren't half bad yourself. Maybe we should go out looking for some men. I hear there is a club downtown that has speed-dating for seniors."

"Not for me."

"Maybe a toy boy?"

"How's your new tenant?" Bridget had seen the man going in and out.

"Works all the time. One good thing about yuppies, they're too tired to make trouble."

She disappeared into the house.

When Angela came back a light breeze rippled the oak leaves as the women sat in a silence that satisfied them both. Humidity still dampened the air.

Angela jumped up. "I forgot dessert. It's ..." She didn't finish before she once again disappeared through the back door.

While she was gone, Bridget remembered how when she stopped by last week for bingo, Angela had forgotten they were going. Maybe she should speak to Susie, but only after making her promise to say nothing to her mother. Angela's temper had not been diminished by years, but like a thunderstorm when it was over it was over. Still Bridget didn't want to be the recipient.

Angela appeared with two large brownie squares topped with vanilla ice cream and dribbling chocolate sauce. Both women spooned into them. "Like the days when we went to Bailey's," Angela said. A drop of chocolate marked her lips.

"What I would give for a Bailey's sundae." Bridget shut her eyes imagining it.

"The silver dish with hot fudge dripping over the edge onto the matching saucer."

"And we never ran out of the fudge before we ran out of ice cream."

Both women sighed in unison.

"And we waited for the boys to come in. Even then Patrick was after you."

"As Liam was after you."

They both sighed in unison again.

Angela's eyes widened. She grabbed Bridget's hand. "I just remembered something. I should have told you when it happened, but I called, you weren't home, then I forgot and when I remembered it was the middle of the night and ..."

"It's all right, just tell me."

"Friday, no Thursday, two men knocked. Said they were the FBI."

How could anyone forget about the FBI, Bridget thought. Then she remembered the time that Angela had told her about a television show so realistically that it was only at the end did Bridget realize that it wasn't real. Maybe this was the same thing. "Your door?"

"It was the strangest thing." Angela leaned over. "I asked for their badges. I know better than to let any stranger into my house." She cocked her head.

"Are you confusing this with something you saw on TV?"

Angela put her hands on her hips. All her life she had been good at puffing herself up. "Bridget Marie Riley Flanagan, I know the difference between TV and reality."

"I'm sorry. What did they want?"

"They asked all kinds of questions about your Peggy."

"Our Peggy?"

Angela nodded. "About the whole family, but mostly about Peggy."

Bridget knocked over her chair as she jumped up. "I need to go home."

* * * * *

Walking the 10 steps between the houses took seconds. The porch light was off. As long as someone was out, the light was left on. Maybe the bulb had burned out. Sean could change it tomorrow. As she stepped onto the porch, she noticed the cut glass swans in the oval door windows were missing. Glass scrunched under her sandals as she stepped through the unlocked front door.

She stifled her impulse to go further: hundreds of scary movies flashed through her mind along with Patrick's statement, "Who would be that stupid to continue into a situation like that" to which she always answered, "Anyone who wants the story to continue."

She ran back to Angela's and pounded on the door. As soon as it opened she raced to the telephone.

"What's happened?" Angela asked as Bridget dialed 911.

"There's a robbery-in-progress at my home," she gasped into the receiver. To bring them faster she sobbed. "My daughter is with them. I'm so scared."

251

Angela stood behind Bridget, one hand over her mouth, the other touching her friend as she gave the address.

"Please, as soon as possible." She hung up. "Angela, watch the back of the house: I'll watch the front."

Although she'd read articles in *The Globe* critical of police response time to 911 calls, a siren came around the corner before she reached Angela's front door. The two women rushed onto the street and hid behind Bill's truck as two cops holding guns mounted the stairs to her house. She realized she'd been holding her breath.

Nothing happened for what seemed like hours. Then lights went on floor by floor. Through the bay windows on each level, Bridget tracked the police's movements. When they came onto the porch, she called, "Over here. It's my house."

The women and the police met at the stairs. The older policeman stuck his gun in his holster. He was overweight. Round wet spots circled under his arms. He took off his hat to wipe his brow. A hat mark outlined his reddish-brown hair and creased his forehead.

Bridget collapsed on the stairs. "My daughter?"

The older policeman sat next to her. "No one's there. It looks as if things have been taken from the middle floor."

"There's been a struggle," the black policemen said. His shirt was double-creased back and front. He had no sweat marks. His antiperspirant worked better than his partner's. "Come show us what's missing." For someone with such a well-developed body, he spoke in a high voice.

"Besides my daughter?"

"Couldn't she have gone out?" the older one asked.

"I doubt it." When Bridget tried to stand, her legs wobbled and she swayed.

The black cop gently pushed her down on the stairs and forced her head between her legs. "Take your time, lady."

As she began to shiver, time was the last thing Bridget wanted to take. She wanted her daughter with her.

Now!

CHAPTER 61

"Salty." Aidan licked Jess' left nipple. His yellow plaid sheets were tangled under them. The yellow basket-weave blanket was on the floor. The discreet covering by bed linens shown in the movies after stars make passionate love was not for them. Their sweaty skins glistened in the early evening light. The buzzing air-conditioner was inefficient.

He lived in a Cambridge Victorian house converted into condos. His bedroom had a fireplace, a 12-foot ceiling, moldings and a rosette in the middle.

The walls were beige: the ceilings were white. The furniture was flat-pack white. The shades at the curtainless windows were white but not the sophisticated white of a loft apartment. This white was just white, thrown together to make sure nothing mismatched but with no thought of nest-building or even of seduction. The sheets and blanket had come from his parents' house.

The first time Jess visited Aidan's place she expected a mess like other apartments of men his age whom she knew. His was neat, although nothing in it said, "Aidan" with the exception of his library/office. There books, computer, photos and framed news stories with his byline marked his territory.

"Of course, I taste salty. We just spent the afternoon playing in the Atlantic followed by a good hour of love making. Did you expect Chanel No. 5?"

He propped himself up on an elbow and continued teasing her nipple with his finger. "I've something to ask you."

"Sure."

"Marry me."

"Marry you?" Her plans were to graduate and open her legal aid center. As a kid she never dreamed of white dresses. She played archaeologist, scientist, lawyer, cop, not wife or mother. The problem wasn't marriage. She just never expected to find any man who would accept and love her as she was. Her opinion of herself was someone too opinionated to settle into a double harness. Jess sat straight up.

"Law Student, think! Legally binding agreement between a man and woman. Love, honor and cherish. No obey. You wouldn't buy that clause."

Jess circled her legs with her arms. "You're serious?" She couldn't look at him, although he stared at her.

"You mean you haven't been thinking along those lines?"

Jess hadn't. She rushed back and forth between classes and work, helping Aunt Peggy's crusade; when she could, she fit Aidan in for coffee, a movie, dinner and maybe sex, which she liked. No, she loved it with him. Some of their lovemaking was passionate, but some was fun as they joked their way through. Time with him raced by, and when she wasn't with him, she often made mental notes of what to tell him when she would be.

"I love you, Jess Kelly. I've never met anyone like you, and I know you won't be a traditional wife, whatever that is. But I am prepared to put up with you."

Jess hit him with a pillow. "Put up with me. That's not romantic."

"I'm not a romantic type, but if you want, I'll fake it." He opened the nightstand drawer and took out a small box. The condom they'd just used dangled from the end of his penis. He got down on his knees. "Marry me."

There must be something wrong with me, she thought. Her friends dreamed of weddings, marching down aisles with white dresses and an organ playing. They thumbed through bridal magazines arguing the merit of dresses. It bored her. She looked into his eyes and saw his intelligence and goodness as well as his nervousness. Taking his head in her hands, she kissed him on the lips.

He rose and sat on the bed next to her. "Is that a gee-I'm-sorry kiss-off?"

"Not at all, but ..."

"But ..." How could she explain that although her parents' marriage was happy, she didn't want to live their way, but didn't know what way hers was. What if they had a handicapped child like Auntie Rachel and Uncle Connor? Aunt Peggy's marriage had been a nightmare, but Aidan wasn't a drunken violent man. Two high school friends who'd married out of college were already divorced. "We need to negotiate the type of relationship we want.'

"Marriage." He used a tissue to pull the condom off. Instead of throwing it in the bin he left it on the night stand, wadded up in a wrinkly ball of white tissue.

"How do we want to live? What do we believe in? Who'll do the dishes? How will we solve conflict?" She wanted to notch this relationship up. Maybe loving him and fighting for social justice were not an impossible combination.

He rolled back on the bed and cradled his head with his hands. "Just my luck to fall in love with a lawyer."

"If you ever go to jail to defend a source, think what you'll save in legal fees."

He grabbed her and kissed her long and hard.

When they broke apart, she said, "I need to think about it. Know this — I do love you."

Her mobile rang.

"Ignore it," he said.

She scrambled out of bed to dig through her backpack. After shaking her hair back she put the phone to her ear.

Aidan watched as she sank into a chair that was covered with their clothes.

"We're coming now." She hung up and reached for her jeans. "There's been a break-in. Aunt Peggy's disappeared."

Aidan was dressed before she was.

255

CHAPTER 62

Hammering sounded in Peggy's apartment as Aidan and Sean nailed boards over the broken window. The blows matched the pain in Bridget's head.

The hall clock struck midnight. Bridget, who sat on her missing daughter's couch, realized that she'd forgotten the clock existed. The sound had always melded into the household noise. Tonight, it was an intrusion.

She'd experienced fear like this once before, when Peggy's appendix burst at age seven. They weren't sure she would live. Now they'd just celebrated her 48th birthday, but the additional years of her daughter's life that Bridget had been given weren't enough. My God, how had her daughter survived losing Jason?

Once upon a time, as fairy tales start, she had four children under five with two in nappies. Without a moment to herself and amidst screaming and jam-sticky tables she dreamed about walking out the door and never seeing them again. Once they were asleep, she looked at them and said a rosary for her bad thoughts.

If asked, she would declare she loved them equally. In her heart of hearts, she knew she loved them differently.

Desmond, from the day he was born, eschewed hugs and kisses and kept to himself. Her pride in him swelled whenever she imagined him walking the Vatican's corridors. He'd been a goody-goody. Sometimes she found it just plain annoying. Desmond was lost to her, stolen by the Church. If she must lose a son, better to lose him to that.

Connor was a good boy, a bit selfish, getting into just enough scrapes to make him more interesting than his brother. With his wit and smile, he explained himself out of most doubtful situations. When he couldn't, he accepted whatever punishment she and Patrick doled out. She hoped he was an honest politician or as honest as possible.

Katie, well Katie had lived a blessed life in finding Bill at such an early age. Her daughter was a bit rigid with Jess, but it was done with love.

Peggy, however, ranked first in her heart if she allowed herself to rank her kids by love. Not just for the hardships she'd overcome, but for reasons making no sense to Bridget. They could sit in silence, Bridget sewing on a client's dress, Peggy knitting, saying nothing but having a great time.

What if Peggy were dead? Bridget had weathered losing Jason, always a troublesome kid. She'd survived losing her Old Goat. Lord knows she'd enough time to prepare. Nothing was like the panic she felt now at her daughter's disappearance.

The police had left to answer another burglary in process. The older cop said over his shoulder that Peggy might have left on her own before the robbery.

If only she'd thought to show them the kitchen white board where Peggy and Jason wrote messages about their whereabouts. When she thought to check it herself, its blankness made a mockery of hope.

Jess paced until Bridget shoved her into a chair. "Sit still."

Sean, followed by Aidan, came into the living room. "Okay, the door is secure."

"Call Connor," Sean said. "He has influence."

"He and Rachel went to the Cape," Jess said. "I already left messages on their phones, but if they don't look ..."

"Let me check something." Aidan rushed out into Peggy's office. Sean, Bridget and Jess followed.

"Look at what they took," Aidan said.

257

"Her computer," Sean said. "So what? We know that."

"But why your mom's computer. That's it. Not the TV, not the DVD, not the piggy bank – only the computer."

Jess opened the drawers of Peggy's new filing cabinet. "And all her files and papers. All of them and the USB key."

"Weird." Bridget hugged herself. If she let go, she would melt into nothing. She always thought she would be able to rise to any occasion, but she was tired of rising.

"Something else is weird." Bridget told them about Angela having the FBI ask about the family.

"What would they want with her?" Sean stared at Aidan.

"She's a war protestor." They all looked at Aidan. "Maybe it was the government."

"Government? They don't steal people," Sean said.

"She's a mother who lost her son," Bridget snapped, although she believed Aidan. She didn't want to, but it was the only thing that made sense. No, it didn't.

Although Bridget wanted to tell everyone to go to bed, she didn't want to be alone. She thought of all the missing persons that made the news: mothers pleading for their children, the interviews on Larry King, an industry of missing people.

"Go to bed, Gran," Sean said.

She read worry on his face but shook her head.

"Well at least stretch out on the couch," Aidan said.

"Good idea," Jess said.

Bridget looked at her granddaughter, who was pinkish but not quite sunburned. She looked healthier than usual, although worry showed through indicating what she might look like in 20 years. Her family worked too much and lived too little. If she could relive her life, she would play more and sew less.

A light breeze came in through the three screened windows behind the couch. Fighting the urge to start searching for her daughter herself, she put her legs up and closed her eyes; later, Jess threw a light blanket over her.

CHAPTER 63

Katie stared at the planes at the Tampa airport. The tarmac shimmered almost like an oasis. If it had melted in the heat, she wouldn't have been surprised. How did the Floridians stand it?

In the week they'd paraded through houses like moles running from hole to hole, only in their case it was from air-conditioned shelter to air-conditioned shelter.

Although the sky was still blue, she had learned in a second it could change to torrential rains so strong that it was necessary for Bill to pull their rental car off the highway. Visibility went only as far as the inside of the windshield: beyond was a solid sheet of water.

The house they had first put in an offer for had been withdrawn from the market. With Patrick's death they hadn't followed up on any others until this latest trip. Katie hadn't realized Bill's house hunting around Boston would seem wonderful compared to being dragged to the bottom of the country as she thought of the Sunshine State.

Many of the houses they had looked at were deserted for the summer, their sane owners having sought refuge in the north. Her husband had mumbled it was better than snow, but his enthusiasm had seemed to wane until they found what he thought was a perfect house.

Almost saved by the bell. He had promised Katie they would look at only one more and then he would give up the idea of moving to Florida.

This place was on a canal, had an enclosed pool, three large bedrooms for when Jess or the family visited. Whoever decorated it had chosen icy blues and greens. Between the air-conditioning and the overhead fans, Bill swore the heat could be kept at bay.

All the arguments about electrical bills and too much house for the two of them melted in the summer heat. They had put a bid in, which, thank God, was refused.

When the real estate agent had told them, she would ask for a counter offer, Katie had wanted to push her into the pool. It needed skimming. Lord, she didn't want to have to care for a pool.

Once again, their trip had been interrupted by a family tragedy. Only this time it was her sister. If Da's death and Peggy's disappearance, both events happening while they were in Florida, weren't omens against this move, Katie didn't know what was.

What her mother had said about kidnappings, FBI and break-ins made no sense at all. Even Aidan, speaking slowly and calmly, didn't clarify the situation. The FBI don't kidnap people like her sister.

In the name of the Father, Son and Holy Ghost, protect my sister. Protect Peggy.

Sean must be going through hell: first his brother now his mother. If something had happened, she and Bill would see him through university. He was as close to being a son as she was going to get. Peggy would protect Jess if the plane crashed, but Peggy was missing.

Next to her Bill fastened his seat belt and then checked hers as if she were incapable of doing it. He caught her eye. "You're preoccupied with Peggy."

She reached over and touched his hand as the hostess prowled the aisles in search of seats too far back and trays not in upright positions.

"She'll be okay," Bill said. "I feel it in my bones."

She didn't need her bones to know Florida wasn't good for them nor that something had just happened to her family that would change things forever, even if her sister came back unharmed.

CHAPTER 64

The biggest of the FBI agents caught Peggy in the dining room, pinning her to the floor, but not before she pushed a living room chair to block him, knocked over the fan, the stacked TV tables and a dining room chair. He sat on her, covering her mouth, muffling her scream. She struggled under the weight of his body. Over his shoulder she saw two other men. Only two had come to her door. Where had the others come from?

"I don't want to hurt you." He spoke in a monotone as he rolled her over onto her stomach and cuffed her.

The metal bit into her skin. Screaming would be useless. The neighbors wouldn't hear over their televisions and air-conditioning.

She forced her body to go limp. The dust from the carpet made her want to sneeze, but she fought it. Forcing herself to try to be calm she whispered, "What do you want?"

"You're coming with us for questioning." He straddled her. His left hand held her cuffed hands high enough that her shoulder muscles protested when he rolled her over. Once she'd wrestled with the boys, sitting on them to tickle. The FBI man wasn't tickling her.

All the men were dressed in crisp suits despite the withering heat. She watched one man carry her computer and another a box crammed with her papers. A file fell off the top, its papers scattering.

"Do you have a warrant?"

"Lady, you're living in the past. We don't need one for anyone suspected of terrorism." The man stood above her, but all she could see was his shoes, black and shined to a high polish.

I'm not a terrorist. I'm a patriot. I've given my son to this country, she thought, but what she said was, "You've got to be kidding." A look at his face, a boyish face, with a hint of grey at the temple, told her he wasn't kidding.

She looked at the other man, the older of the two who had come to the door. "I've a gun. If you promise to be good, we can uncuff you. You wouldn't want the neighbors to see you like this, would you?"

Yes, she would. They could sound an alarm, but to whom? The FBI? The police? "I'll go peacefully," she said.

The man, who had sat on her, pulled her into a standing position. She heard a click of the key turning in the lock of the cuffs. They left imprints of scraped lip-pink skin. Her wrists hurt. As much as she wanted to rub them, she wouldn't give the men the satisfaction.

The man, who carried her computer, stood in the doorway. "We've got everything."

If I can just get out the front door, I can break for Angela's, Peggy thought. One of the agents was in front of her, one on each side and one was behind her.

Peggy's brain scattered her thoughts.

Run!

No, don't run!

Break left ... get to Angela's ... no, that would frighten her mother ...her mother would be more frightened to discover her gone ... Sean?

Outside the heat was at least 90 degrees despite the sun hovering so low behind the buildings that it was almost dark. The streetlights were surrounded by insects.

Peggy glanced at the house next door. No one was visible in the windows. The same for the houses across the street. Even Angela's place looked deserted. No cars drove by. Too bad Delle Avenue was so short. Because of how it was situated on Mission Hill, the bar of the 'H' between streets that went up and down The Hill, only residents, their guests, the garbage men and street cleaners drove down it. Peggy cursed herself for all the years she'd appreciated the lack of traffic which allowed her boys to play ball in the street.

As she moved to the right to see if there were a getaway route, the man who had sat on her said, "Don't even think of trying it."

Like in countless detective shows an agent put his hand on the top of her head as they pushed her into the back seat of a dark car. Three of the four men went with her, one in the front and two flanking her in the back. The car smelled new. The fourth man drove away in an identical car.

"Where are you taking me?" When they said nothing, she said, "I want a lawyer." God, it sounded like a line from a bad TV detective show.

The inside of the car was suffocating. Peggy noticed Hertz rental papers on the glove box between the driver's and front passenger's seats. By the time they turned left onto Route 9 from Tremont, the air-conditioning kicked in. Peggy took great gulps of air.

The first red light was at the gas station at the Boston-Brookline Village border. Three cars waited in line for gas. Peggy tried to inch her hand to the door handle.

One of the agents noticed. "The doors can only be opened by the driver. A safety feature so kids don't fall out," the one who spoke in monotones said. "Cuff the prisoner."

The word prisoner was almost as shocking as the word terrorist. Good God, what was she caught up in? Breathe in, she thought. Keep oxygen in the brain, that's what she had been taught in her first-ever computer class. "When people get tense, they hold their breath, slowing their thought processes," the instructor had said as he put his hand on her shoulder. "Breathe."

Help me, God.

The agents on each side pulled her arms together in front of her then snapped on the cuffs. Once again, the metal dug into her wrists, but at least her arms were in front of her.

They pulled off Route 9 somewhere after Natick. The car turned into a parking lot of a one-story motel, not a chain motel but a light stucco building with green doors. The man in the passenger seat jumped out and opened the door.

"Don't do anything stupid," Mr. Monotone Driver said as he got out of the car. He looked around. He came to the back. "Out," he barked, grabbing her by the wrist.

Peggy felt herself propelled out of the car, across the pavement and into the room. Two double beds had cheap green chenille spreads that didn't match the drawn blue-striped curtains.

"There's no use screaming. We've rented the rooms on each side," Mr. Monotone said.

She was thirsty. She nodded. "Some water, please."

"Not until you tell us what we want to know," the biggest man said. He reminded her of a boxer. His body was fit, but his nose looked as if it had been broken and had healed at a slight angle.

"Aw, give her some water," the smaller one said. Smaller, yes, but not small. He was probably at least 5-10.

Maybe good cop/bad cop wasn't just Hollywood fiction.

Mr. Boxer rolled his eyes. "Go on, but not too much."

Mr. Small disappeared. She heard water running. He came back with a glass, which he held to her mouth with his hand under her chin as someone would with a baby learning to drink from a cup. Maybe he had kids.

"What do you want with me?" she asked.

Mr. Boxer slapped her. "We ask the questions."

Her face stung, although it wasn't a very hard slap, merely enough to show who was in control, not that she had any doubt.

What she wanted was to get out alive. Her recent reading had taught her about "the disappeared" in Chile during the time of Pinochet, but Holy Mother of God, the U.S. hadn't come down to that yet, or had they? Vaguely she remembered Monica Lewinsky talking about being held in a hotel room. The girl that nearly brought down the president of the United States had said she hadn't been allowed to call her lawyer.

The next three hours they asked about her plans to help terrorists and the names of people planning to overthrow the United States government. They asked her if she planned to travel to the Middle East.

"I don't even have a passport. You should know that."

"You could have gotten a passport through nefarious channels," Mr. Monotone said.

Nefarious? Channels? She barely could spell the word, much less find that type of channel.

They wanted names and addresses of people on her mailing lists.

"I only have their e-mails."

They showed her photos of her burning the flag. "Why?"

"Because I wanted people to know my son died for nothing. I wanted to stop the war that would kill other women's sons."

The questioning went on and on in the same vein.

The pressure in her lower intestine mounted. She forced her sphincter muscle to stay shut. She wasn't going to give them the satisfaction of messing herself. She forced pictures from Abu Ghraib out of her mind. "I have to go to the bathroom."

They let her go alone. The tiny room had bilious green tiles, including the floor and ceiling, a toilet, sink and stand-up shower. A window was so small that not even an anorexic model could crawl through. Thank God her hands were cuffed in front so she could unzip her shorts. She made the toilet in time, expelling nerve-triggered diarrhea.

But there was no way to wipe herself totally clean with the limited movement of her cuffed hands.

Thump! Thump! Thump! Thump! This was no knuckle-rap knock. Whichever FBI man was hitting the door had to be using his fists. "Hurry up."

She used her elbow to flush and wished the men would need to use it before the smell dissipated.

She worked her pants up, holding them in front of her and moving them side to side. As she walked back into the bedroom under the men's glare, she heard a clock between the beds ticking. Without her glasses she couldn't see the time, only fuzzy red numerals.

The questioning went on and on. Light shone through the crack in the curtains.

"You know we can put you in prison and forget about you," Mr. Boxer said.

Peggy wanted to say her family would search for her, but she wasn't sure how successful they would be. What happened to the need for warrants? Had she moved into a parallel universe without being aware of it? Although she thought she'd experienced fear for Jason, she had never experienced such devastating fear for her physical self.

Vaguely stories about hostage situations came back to her, people held on planes, people trapped by Mid-Eastern governments, something during the Carter administration. How did they survive day after day, week after week, when she doubted if she could hold on to her sanity after only a few hours?

Mr. Small disappeared and came back with coffee and a Dunkin Donut box. She smelled the coffee as they ate and drank in front of her.

Two new men took over from Mr. Small and Mr. Boxer. "Get some sleep," one of the new men said to them. She didn't give these new questioners nicknames: she was too tired. They told her of phone calls she had made, repeating parts of conversations. Even though she deleted most of her e-mails rather than jam up her system, they knew the contents. How in hell had they gotten that information? Wiretaps don't happen in the United States or was that something that went away with the Patriot Act.

"I am *not* a terrorist, but this war has got be stopped," she repeated to every accusation.

The questions became verbal clubs battering her. When Peggy closed her eyes, someone threw water on her. And on and on and on and on and ...

CHAPTER 65

Bridget's face touched the scratchy couch cloth in place of smooth sheets. The waistband of the lightweight slacks she wore yesterday dug into her stomach. Her bra had twisted, binding one breast while freeing the other.

Why wasn't she in her own bed?

She sat up. In the dawn light she saw Aidan asleep on the rug. Jess slept in the chair. Sean's baseball cap sat on the coffee table.

Then she remembered the break-in and the police saying they would come back. They hadn't. Aidan's last call to the station produced nothing even though he said he was a reporter.

The dispatcher had said they had too many other calls and it was too soon to list Mrs. Doherty as missing. When Aidan yelled saying that the person had disappeared during a robbery, they didn't hear because the dispatcher had already hung up.

Sean entered the living room dressed only in navy blue jockey shorts. His chest was covered with a soft mat of hair. "Anyone hear from Mom?" he whispered.

Bridget adjusted her clothing. Putting a finger against her lips then pointing to the sleeping Aidan and Jess, she rose despite her stiff bones.

She stepped over Aidan.

Sean followed her into the kitchen. "We've got to do something."

"We'll call Connor's office as soon as they open. They'll know how to find him. He'll pull strings." Her imagination gave her a scene with her son playing puppet-master as police marionettes danced, looking behind trees. "We'll find her."

"You're saying that to make me feel better, Gran."

Bridget hugged him. "I said it to make *me* feel better." Inside she forced herself to be strong for her family. Their survival above everything was all she cared about, all she had ever cared about, all she would ever care about.

They sat in silence at the kitchen table, their hands folded. Silence in the Flanagan households was a rare commodity. Bridget refused to turn to look at the clock, because she was more aware of time than she had ever been in her life.

Jess appeared in the kitchen doorway. "If we call Connor's office now and ..."

Bridget looked at her watch. "My God, nine already."

For once no one made tea or coffee. This was the first beverageless Flanagan family crisis. It struck Bridget that it was too serious to consume anything. Worry filled up the place where anything could be soothed.

It was worse than Jason's death, because they knew he was dead. The next step had been clear: wait for the body.

She started shaking. Although she wanted to hide it from Jess and Sean, she couldn't. If God had told her to walk out of the room, she wouldn't have been able to stand.

The morning dragged on. They left messages at Connor's office, but he didn't call. Perhaps no one had located him.

No one knew what to do next. Break-ins and disappearing family members were in no one's frame of reference.

Aidan paced until Jess grabbed him by the shoulders and hollered, "Sit."

Sean had made a Stop&Shop run to pick up food from the deli counter, but they all pushed the potato salad and cold cuts around on their plates.

At 3:00, Aidan stood up. "I am going to the police station; they can't hang up on me if I'm in their face." He left the kitchen. The others heard him shout, "Come here!"

They did.

Peggy, her face bruised, cried as she fell into her mother's arms.

Nothing she told them made sense, including being shoved out of the car at the light on Route 9 when the car crossed from Brookline into Boston.

CHAPTER 66

Three days after Peggy's kidnapping, Jess paced the lobby of the bank where her aunt last worked. The building made her feel almost claustrophobic. No way would she ever be able to work for a big law firm that thrived on this type of pretentious office space.

Her short denim skirt and pink T-shirt contrasted to the dress-for-success people milling around. Somewhere she suspected a giant machine spat out little businesswomen and businessmen dolls with suits in grey, blue, black and, for the daring – brown.

Her vision was a storefront where she could help people, real people, people who had been screwed by the same people running around this lobby.

A man with a briefcase demanded the receptionist call Mr. Barnes. No good morning, no please, just a tone that said, "Peon, do my bidding." The receptionist put away her smile and picked up her telephone.

Jess took several deep breaths. She wasn't here to give courtesy lessons to assholes.

How could she help her aunt if she lost control?

When the FBI, if it were the FBI, had dropped her aunt off, they had left her shell. They must have kept the woman with the sense of humor who never failed to give a hug or have time to listen. Jess searched her mind for the right word to describe her aunt, because she never remembered seeing her as she was now, not when her husband died, not when she lost her job, not when Grampy died, not even when Jason died: zombie, broken, defeated, lost, scared – all worked.

She looked at her watch. Where was Aidan?

Another robot, this one a female, walked by carrying folders and stood by the elevator door, tapping her foot. Maybe foot tapping was built into her database.

Another woman walked in wearing Nikes and carrying her jacket. As soon as she felt the air-conditioning, she put on her jacket. Spying a chair, she sat, removed a pair of high heels from her briefcase and slipped out of the sneakers. Jess saw nothing else in the briefcase. How much energy did that woman expend pretending to be carrying something important?

Okay, Jess told herself, she wasn't being fair. Most of the people here were ordinary men and women who wanted to buy a house and to give their kids an education. After work, they probably went home and watched American Idol or quivered as Donald Trump said, "You're fired," while being thankful it wasn't them.

What they should be doing was watching their government. With this thought, Jess was convinced she was being fair in disparaging them. She was blaming them for not realizing that something was terribly, terribly wrong.

Get control, get control. Letting her emotions yo-yo did nothing to help her aunt.

She looked at her watch again, which hadn't seemed to move. Staring out the window, there was still no sign of Aidan. She reminded herself that he had spent all his free minutes trying to find out more. He'd talked to local FBI offices which denied any knowledge. The police couldn't find the report about the break-in. If the window hadn't been broken, if the computer hadn't disappeared, it was as if it never happened.

"Sorry, I'm late."

Jess jumped at Aidan's voice. "What happened?"

"I tried again to sell the story. My boss says there's not enough proof that your aunt was kidnapped and beaten by the FBI. By the way, how is her face?"

271

Beaten was exactly the word. "The bruise is down."

"My boss insisted the FBI would have a warrant if it were true."

"Did you get the next couple of days off?"

"Today only, unless I can grovel big time and ask a co-worker to switch, which will piss off my boss even more."

"This should be a big story." Jess noticed one of the security guards staring.

"My boss asked if your cousin's death unbalanced your aunt." He put his hands on her shoulders as if to hold her in place. "When I said no, he asked if she were menopausal."

"He what?" Everyone in the lobby turned to look at the yelling woman in the denim skirt.

"Calm down. He's old school. You gotta remember I'm just this kid reporter, a baby in his eyes."

Jess didn't want to calm down. She wanted to march into the paper's city room and slap Aidan's boss. "So, what's our game plan?"

"We'll talk to your aunt's friends and co-workers, starting with Mary Ann. Wasn't that what we agreed on? If the FBI talked to the neighbor, they probably talked to others."

Even if they got the information, she wasn't sure what they could do with it, but she hoped it would help her aunt. "Stupid, I mean how do we talk to them? Do we just ask: 'Hi, did you talk to the FBI about my aunt?'"

"Well, Angela reported someone stuck an FBI badge in her face."

"Angela is half dotty."

"Your aunt isn't. Let's get going."

The security guard stood close by as Jess asked the receptionist if they could speak with Mary Ann.

"You must make an appointment to talk to HR."

"I'm the daughter of a friend, please call and tell her Peggy Doherty's niece is here, and it's really, really important."

The receptionist picked up the phone, said what she had been told to, listened and hung up. "She's tied up all day." Her expression said I-told-you-so.

Aidan propelled Jess out of the building. "Stop sputtering. We need to strategize." They settled on a Boston Common bench near the two white buildings sheltering the entrance and exit of the Park Street T-station.

Ignoring the sun-exposed wood burning through her thin denim clothing, she rummaged in her bag to find her phone. A second search brought out her address book. "We don't need strategy, we need attack. I'm calling her direct line. My aunt gave it to me after Jason died, and I saved it, never dreaming I'd need it for this."

When the recorded message finished, she said, "It's Jess Kelly, Peggy Doherty's niece. It's an emergency. I must talk to you. I'm in the vicinity." She gave her phone number.

"Give it one more try through the system," Aidan said.

Jess pressed the numbers she needed to press until a human came on the line. At least there was a human somewhere in that building that could pick up a telephone. "It's urgent that I speak with Mary Ann Hutchinson."

"She's not available."

"It's an emergency. Please tell her it's Jess Kelly, Peggy Doherty's niece."

Jess put her hand over the receiver. "They're checking with her."

The voice that came back could have reduced Jess's body temperature. "She's in a meeting and can't be disturbed."

"May I leave my number?"

"If you must, but she's in meetings all day."

Jess gave her cell number and hung up. "She didn't write it down, I know it."

"You know what Mary Ann looks like?"

Jess nodded.

"We'll wait for her." They doubled back to stand in the doorway of the store across from the entrance to the bank building.

A security guard eyed them. Eventually he ambled over.

"We're waiting for a friend, who's always late," Aidan said.

The guard shrugged and wandered off.

By 1:38 Jess wanted to quit. Even if Mary Ann wasn't hungry, she was starving. Low blood sugar turned her from a sane person into a mega-bitch. When Aidan spoke to her, she snarled at him.

"Maybe she went to the company cafeteria," Aidan said. "I'll get us something to eat. Gotta feed the grouchy animals."

She glanced across the street to see Mary Ann leave the building and walk toward Downtown Crossing.

Jess zigzagged across Arch Street. "Mary Ann! Wait!"

Aidan sprinted after them.

Jess passed Mary Ann and turned, blocking her passage.

"I'm sorry, Jess. This is a really bad day." Remnants of red lipstick marked the corners of Mary Ann's mouth.

"Why won't you want to talk to me?"

Mary Ann looked everywhere but at Jess.

"Are you on the way to lunch?"

"I'm buying something to bring back."

"We'll go along. This is my fiancé, Aidan." She ignored Aidan's raised eyebrow at the word fiancé. She still hadn't told him yes, nor had she worn the ring.

Rather than acknowledge him and despite high heels, Mary Ann took off. They followed her to the food court near Filene's. Because it was almost two o'clock only a few of the tables in the center of the large space were occupied. The trash bins overflowed with paper plates and cups. A man with grey hair and an emaciated body emptied a bin, spun the black garbage bag, then tied it with a pink plastic string.

Jess grabbed Mary Ann by the elbow and steered her to a seat in the middle. "Tell Aidan what you want. He'll get it while we talk." Mary Ann started to protest. "Please, I can't stress how important it is."

"Noodles. From there." She pointed to the Oriental counter.

"Ditto and a Coke," Jess said. "Take your time," she mouthed over Mary Ann's head.

Aidan wove his way around the tables toward the counter where no one was in line.

Jess sat opposite Mary Ann and put her hands on the tabletop, avoiding a spot of something that could have been Coke or coffee.

Mary Ann looked over her shoulder for the third time and then crossed her arms. "I don't know what this is all about."

"Don't you? Why avoid me then?" With a glance Jess saw Aidan pay. However, he was back so fast that she didn't have time to go ahead.

"Are you afraid to be seen with us?" Aidan put down the Styrofoam boxes and Coke cans.

Mary Ann bit her lip. "Why would I be?" She glanced around the food court again.

"Because you ignored me, refused my calls." When Mary Ann said nothing, Jess continued. "You and my aunt were friends for years. You studied together, took notes for each other. If you know anything that can help us, please, please tell me."

"Help you? I don't know what your problem is." Mary Ann picked up her bag. Aidan stopped her as Jess told about her aunt's kidnapping by FBI agents.

"She's terrified. She won't leave the house," Jess said.

"That's not like her."

"In the last year my aunt lost a son. She lost her father. She lost her job, twice, but nothing stopped her. She went on a peace march at Fort Bragg, something she never would have done earlier. She's fighting to stop a stupid war, but she's done nothing to merit what happened to her. Now tell us ..."

For the first time Mary Ann looked directly at her. "Jess, I support three kids. My ex doesn't believe in regular child support payments."

"I don't understand." Aidan said.

Mary Ann started to cry. The speed with which Aidan produced a handkerchief amazed Jess. Maybe it was part of being a reporter to be ready for tears.

"All her employment records were turned over to someone. I don't know who. My boss told me she was a dangerous woman and we were well rid of her."

"Why didn't you call her? Warn her?" Jess asked.

Mary Ann shook her head. "I need to go."

"You've a son, don't you?" Jess asked.

Mary Ann hesitated.

"My aunt is fighting a war based on lies. She lost a son, next time it could be yours."

Mary Ann shrugged. "There's no draft. He's safe." She left without taking her lunch.

"Yet," Jess called after her. Mary Ann faltered for a nanosecond before racing away.

"Now what?" Jess asked. She opened her box of Japanese noodles and shoved them into her mouth using the chopsticks.

"How many other friends does your aunt have? Real ones?"

"Aunt Peggy spends most of the time with us." She drained her Coke.

Aidan rocked back in his chair. "Let's talk to the funeral director."

"Why?"

"Reporter's instinct."

* * * * *

Ed Halligan hugged Jess when he found her at his door. "Nothing has happened to your grandmother, I hope."

"She's as feisty as ever."

Ed mopped his brow of non-existent sweat. "Whew for that. You're looking good. Pauly should see you now." He ushered them into his office and shut the door, cutting off the smell of too many flowers.

"How is Pauly?" Jess asked.

"Great. Just started an SAP project in Austin. Some kind of computer stuff. I don't understand what my son does, but he does."

"Pauly was part of my gang at Latin, half football hunk, half computer nerd. Aidan is my fiancé." Jess ignored his smirk at her second use of the word in about as many hours.

"You were at both funerals," Ed said. "So, you're here to introduce Aidan?"

Jess blushed. She didn't keep up with her high school chums' parents. If they ran into each other they exchanged news. Whenever

276

she saw any of them, she felt the need to rush home and study for a Latin exam. All the parents had been strict, even the non-Catholics.

"You kids certainly didn't come to chat about the old days."

Jess wondered how to get into the subject. It was just too weird to ask about FBI agents. With Mary Ann's strange behavior, it was obvious that something was going on, but Ed was a neighbor. She looked at Aidan.

"Has anyone asked you about Jess' family?"

Ed rubbed his chin. "Strange question." When Jess opened her mouth to speak, he held up his hand. "You know most of my business is repeat?"

Jess resisted asking, "You mean you bury the same person twice?" More than once her professors, especially the ones that took themselves seriously, rebuked her for irreverence. She thought of it as realism.

"I mean the same families come back. Uncle Joe dies, let's call Ed. He did such a good job with Aunt Wilma." He tapped his fingers together, shut his eyes, frowned, opened his eyes and pointed with his forefinger as if lowering a gun to shoot. He opened the bottom desk drawer and took out a folder then picked up the phone. After listening he nodded without speaking and hung up.

"What's that?" Jess knew she should be patient: patience wasn't one of her qualities.

"It's my file of people who don't complete the process. It doesn't happen often. Buying a funeral isn't like buying a house. The bereaved family knows who they want. They're in no shape to look for deals." He opened the folder.

"But sometimes they do?" Jess asked.

"When it happens it's usually because there's some family dynamic, which is just a fancy way of saying they are fighting like mad over something that makes sense only to them." He stared at the ceiling. "Deliver me from those situations. I can deal with grief, but the fights about heaven knows what ...?" His shrug said more than finishing the sentence.

"Is there a connection to what we asked you and this file?" Aidan asked.

"About two weeks ago, maybe a little less, two men came in. Their kid brother had been killed in Afghanistan, they said. They asked if I'd done military funerals. I said I had. They asked for references. References?"

"You don't usually get asked for references?" Jess asked.

"Strangely enough, no." Ed handed her the form labeled intake sheet.

On it was written the names, the address, telephone, name of the deceased, where the body was, etc. Still empty were the details of what type of funeral.

"I said the last military funeral I did was in February, a kid from the neighborhood."

"Was that the one where the mother burned the flag?' the older one asked me. Anyway, all they really wanted to talk about was if I knew in advance about the flag burning, what did I think, how well did I know the family, yada yada, yada. I thought it weird, but I was really busy so when they said they'd get back to me, I just filed this."

"No follow up sales work?" Aidan asked.

"Not really. It's an intrusion into the family. But again, most people come in and that's it, and I was busy." He took the file from Jess. "Ninety percent of my business is from this neighborhood. The other ten percent is from people who used to live here. Families tend to have family funeral homes much like family dentists."

He pointed to the address. "This address is from Southie. I never had a client from Southie, but at the time, I thought maybe they had been here to a funeral. But I called and the phone number they gave me. It doesn't exist."

Aidan took Jess's hand. "I guess that answers what we were looking for."

"What's up?" Ed asked.

"We're not sure," Jess said. "Next time you talk to Pauly give him my love."

"I wish you kids the best. It's nicer planning weddings than funerals. Maybe in another life, I'll choose a different profession." Ed walked them to the door. "And I think your Aunt Peggy was great doing what she did." He hugged Jess and shook Aidan's hand as the first people arrived for visiting hours. "You're getting a great girl, Aidan," he called after them.

* * * * *

Aidan's car was a 10-year-old Honda. Where the green paint had chipped, he had spray painted until it resembled a bad attempt at camouflage.

"I gather you've accepted my marriage suggestion," he said as she got in. The seats were cloth, but she felt like a cookie being shoved into an oven.

She looked at him. "We'll be good together."

He went around to the driver's side, which was open, because she unlocked it. "So? you'll wear the diamond?"

Chains descended on her spirit. The idea of trying on dresses, looking for halls, florists, music and all the other details that went into a wedding each created a separate link until she felt encircled. However, coming home to find Aidan waiting or studying at his place and hearing his key in the lock, well, that appealed more than anything in her life outside of her work.

They rolled down the windows to replace the air inside the car that was searing their lungs and wilting their bodies. In perfect choreography they fastened their seat belts. Aidan pulled out onto Tremont Street. "Where to?"

"Your place. We can talk about the next move. Do you want a big wedding?'

"Not very. It's a girl thing."

"Good."

CHAPTER 67

If anyone had asked Peggy how she felt, she would have replied that she was swimming in a cup of milky tea. She wasn't usually given to poetic language, but this was her truth. She hadn't left the house since her kidnapping.

She sat on her back porch with *Good Housekeeping* open in her lap and her eyeglasses on top of her head. The flowers in Angela's backyard below were a blur of color as were the magazine pages. When she shut her eyes, the memories of the motel room appeared on the eyelid screen.

Connor had said, "Impossible, the FBI doesn't do that to citizens." She knew it was possible. In her heart of hearts, her mother's oft-used phrase, that was exactly what had happened.

A bird landed in the birdbath almost hidden in the corner of Angela's garden. Peggy watched him walk around the dry sandstone circle. In the old days Angela never forgot to fill it. The old days were gone. Peggy envied her neighbor's ability to forget.

Without having read anything in the magazine, she turned the page. She should work, but she'd cancelled her contract at the Education Department. The agency probably would never offer her a contract again. Another agency called earlier that morning. She'd told them she wasn't available for a month, although she wasn't sure she could face the world by then. Her creditors were out there waiting. Maybe the FBI was out there waiting too.

The house didn't seem any safer. She hated the rug where she had been forced onto her stomach, her face next to an agent's shoes. In her mind she felt the carpet irritating her cheek, the dust in her nose and saw the shine on the agent's black shoes.

Bill had secured the house's doors with police locks. Their long iron bars from the door to the floor meant that the door would have to be broken down for entry. Each time Peggy saw those police locks, she shuddered.

Below her, two workmen carried iron bars that Bill was having installed on all three floors and basement windows. She had insisted he stay home until they came in case ... she wasn't sure of in case of what and said so when he asked. Still, he'd done what she asked.

Before he left for work a little over an hour ago, he'd come up, downed a cup of coffee, and reassured her that the men were okay. The clacking of metal and their voices broke the quiet of the morning.

Peggy tried to force herself to stop being afraid. She had to get back to normal. Had to, had to, had to ... But how? Nothing would bring Jason back. Nothing would return her father to his chair. Nothing would restore her belief that her government was the good guys.

Bill and Katie offered to buy her a new computer. She'd said no. With the loss of her laptop and USB key came a loss of her contacts. If there were any energy left in her body to start over, she couldn't find it. Whenever Jess brought it up, saying that the people in her network needed to know what had happened, she left the room.

I must go out. I can't be like those people, usually women whom she'd read about that wouldn't venture beyond their front door, she told herself over and over. She wished she could remember the name for the syndrome, but then if she named it, the problem would never go away.

It took until mid-afternoon most days to find the energy to dress. "Today, I'll do it," she whispered to no one. "I'll pick up some things for supper." As she walked down the stairs she repeated a mantra, "Buying bread and broccoli are no big thing, buying bread ..."

She reached the new hard clear plastic pane, almost axe-proof, which had replaced the frosted swans. It was about the only thing clear in her life. As for the swans that she had seen every time she had come home from the day she was born, their loss seemed a message, but what the message was, was unclear. Her hand reached out to unlock the door. She couldn't force herself to do it. Sean could run the errands later, or maybe she could borrow something from her mother or sister.

CHAPTER 68

Aidan's apartment was cool. Maple leaves covered the windows in the living and bedrooms, providing shade. He went to the fridge and opened two beers and handed Jess one. They sat at his kitchen table, a small blond wooden square with thick turned legs.

She held the beer bottle against her head before drinking. "Can we talk about this marriage thingie?" She twisted the diamond ring, not quite her ring yet.

"Marriage thingie?" His voice carried his nervousness.

"I can imagine spending the rest of my life with you."

Aidan sat down. "I hear a big but."

"No but. I don't want all the fuss of a wedding. I just want us to get on with it." She never wanted a Barbie wedding dress. She wanted Barbie to go on adventures, not hang around with silly Ken. "I want to live with you. At some point we'll sneak down to City Hall and get a license and get married."

"And what about your very Catholic mother? She'll need Ed's services."

It felt good that he cared about his future mother-in-law's reaction, but she also wished he planned the practicalities. Although she wanted to spend tonight and all her nights with him, she wanted to test it, a moot court. Not that she wanted a long test, but nevertheless, a test was necessary.

What was he like when he had the flu, or when she had the flu?

How did he handle money? Would he really be supportive of her work long-term? When she did promise God that he would be her husband until death do them part, she wanted to make sure she could keep the vow. She might not have her mother's religious fervor, but a vow was something to take seriously. Dating was different from living under one roof.

"No white dress?" he asked.

She shook her head.

"No five-tier wedding cake with a plastic bride and groom on top?"

"No bride and groom. How about chocolate cupcakes?"

He took her in his arms. "I like chocolate. But I also like the idea of a priest sanctifying our marriage."

"That we can do." She wanted that.

CHAPTER 69

Bridget sat in Patrick's chair. She didn't miss her Old Goat: she missed the man he'd been before he became an Old Goat, when they were partners in raising kids and building their lives.

As if each of her memories were a stamp and she were a collector she examined each one. Her decisions had been made to protect the family, to prepare them to be ... to be what?

Good Catholics: check. Three of her children went to Mass regularly. Even if Connor had left the Church, she still prayed that someday he would go back.

Good parents: check. Katie was a bit rigid with Jess. Ashley was coming along fine. Rachel, more than Connor, knew how to handle Jamie. Her only worry about Sean was that he would be too protective of his mother and not lead his own life.

Good Americans: she began to tremble.

What had happened to her country?

It seemed to have melted away. Just thinking that while sitting in Patrick's chair seemed so wrong that she stood up. It wasn't that she was ashamed of thinking it, Lord knows, she always handled reality, but to do it in his chair that was still dented with his presence was almost sacrilegious.

Jason, as a good American, served his country. It had killed him. She wished she'd never read the e-mails he'd written Sean. Good God! What would have happened to his head had he not been killed, and he had had to live with ... she didn't want to think about that.

Sinking back into the chair she tried to work out just what it was she needed to do next. Throughout her adult life she had done whatever was necessary to live a good life and to protect her family. The old rules seemed useless, but what were the new rules?

CHAPTER 70

"I won't have it." Katie screamed as Jess threw clothes into a Chiquita Banana box.

The blouses on the bottom were neatly folded, but the ones on top gave new meaning to the word muddle. Between her mother's glare and banshee imitation, she just wanted to get out as fast as possible. Neatness didn't count.

Katie grabbed a blue T-shirt from the box and put it back in Jess' top drawer where her underpants belonged.

"You're not going to live with that man."

Bill entered the room, but neither woman noticed. "It is not up to you, love." He put his hand on his wife's shoulder.

Katie spun around. "What!?"

"Jess is just doing what most women her age do."

"Living in sin is wrong, wrong, wrong!" Each wrong was slightly louder.

"Not by today's standards." Bill kept his voice low.

"God doesn't change his standards."

Jess took her father's attempt to distract her mother as an opportunity to open another drawer. She couldn't remember the last time her parents had fought. It didn't mean that they didn't disagree.

Katie usually said yes, then implemented her own agenda in a manner to which Bill was oblivious. Although Jess wouldn't admit it, it was a tactic she had often used with her mother, like taking a sweater that Katie insisted she would need and then not wearing it. But this fight was more serious than a possible drop in temperature leading to a chill.

Katie shifted her attention back to her daughter. "If you ever marry, you won't be able to wear white."

"Considering all the loose-stomach white wedding dresses your mother makes, I doubt if the Church will say anything," Bill said.

"Stay out of it."

Jess had never heard her mother hiss like that. She tried to concentrate on which books she needed. Too bad that her parents had decided not to go to the movies. She wouldn't have snuck out, but after her announcement yesterday of her intention to live with Aidan the battle had raged whenever the two women were in yelling range.

"Mom, when I do get married, I want to make sure it is right, and the only way I can do that is to actually live with Aidan as a trial." Jess had said all that the night before, but her mother hadn't been listening. In fact, she'd put her hands over her ears.

"Your father and I didn't ..."

"Different time." Bill and Jess said this at the same time.

"If Aidan throws you out, don't expect us to let you back in."

"You're acting like Rachel's parents. Look at what they lost out on," Bill said. "Jamie, Ashley. When the kids have their kids, you'll want to be a grandma."

Tears wet Katie's cheeks. "I think I understand Rachel's parents for the first time." Katie stepped aside as Jess started carrying her boxes to the front door. "Your key."

"Katie!"

"Don't Katie me, Bill Kelly."

Jess snapped the key off its ring, picked up two boxes, one on top of the other, and carried them to the front door. Bill looked at his wife then did the same.

"I'm praying for your soul." Katie ran to her bedroom and slammed the door.

"I'll take care of my own soul, thank you very much," Jess yelled at the barrier.

Her father helped her carry her things to Aidan's car. He was now forbidden to "darken their door" as Katie had put it. Sometimes Jess wished her mother didn't think in clichés. Maybe if she could let go of them, she might get beyond the patterns. Or maybe she would have to accept that her black-and-white mother could never turn into a rainbow.

Bill whispered to her, "Don't worry, it'll all work out." He glanced back toward the house as if afraid that Katie could read his lips from several blocks away.

"Bad, huh?" Aidan asked as he arranged the boxes. "We don't have to do this."

"Yes, we do. My mother hates the idea I'm having sex. We'll have sex whether we live together or not."

"I like calling it making love," Aidan said as the couple got into the car.

"And they say it's women who are romantic." Jess smiled for the first time since Katie had stormed into her room during the packing.

* * * * *

Aidan watched Jess unpack silently.

She put her computer on the kitchen table. Two pairs of jeans went on the couch, a top over a chair. Papers from one box were put into another which contained underwear.

As she was bent over a box that was falling apart, he pulled her into his arms.

Enveloped in the warmth of someone who loved her and wasn't thinking she was destined for hell, a place she doubted existed, Jess started to cry.

"Don't cry. I don't know what to do when women cry." He didn't take his arms away and he patted her head. He reached for her chin, "Do you cry a lot?"

"Only when I move out of the house and my mother acts like I'm a whore."

"That's good news."

"And at sad movies."

"Not so good. And ..."

"When animals are hurt."

"And ..."

By now she was giggling. "And when I discover that the man I'm about to marry doesn't like crying women." She reached into his pocket and took out his handkerchief. The discovery starts here, she thought, but not with fear of the future – more like a treasure hunt.

"Change of subject." He disengaged himself and tripped over a box. "My best friend when I was kid is with the FBI. He'll talk to us, if you want."

"Do you think he knows anything about what happened to Aunt Peggy?"

"I don't know, and even if he does, he might not be able to tell us anything."

CHAPTER 71

Katie cut through Wigglesworth Street then waited as the E train rattled down Huntington before crossing into the Harvard Medical School complex. Heat rose from the large marble tiles that formed the courtyard. The smell from too many cars hung in the air.

All the cold water she had put on her face reduced the puffiness. Bill had held her as she cried herself to sleep. She didn't remember dropping off.

She spurned his suggestion to call in sick. Two technicians were on vacation: the lab assistant was at a conference. It would only be her and her boss.

She walked up the stairs to her office. She had a wooden desk circa 1940s with the latest model computer and flat screen. Through the lab doorway she saw her boss, Dr. Audrey Adams, bustling around in her lab coat, holding test tubes to the light and tapping them. The woman glanced up as Katie entered. "You look like the wrath of God."

"I feel like it." She slipped her pocketbook into her bottom desk drawer. Unlike most days, she had no sandwiches. Making them took more energy than she could summon.

Katie liked working with Dr. Adams, who was the type whom no one would cough around because she would stick a thermometer in their mouth. In her late 50s, she pretended to be a terror.

Everyone called her Doc Adams or Doc, although titles were rarely used. "The Doc" carried a certain affection mixed with equal parts of awe. "I don't get ulcers, I give them," she once announced. No one, least of all Katie, believed her.

When it came to her work there was no detail too small, which was why she was tops in her field, bringing in maximum grant money. In turn, university officials bowed to all her requests for staff, equipment and space.

As brusque as she was, she remembered everyone's birthday with small presents, knew everyone's children's names and gave time off so parents could attend a school event.

Doc Adams put the test tube back into the middle space of the holder which held seven others. She wiped her hands on the lab coat. "Want to tell Mother Audrey?"

Katie would sooner call Father Robert "Bobby Boy" than call Doc Adams mother anything. And while everyone in the lab blabbed about their marital or kid troubles, Katie kept her family life to herself. The other staff teased Katie that her only problem was she had a husband with a house-hunting hobby, or they did until the deaths of her nephew and father.

When she sat at her desk, Doc Adams perched on its corner. Sometimes, Katie thought that had her own mother had the education that Doc Adams had, she would have been an executive or even a doctor like the Doc.

"I know you never talk about the negative stuff, but unless you lead a very strange life, shit happens to you too – so give."

Katie looked hard at this woman with the white hair that looked as if an electrical charge had gone through it. Without wanting to she started to cry.

Doc Adams wasn't the hugging type, but she was the type that kept tissues in her pocket. She gave Katie one.

"You'll think it's stupid."

"Try me."

"My daughter is moving in with her boyfriend."

Doc Adams walked over to the coffee pot next to the copier. She filled two mugs and handed one to Katie. "Is there something wrong with the boy? Is he abusive? A leach?"

Except for the fact Aidan had slept with her daughter outside of wedlock and helped her commit a sin, he was a perfect husband candidate.

"No."

"Then what's the problem?"

Katie regretted saying anything. As a proclaimed pagan, the Doc wouldn't understand. "They should get married first."

"If I had a daughter, I wouldn't let her get married unless she lived with the guy first. Might save a divorce later. Best thing to do Mom, is butt out. You're only going to alienate her." With that Doc Adams picked up another test tube.

Katie wondered how she could ignore the fact that her daughter was sinning.

CHAPTER 72

Bridget wiped her filthy hands on an old ragged towel as she finished shifting dirt from the five-pound bag bought from the Stop&Shop plant section to the two-foot cement planter. Peggy had painted it dark green and stenciled it with white Pennsylvania Dutch doves. It had been her Christmas present last year when things were normal. Normal meant Jason and Patrick were alive. It meant the FBI didn't kidnap her daughter. Jess and Aidan had told her what Mary Ann and Ed had told them, so she believed her daughter's version.

Bridget never remembered feeling so frightened. The fear was not that of the first day of school or when she walked down the aisle to join her life with another. Those changes were mere discombobulations, blips and discomforts, good and bad. Even the stretch when Patrick had a series of insecure jobs before he went to work for Polaroid, and they weren't sure if they might be short of food by the end of the week, had not left her as afraid as she was now.

In the past, she felt she could work through the discomfort, be a better wife, find more clients, pray. What was happening now, prayers wouldn't solve.

To one side of her left knee, marigolds waited to be transplanted.

What was her government doing? Usually she was too busy with the children and earning a living to pay much attention to what was going on.

Until the four kids were shot at Kent State, she hadn't noticed

Vietnam. She chalked up Watergate, Irangate and Monicagate as just politics.

But when the FBI came for her daughter, something broke inside her, wiping out the years at school when she pledged her allegiance to the flag. The last time she heard the "Star Spangled Banner" played at the beginning of a Red Sox game, instead of pride, she felt sick.

The things Peggy had been saying before the kidnapping, for she thought of it as a kidnapping and not as an arrest, she had poopoohed. Now, they woke her at night.

She'd hadn't protected her family.

She looked at her dirty hands. She was a fanatic hand-washer. Only once did she ruin a piece of expensive silk because of ink on her fingers from writing a check. The stain was in a place that prevented her from any type of creative cutting to save the fabric. She'd used it to line one of her own skirts. That was when the kids were still little, but every little piece of fabric wasted cut into her profit margin, although that wasn't a term she thought of then. In fact, Sean had used it when he was talking about one of his courses. Still, she had understood the term long before she had words to describe it, only she called it, "waste not, want not."

From the day of the stained silk she washed her hands so often the skin was dry. Bridget tried to shove her fears into a place where they couldn't touch her.

Concentrate on other things, she told herself, like finding a new brand of lotion because her favorite had been discontinued. Katie joked her mother's brand was On Sale. When she sewed, she didn't use the cream for fear the oil would mar the fabric. It was an ongoing battle. Dry chapped fingers caught threads. Cleaned oily hands created other destruction.

Today's planting chores called for dirty hands. Like a bad little girl told to keep clean, she found perverse enjoyment in seeing the cracks in her palms embedded with soil.

She held her right hand to the light. Once it had been beautiful. Now it was veined: at least dirt minimized age spots. Her Irish-born mother swore that by using Porcelana cream the spots disappeared. Like her sense of well-being, it had disappeared.

No, don't let the scary thoughts in.

A client told her how she had her spots removed by laser. Bridget wasn't a woman to spend good money for vanity. If she had extra money, it would go to charity or to her family. Her spots were like friends. Someday she might even give them names. She'd loved naming her children. Thank goodness she didn't have one child for each name she thought of. The house would outdo the old woman in the shoe.

The early morning air on the back porch was mellow. An oak tree grazed the porch, making her feel as if she were in a tree house, not that she ever had one. That was for suburban or country kids. When she looked over her wooden railing, she did have her little bit of country with the garden.

Bridget stared at the trowel. For how long had she been frozen? "Oh my, this is getting nothing done."

Sean appeared at the door. "Come downstairs quick. They've bombed London."

Bridget followed her grandson.

Peggy was listening as CNN talked about a bus in King's Cross.

A red double decker looked as if Godzilla stomped on it. People mulled around. A yellow and green ambulance drove away with its siren screaming.

"At first they thought it was a power surge that caused it, but power surges don't blow up buses," Peggy said. "It happened about six hours ago, but I just turned on the television."

The screen switched to Tony Blair walking away from world leaders to a bank of microphones. "He resembles an elf." Bridget said.

"An evil elf," Peggy said.

Bridget wasn't all that crazy about the British, although she was nowhere as vehement as her Irish-born mother, who felt the only good Englishman was a dead one.

"Listen to him prattle about values and not cowering to terrorists.

What do you think we did to Baghdad? They've four little bombs, and its terrorism, but Brits and Americans bomb Iraqis night after night and that's bringing liberty and democracy." Peggy started to cry. "I can't do this anymore."

Sean gave a you-take-her-this-time shrug. Bridget gathered her daughter into her arms as she did when the children were small. Grown-ups needed to be held sometimes too, but never had she felt her daughter tremble as she was shaking now.

"I want to run away," Peggy said. "This is insane."

Bridget didn't ask what *this* was. Life had grown insane. Never had she had trouble adjusting. She was always willing to try something new, and if she liked it she would keep it.

Everything was topsy-turvy. Families didn't have time for each other, gang killings racked the city, everyone was in debt, people were getting poorer and poorer. All you had to do was walk by the soup kitchen at the Church with its ever-lengthening lines to know how much trouble people were in.

"It gets worse," Sean said. "Hurricane Dennis is going to where Aunt Katie and Uncle Bill want to buy a place."

"Sorta like Californians buying on top of an earthquake fault," Bridget said.

Peggy sat up. "Mom, I don't know what to do next. I really, really don't."

CNN showed a wounded man. As Sean turned up the volume, the man said that he pitied his attackers.

"At last," Peggy said. "Someone who doesn't say kill, kill. Someone has to say stop."

The news recycled with little new information dribbling in. Peggy shut it off saying she couldn't stand it and went into her bedroom.

* * * * *

Back on her porch Bridget finished transplanting her flowers, packing the soil tightly, but not too tightly. Her old and battered tin watering can was on one side; it had been her mother's. No need to throw out something good. Plants had been nourished from that can for more than 80 years.

Bridget sat in the egg-shaped hanging chair, enclosing her in a wicker womb. Until now this house made her feel safe. Mother of God, she crossed herself. She called it her house, not her home.

Terrorists weren't scaring her. Terrorists were like bad weather – they existed. Nothing could be done about them. What was being done now certainly wasn't helping. Vengeance is mine, sayeth the Lord, not man. She couldn't think of one vengeful act that hadn't led to another. As a kid she loved history and wanted to teach. The money hadn't been there even for the cheapy state teacher colleges.

Last night she watched a program about elephants. Each herd had a matriarch elephant, the oldest and wisest, the narrator said. Bridget felt that she was the old wise elephant of this family. There had to be a way back to safety for the others.

She got up from her break to admire the plants. Whatever pain they felt at being uprooted would go away as their roots spread through the new soil.

Looking down, she saw Angela sitting in a deck chair. Something Angela said the night of Peggy's kidnapping niggled in her mind. Then she remembered. She almost tripped on the step up to the kitchen as she tried to reach the telephone and find the number of the Irish consulate.

An Irish lilt, an accent far stronger than her husband's, answered.

"If you have a parent who is an Irish citizen, you're entitled to an Irish passport," the woman almost sang. "I can't tell you how many requests we have had in the last three years, but the numbers are way up."

When Bridget hung up the phone, she called Mavis, a neighbor who had moved away; moved away meant leaving a Mission Hill triple decker. Mavis moved all the way to Brookline, 10 minutes door-to-door, but it was still away in the sense that the South Shore, New York, Florida or Ireland were away.

They stayed in touch, though not like when their children played together and got on the same school bus. Mavis, after her last was in high school, threw her drunken husband out, got her real estate license and now ran her own agency. Bridget looked up her phone number.

"Long time, no hear," Mavis said. "Lucky you caught me in."

"Can you come over and look at my place?"

"You're not thinking of selling? It's only been a few months since Patrick ... you know the advice about waiting a year before any big decisions."

A true friend, Bridget thought, putting my needs before a commission. "I just need some ideas."

"For you, anything," Mavis said.

Bridget kept her hand on the receiver after hanging up and looked at the dirt caked under her nails. The white Princess telephone must be at least 35 years old. If the phone had broken, she would replace it with a portable.

Life changes, she thought.

CHAPTER 73

The night of the London bombing, Katie thought her own heart had been bombed. She wanted to throw up each time she thought of Jess, her all A student, the future lawyer, the righter of wrongs in the world. This was her punishment for giving in when Jess wanted to go to Boston Latin rather than Catholic school.

At least, Jess ran with a good crowd, even if there were Protestants and Jews and even a Chinese girl of God knows what faith. She took several deep breaths to gain control.

Bill pushed his kitchen stool aside. He put his hand on her arm. "Jess is a grown woman, Sweetie."

"I know she's a grown woman, but ..."

"And wanting sex is normal. Think how we were."

"I know what's right and wrong and that has been true since Christ walked the earth."

Bill reached to touch her hand, but she withdrew it as if it were a lit match.

"They'll get married eventually."

Katie turned so quickly she knocked over the glass coated with the last of her milk from dinner. "Whose side are you on?"

"I'm not on anyone's. I've a daughter who wants to get married, and she'll live with her fiancé for a short time before they do. It's done all the time these days and even if we don't approve, and although I wish they would do it in the reverse order, it is not worth antagonizing them over."

"Well I forbid it," Katie said.

"I forbid you to forbid it," Bill said. 'Besides, she's already moved out."

Katie got up from the table, leaving the glass on its side. Somewhere there might be a time machine she could enter where she could turn back the clock and make her daughter a virgin again. And while she was there, she would tell her nephew not to join the Marines.

CHAPTER 74

Mavis walked around Bridget's apartment. She was in relatively good shape for a woman in her 70s, although her lilac suit was chosen to camouflage a thick waist. After a welcoming hug, Mavis took a leather folder with a pen fastened in the middle. On the right was a white, blue-lined tablet, half used. The other side was a form with lots of boxes.

"Would you like some tea first?" Bridget asked.

"Business before pleasure, then we'll catch up. Let's start in the bathroom."

Mavis looked under sinks and turned taps on and off. She opened and shut every window and smiled when she checked double-glazed combination windows. On the back porch she stamped on the floor and pushed against the wooden bars supporting the plant-laden banister. She turned on the stovetop burners, holding her hand over the flame.

Check, check, check, Mavis marked her form and with each check her head nodded up and down. When she finished, she smiled, "Everything is in good condition, but a bit old-fashioned. It might be harder to show with your sewing room in place of a living room. I'd suggest you rearrange if you're serious about selling."

"Katie's place is modern, Peggy's is cozy." Bridget led her friend to the bottom floor. No one was home at Katie's, thank goodness. Bridget wasn't ready to reveal her plans to anyone until she found out as much as she could. They might think she was crazy – or worse – senile. Mavis trailed behind her, stopping to tap the wall between the floors.

"Are they separate condos, or are you selling as a unit?" Mavis opened Katie's bedroom closet. Bill had enlarged it so it wasn't the narrow little hideaway that held the limited wardrobes of the early 1900s.

Bridget didn't know. She had only thought of running away to make Peggy safe. "I guess both are possible." They went into the kitchen.

Mavis turned 360 degrees. She peeked out the window into the garden. "This is incredible. I'd list it for four hundred fifty thousand. There's three huge bedrooms, the kitchen is out of *Homes & Gardens,* and the back yard with all the flowers right here in the middle of the city, well it's a hideaway."

Bridget swallowed. "The house is worth that much?"

"No, just this unit."

Bridget put a hand against the kitchen counter to steady herself. Patrick had worked 15 years and still hadn't made that amount of money.

Mavis helped her friend to sit. "Are you all right?"

"I'd like some water."

Mavis ran cold tap water and gave the glass to Bridget, who held it against her forehead before drinking it down. "I had no idea that it would be that valuable, I mean that, but ..."

"When you're up to it, let's look at Peggy's."

"Put your notepad away. I don't want her to know."

Mavis frowned but followed her friend upstairs.

Peggy answered the door. She was in cotton slacks and a loose top. Her hair was fastened back, and she wore no make-up. Circles were under her eyes. "Ma, Mavis. This is a surprise, Mavis, not you Ma."

Mavis came in. "I was in the neighborhood ..." She walked in a circle. "This is adorable. Can I see the rest of it?" When Peggy turned to lead the way, Mavis winked.

As soon as Bridget and Mavis were upstairs and seated in the TV room, Mavis started checking boxes. She took out her calculator and let her fingers dance over the keys. "My desire would be to ask three-fifty for Peggy's and three hundred thousand dollars for yours. You may have to come down a bit because of the old-fashioned bathroom and kitchen. You say the separate furnaces and hot water tanks for each apartment are all under five years old?"

"It pays to have a plumber for a son-in-law." Bridget toted up the prices: over a million, more than enough to start a new life for all of them if they wanted it. It could happen so fast. Life went on for years and years and years without a change and then in months, weeks, days, everything was swept away to be rebuilt. Neither woman heard Jess come in.

"Definitely, you should go condo."

"Go condo?" Jess popped her head into the television room. "Hello, Mavis. Gran, what are you up to?"

"Oh dear," Bridget said.

Mavis shoved papers into her briefcase and almost backed out of the door. Her heels clicked on the wooden hall floor. "I must be on my way. Tea can wait for another day."

Jess stood with her hands on her hips. It was how Bridget stood when she caught any of the kids doing something they shouldn't.

"You playing outraged-gran these days? You're not very good at it. Haven't had the practice I've had." Bridget gave what she hoped would be a disarming grin. When Jess only raised an eyebrow, she said, "How's life with Aidan?' She heard the door downstairs close behind Mavis.

"Changing the subject?"

"I've been listening to your mother not cope with the fact that you're no longer her fair-haired girl."

A smile played around Jess' lips. "Oh, you're good, Gran, really, really good. Let's negotiate. I'll tell you mine if you tell me yours." Both women burst out laughing at the old family joke.

"You first." Jess.

"No, you."

"No, you."

"Rock, scissors paper?" Bridget raised her fist.

Jess matched her.

"One, two, three." In unison.

Jess' fist came down flat, covering Bridget's rock.

"Darn." She told Jess everything, about selling the house and starting over in Ireland.

"You certainly beat anything I've done. How thoroughly have you researched it?"

"I know what papers I need to get passports. I know we can make a lot of money by selling out to start over."

Jess nodded. "I suspect you haven't approached anyone in the family."

"I wanted all the details worked out."

"Let me research more stuff: job opportunities, housing prices, moving costs. When you talk to the family, you'll have the answers to their questions."

"How do you think they'll take it?"

"Mom will freak. Dad will look upon it as a message from God that it really is time to move. Peggy will be scared, and Connor will bluster." Jess stood up. "You really should think about taking a visit over there, before finally deciding."

Her niece was right. The idea of getting on a plane and seeing Ireland suddenly seemed real. Before it had been an idea. Now it was a goal with steps to make it happen. "And now your turn ... You and Aidan?"

"We're getting married sometime next year if this living together thing works out." Jess was almost running down the hall before Bridget could ask for any more details.

"That's not enough information," Bridget called to her granddaughter.

Jess stopped, turned, waved. "Next time. I promise."

CHAPTER 75

"Want a beer?" Aidan asked Rob Holmes. The man was Aidan's age with short-cropped blond hair, but he stood half a head taller. He was dressed in khaki shorts, a Boston Red Sox t-shirt and tennis shoes.

"Sure."

Jess entered Aidan's flat, which she still didn't think of as her place, followed by a whirl of hot air. Her hair was sticking to her forehead and wet circles darkened her white blouse under the arms.

"Shut the door, don't let the air-conditioning escape." Aidan walked over to kiss her. "Let me introduce my old buddy since kindergarten, P. Robert Holmes. We called him P-man." He feinted a punch. P-man returned it. They boxed the air, exchanging six fake blows.

Jess assumed this was a ritual only they understood. "You were really friends that long?"

"Yup, we were like twins, born from separate wombs," Aidan said. "Now I'm a big grown-up reporter and he's a big grown-up FBI agent."

"Soon to be ex-agent," Rob said.

Aidan's eyes opened wide. He motioned for P-man to sit. "Don't tell me yet." He disappeared and returned with three Sam Adams still in their bottles and no glasses.

Rob frowned. "I hate my job."

Jess sank into Aidan's big leather chair that reminded her of a newer model of her grandfather's. What was it about men and their chairs? Her skin stuck to the leather. She realized if she moved, she might make an embarrassing sound, but she didn't care. "But why?"

P-man took a long sip of his beer. "Let me fill you in."

"This I want to hear. All you talked about since you were a kid was to be a modern Eliot Ness," Aidan said.

He looked at Jess. "It was because of my parents. My dad was a peacenik hippie artist; my mother a nurse. They had the last farm in Reading, grew their own food, nothing but organic, etc. My sister and I were dragged to protest marches like some kids are forced to take piano lessons."

"I always liked his parents." Aidan settled on the arm of Jess' chair and put one hand on her shoulder. "They never worried if we got dirty."

"You weren't forced to write essays on the big bad government.'

Jess watched this six-foot muscular man stare at his hands. 'So, you rebelled by joining the FBI?'

"My parents used to say how they could always tell the FBI guys at the anti-Vietnam protests because of their short hair and pressed jeans."

"He graduated high school National Honor Society, university Magna Cum Laude and was in the top five percent at Yale Law. And he got me through trig in high school. I'm a wordsmith, not a numbers man." Aidan swigged his beer.

"I love you anyway, you wordsmith." Jess turned to Rob. "What changed?"

P-man rolled the beer bottle between his hands. "Is this off the record, ace reporter?"

Aidan nodded.

Jess guessed that Rob's frown went all the way into his heart. Tonight, in bed, she and Aidan would talk about it. The day that she'd discovered how observant Aidan was of body language made her happy. Maybe that was part of his being a reporter, but she didn't care why, just that it was.

P-man handed Jess a dollar. "You're my lawyer, bound by confidentiality, and it doesn't matter that you haven't passed the bar yet." He stood up and began to pace. "I'm calling on our blood oath, Aidan, Buddy."

"We did the blood oath thing when we were eight," Aidan said. "My word is my word with or without blood."

P-man turned to Jess. "My job was surveillance of what was termed threatening groups."

"Muslims?"

"Americans. Peace groups. I trained local cops to infiltrate, sometimes in their own towns, sometimes in neighboring towns. Or they identified people who were super patriots to work for us. Which is how I met Jocelyn."

"A super patriot?" Jess asked.

"She was a super-against-Bush, super-against-the-war and an economist to boot. Followed Stiglitz. We started with coffee." He smiled. "You'll get the wedding invitation next month."

"Wow," Jess and Aidan said together.

"She converted me into my parents. I hope we four can get together soon. I hear there are wedding bells for you, too."

"Probably sometime next year. I'll graduate, take the bar and then I'm setting up a storefront practice with a friend," Jess said.

P-man laughed. "That's what Jocelyn says I should do. She works for a progressive think tank and can support both of us."

The look that Jess and Aidan exchange said they thought they found their first friends as a couple.

"So why did you ask me here? You said you had a problem.'

Aidan told him about Peggy's experience.

"I don't know anything about your aunt's case." He looked at Jess. "My guess would be after they looked at her computer, they concluded she was a harmless nutcase, although I bet, they followed up on all her contacts."

"But there are no warrants," Jess said.

"The government doesn't need them. Since the Patriot Act, we just do what we want to get the information. You should know that, Jess."

"I want a story," Aidan said. "Who should I talk to?"

"You won't get one. There'll be official denials out the ying-yang."

The three sighed as one.

"This stinks," Jess said.

The two men nodded. "Even without Jocelyn, I can't be part of this anymore."

They finished their beers.

"What's the P for?" Jess asked.

"Peace. My hippie parents. At least they gave me a normal middle name."

CHAPTER 76

Peggy sat with her old yellow legal pad and pen. It was the first time she had picked them up since her kidnapping.

Instead of plans for posters, senators to call, messages or website additions, she wrote, corn, hamburger, milk. The sounds of a cabinet closing and a refrigerator door click were the only other sounds in the apartment.

Sean would leave after eating. Katie and Bill were at work. Jess was living with Aidan. If she'd more energy, she would tell Katie to relax.

Upstairs she heard her mother's footsteps. For years, she had never noticed them. Now they told her she wasn't alone.

Since her return, someone was always in the house with her. Although they never discussed it, she knew it was no accident. Sean no longer hung out with his buddies. Rachel came at least every two days, something she had never done before. Maybe there was a family guard-Peggy schedule somewhere.

Sean sauntered into the living room and bent to kiss her goodbye. His breath smelled of coffee, so different from the milky breath when he was a baby. "I'm working until three. I'll be home right after."

"I've a list of things we need." She held up the paper.

He shook his head. "Nope. It's time you went out."

She imagined herself walking out the door to be wrestled into a car never to be seen again. "I'm not ready."

"The longer you wait, the harder it'll be."

"Maybe Ma can go."

"I've told her to make you go. Sorta like when I failed my first Little League tryouts. You made me try the next year. You said I should never quit."

She threw the pad at him. "I hate it when you throw my words back at me."

The pad bounced off his hip. He gave it back to her. "Mom, you can do it three ways: one, go by yourself; two, ask Gran to go with you; or three, wait until I get home when I will throw you out of the house." He blew her a kiss. She didn't try to catch it, not to be mean. Her arms felt too heavy.

Instead of getting up, she curled up on the couch and closed her eyes, trying to find the sleep hiding from her nights. She was tired. For a short time, she napped. She woke to see her mother.

"Your son called and told me you were going to the store. Want me to go with you?"

"I'm not going." It was a snap, a tone which no one used to Bridget.

"You can't hide forever."

"God, now you sound like Sean." Peggy stomped into her bedroom. The easy chair, where she'd read to her kids when they were little, was buried under clothes. She slipped on a pair of slacks that weren't too dirty. Once they had been tight, now they zipped without her pulling in her tummy. A U-Mass t-shirt that Sean gave her for her birthday was wrinkled, but she didn't care. Stop&Shop wasn't a fashion parade.

"That's my girl," Bridget said as Peggy picked up her pocketbook. "Take your cell. If you're uncomfortable, call."

"I'll be okay." Never too late to lie to your mother, she thought.

Bridget had hung new sheer curtains over the new Plexiglas front door windows that would withstand another axe battering. No one could see in, but Peggy could peek out.

She opened the door at the same speed she would have if there were a troop of marauding missionaries waiting on the porch. Pausing at the top of the eight stairs leading to the sidewalk gave her a chance to check the street. Fewer cars were parked during the day than at night. All were empty.

So far so good.

When she turned to look back at her house, Bridget waved from her bay window.

The day with its blue sky against the red bricks of the apartment building on the corner and the green leaves of the tree would have been beautiful if fear didn't muddle the color. She forced herself to walk, not run, down Tremont Street until she came to Stop&Shop.

Once inside she felt better. People weren't kidnapped from supermarkets. As much as she hated to admit it, her son was right. She had to get on with her life. But could she?

CHAPTER 77

"You have to tell them soon, Gran," Jess said.

Bridget nodded even though Jess couldn't see her through the telephone.

"I mean they'll notice buyers coming through."

"How about I call a family meeting, tomorrow night?"

"You could do it at Sunday lunch."

"It's too important for a lunch. Will you and Aidan come and bring everything you've found on Ireland?"

Jess snorted. "Did you imagine I wouldn't? I've a PowerPoint presentation complete with graphs of housing costs, want-ad information, universities for Jamie and Sean and schools for the handicapped in different areas. I've got photos."

One by one, Bridget summoned her family for a powwow, as she called it, for Friday night.

"Are you sick, Ma?" Connor asked over the telephone.

"Is it about Jess?" Katie asked when she answered the call.

"Sure," Peggy said.

Rachel and Katie e-mailed back and forth trying to guess what Bridget had on her mind. They played 100 things that could be on Bridget's mind.

"Ask her," Rachel telephoned after the 10th e-mail from Katie. "You're her daughter. I'm only the daughter-in-law. And you're only a few stairs away."

"I did. She said she wanted us all together."

"Since she told Connor she wasn't sick, it can't be cancer," Rachel said.

"She wants Ashley and Jamie there as well. And it is after dinner. This family always talks over food. You'd think you were all Jewish."

* * * * *

Friday night was hot and sticky. The smell of pollution filtered through the windows. Bridget was downstairs in Katie and Bill's flat waiting to spring her news.

Katie sighed as she stared out the window. "I don't want Aidan here."

Bridget followed her daughter's eyes. Outside Aidan angled his car into a parking spot. "I invited him. If you insist, we can go upstairs to my apartment and leave you here, but alienating Jess is stupid."

"Now you sound like my husband and my boss."

"They make more sense than you do."

She hoped the kids used birth control, but she wasn't going to open that can of worms with her daughter. She hadn't been to confession since Jason died, but she still zipped into the Mission Hill Church for a quick prayer almost daily.

When she met her reward, she wanted to discuss one or two things with God about the way he let this planet go to hell. She had a list of people she thought he would do well to zap and send to a place where they would be very warm for eternity.

Aidan walked in before Jess with a laptop case slung over his shoulder. Her niece carried a pile of papers. Bill kissed his daughter and shook Aidan's hand.

Katie said nothing.

Connor, Rachel and their girls were late. When they did arrive, Connor apologized.

"A committee meeting, unofficial," he said.

Bridget sat without saying a word until everyone stopped talking.

"This is probably the most important meeting this family will ever have."

All her children and grandchildren stared at her.

"This has been one of the worst years in all our lives."

Everyone nodded.

"With the Old Goat gone ..." she paused. It didn't seem quite right to call him that, but he had been her Old Goat, and she'd loved him. She should have shown it more, but she couldn't undo the past. "With Patrick gone, I'm the head of this family."

Connor shifted in his chair. "I thought I was as the oldest son."

"Women's lib," Jamie said. She looked at the floor when Rachel glared at her.

"The idea came from two things. One was from something Angela said that I remembered as I was transplanting my flowers."

"Ma, can you get to the point?" Connor said.

"This country isn't what it used to be. We lost a family member for no reason. Medical care is a disgrace."

"It's a good thing Da isn't here to hear this," Connor said, "or my constituents."

"For once can you shut up about your damned constituents," Rachel said. "I would put whatever your mother wants ahead of them any day."

Jamie clapped.

"Enough," Rachel snapped at her.

"Da didn't see the changes as permanent, but a lot of the Irish have. They're moving back. It's time we did too."

No one spoke. Then everyone spoke.

"Back? We never lived there." Katie said.

"How can we do that?" Peggy asked.

"Alzheimer's, she has Alzheimer's!" Connor said.

"Cool." Jamie and Sean said together, then Sean added, "Moving, not Alzheimer's."

"Ma, if the papers find out my career would be ruined. They'd say my family deserted the country in its hour of need." Connor started pacing.

"Connor, shut up. Sit down!" Jess said.

He did.

Bridget cleared her throat before speaking. Her first words were hesitant, but as she continued, she became more forceful. "Jess has researched everything: the price of houses, schools for Sean, Jamie, Ashley, housing costs, plumbing requirements, etc. We'll be eligible for passports. Jess has all the applications."

"And more info." Jess opened her laptop. The family gathered around as best they could. She kept rotating the laptop so everyone saw the details. When she finished, she asked, "What do you think?"

"You should have told me what your grandmother was up to," Katie said.

"You weren't speaking to me," Jess said.

Peggy hadn't spoken for the entire time Jess was going through her presentation. "This is about what happened to me, Ma, isn't it?"

"I want this family to be safer than it is now. Sean, I don't want you drafted if there ever is another draft. From what I've read, Ireland isn't perfect, but it is in better shape than we are. We've got roots there."

"My roots are here," Connor said. "This is nuts."

They talked on and on, often referring to Jess' charts, debating the advantages of Dublin against Galway against Killarney as possible places to settle.

"Look at that. Ireland has a special savings account where the government pays twenty-five percent interest on the money. How about introducing that in the State House? Now that would do some good," Peggy said.

"Get real," Connor snapped.

Bridget clapped her hands. "Do we go?"

"If Ma is brave enough, I'll go," Peggy said. "Someone has to look after her anyway."

"Me too, even if I lose some school time," Sean said.

Katie looked at Bill who said, "Ireland has a terrible climate."

"But good health care," Jess said.

"Katie and I can move to Florida without feeling we are deserting you," Bill said.

"We'll talk about *that* later," Katie said. "I hate the idea of my mother and ... and ... my daughter being on the other side of the Atlantic."

"Aidan and I are staying. I want to work to make changes here," Jess said. "At least for a while, but I'm applying for the passport, too."

They all turned to look at Connor. "No way. I'll repeat myself. How would it look if everyone thought my family deserted their country?"

"The country deserted us," Peggy said.

"I've a suggestion," Aidan said.

Katie glared at him.

"Hear him out," Jess said. "It makes sense."

"Before doing anything final, take a trip over there and look around."

"And I just happen to have cost estimates for tickets," Bridget said. "We could do it right before school starts in September."

CHAPTER 78

"Florida, not Ireland," Bill said from his side of the bed.

Katie stared at the ceiling. "I don't want to be so far from my family."

"Your mother and sister aren't going to be here anyway."

"They haven't decided one hundred percent. Nothing has been sold. I don't believe they'll do it."

"We need our own lives," Bill said.

"We always had our own lives," Katie said.

"Not the way we should." Each subsequent comment increased in intensity. Their screaming continued, one of the few times they had fought in their entire marriage at a volume higher than conversational. Their voices rang through the upstairs apartments.

Bill slept on the couch for the first time in their marriage.

Katie stayed in bed and felt as if she were plastered against the front windshield of a high-speed train. No matter how she yelled at the driver to stop, he wouldn't.

* * * * *

Bill put his business up for sale against Katie's wishes. She agreed to at least go back to Florida one last time to look. They had lost the house they had chosen when they had to rush back because of Peggy's kidnapping. "I don't want to be so far away from everyone," she told anyone who would listen, but packed her bag and went to the airport with her husband relishing the cool breeze that said autumn was coming.

At Logan Airport people swarmed around the departure board. Flights were cancelled. Another hurricane was due to hit the region. They caught a cab back to Delle Avenue.

Then Hurricane Katrina hit New Orleans before they could book another flight.

Bill sat on the hassock watching CNN's Anderson Cooper stand in water. He saw the people huddled on the street. Katie was beside him on the couch with her feet resting in his lap. He put his hand on her ankle. "I'll make a deal with you."

She cocked her head.

"We go to Ireland with your mother and sister, but you make your peace with Jess."

Katie let the alternatives dance through her mind. She missed her daughter. She thought of herself away from everyone she loved. She saw herself in a rescue boat with an alligator swimming by. "Deal."

"But we have to have our own home."

"Not too far from Ma and Peggy."

CHAPTER 79

Peggy felt like a sardine in the small limo that they'd hired to take them to Logan Airport. Their luggage had been crammed into the trunk.

Despite Bill's cajoling and reminders of her promise to make-up with their daughter, Katie had refused to let Aidan and Jess go with them to see them off, but Jamie, Connor and Rachel followed in their own car.

The sky was the bright blue that only happens in autumn, contrasted to the red and yellow leaves along the banks of the Charles River. Peggy prayed that these were not the last hours of her life. She thought of the photos of Princess Diana going through the hotel doors in Paris and being unaware that in a few hours she would be dead. She told herself that more people died in car accidents than plane accidents. It did not calm her nerves.

"We're here," the driver said, a black woman with corn-rowed hair, as she pulled up at the curb of Terminal E under the Aer Lingus sign.

Bridget, to mark her first flight, emerged dressed in her Sunday best dress. "Even in economy, I want to look first class," Bridget told them as they left Delle Avenue.

As for Peggy, the idea of getting into a metal cylinder to be hurled across the ocean was so daunting that she felt she wanted to be well-dressed, just in case the plane plummeted into the Atlantic, although who would she be impressing? Sharks? Whales?

Katie, dressed in a maroon Harvard sweatshirt, blushed.

Jamie said, "That's okay, Aunt Katie, it makes you look like an intellectual slob," Since she hadn't had the money for Brandeis and had to enroll at U Mass Boston, she put down every private university.

After Connor pulled his car in behind the limo, he and Bill went in search of a couple of baggage carts.

A state trooper, freckled and blue-eyed, wearing jodhpurs, marched over to tell the limo to move along.

"My family is going on their first flight ever," Jamie said, tilting her head and smiling.

He took off his hat, revealing a crew cut of red hair, as he watched each person emerge.

Peggy thought if Connor were with them, he would have pulled out his identification as a state rep and given the cop a hard time. Since her mother had come up with this crazy idea to move to Ireland, she felt as if she were being swept away by a river, bouncing along with the current. She'd been in that river much too long, even before her mother's plan to uproot the family.

"Well, have a good flight," the cop said.

"And may you have a good day, too." Jamie flashed a smile unlike anything she would show her family.

Bill and Connor returned with carts and loaded the luggage onto them, refusing to allow any of the women to lift anything. The line was minimal at the Aer Lingus counter. They had come almost four hours early to avoid the lines like the one at the Lufthansa counter. When it was their turn, the men heaved the suitcases, one by one, onto the conveyor belt next to the ticketing desk.

Peggy stayed back, letting the others go ahead. Bridget and Katie plunked their new Irish passports down on the countertop and received their boarding passes. Then Bill showed his American passport and got his.

Sean and Jamie were staying in Boston for this look-see trip. Connor had said he would consider letting Jamie transfer in her junior year, if the family didn't return home with their tails between their legs. Sean wanted to check out Trinity College, but Peggy had nixed the idea, telling him to finish the year in Boston.

Peggy's turn was next. Too late to back out. The chunky woman in her Aer Lingus uniform took Peggy's American passport, hit a key, frowned, then tapped more on the computer.

The family had applied for American passports at the same time as they'd applied for the Irish, figuring one or the other would surely come in time to take the flight they had booked. Peggy's Irish one had not come.

"I hate these," the counter agent mouthed to the woman working at the next in-take window. She turned to Peggy. "I'm sorry, you're on a no-fly list. We can't board you."

"What? Why?"

"I'm sorry, we don't know."

For the first time Peggy wanted to get on that plane even if it never arrived. How dare the government muck her about again? Good God! First, she wasn't sure she wanted to leave the country and now she couldn't when she wanted to.

"I want to see your boss," she said as the few people in line shifted from one foot to another, failing not to stare. Those in the very back strained to hear.

"It isn't the airline," the agent said, her face showing distress.

Bill, too far away to hear from where he waited with the others, saw something was wrong and strode back to the counter. Peggy stuttered out what was happening.

"Are you sure?" When the agent assured him it was real, he began fighting with her. His voice grew louder.

"I'm not a terrorist, I'm a patriot." When Peggy yelled at them, the other early-bird travelers looked at their feet, the ceiling, each other, anywhere but at her.

"Don't make me call security," the agent said.

Bill tugged at her sleeve. "Let's go." She left, pulling her suitcase behind her, and went over to where the rest of the family stood. Bill followed.

"What is it?" Bridget asked.

Peggy told them.

"We'd better cancel the trip," Katie said.

"Let's go over there." Bill pointed to the area next to the bottom of the escalator leading to departure gates, where there was enough space for them to talk without blocking anyone and without being overheard.

People of all ages, races and shapes, carrying laptops and over-the-shoulder bags, rode the escalator. A woman in a black veil shuffled three children, including a teenage girl in jeans and no head covering, up the stairs.

An Au Bon Pain cart under a gaily striped umbrella sold three croissants to an obese woman.

Peggy watched rather than process what had just happened, but as her family were all talking at once, she forced herself to listen.

Bridget watched her family's faces. She held up her hand, but no one noticed. "Quiet." No one paid any attention. "QUIET!" The woman buying croissants turned.

"This is even more reason for us to do this move. Bill, Katie and I will go to look over everything. Peggy, you'll go home and wait."

"I could drive her to Montréal. She could fly out of there," Rachel said.

Peggy's anger at the counter, like a fire that flares too fast, burned out as quickly. The idea of her going to Montréal and getting on a plane without anyone she knew or loved with her was impossible to picture. "What if I can't get back and get stuck in Ireland?"

"Peggy will stay here," Bridget said. "However, when we do make our final move we will all fly out of Canada." She turned to her daughter, "You'll use your Irish passport."

Peggy wondered how her mother got so sophisticated so suddenly, but then she knew her mother was filled with reserves to meet any situation. Peggy only wished there was some DNA that she could have inherited to be as strong, because even though she was leaving the house, even though she was back to work, she exhaled fear with every breath. Maybe she could pretend to be as strong.

CHAPTER 80

The first few days in Ireland left Bridget thinking of the kaleidoscope she had gotten for Christmas the year she was five. Her family only had money for one present and that was hers, although each child received an orange, a treat beyond imagination. None of her brothers and sister ate them at the same time, but they were all there to savor the smell when the fruit was peeled. Bridget never peeled hers. She asked her mother to cut it in quarters, and she bit into the fruit, tearing every bit off so only the white lining was left. And as she ate, she looked into the kaleidoscope, twisting it, listening to the small stones click into hundreds of patterns.

Dublin was like that, hundreds of patterns, some new, some old. "I know why so many Irish came to Boston," Bridget said as she strolled through St. Stephen's Green with her family.

"Why, Ma?" Katie asked.

"Look at it: it's a bit like Boston, the houses, the green areas."

And it did. Areas were like Newbury Street or Back Bay; the parks were like the Emerald Necklace circling Boston with nature. The family rode buses to all their destinations. Some were like Southie or the South End. Some had their own feeling. They took a tour bus and saw Oscar Wilde's statue lounging on a rock across from where he had lived, decided not to tour the Guinness brewery, saying they would have more time later once they lived there. Katie smiled when Bill said, "It'll make a great weekend excursion."

The guide told them where the big battles against the English took place. Bridget felt the same pride she felt when she walked across the Minuteman Bridge in Lexington, the site of the first battle of the American Revolution.

Jess had told her about an article reporting that all the Irish were descended from only seven men. Besides admiring their virility, it made Bridget feel as if everyone she passed was kin, be it the man in the business suit or the bum sleeping on the bench. Although she preferred to think of the man in the business suit at her table, she put a Euro in the bum's donation cup.

The accents lulled Bridget into memories of her parents, aunts, uncles, and newly arrived neighbors, and yes, Patrick, especially when he was speaking with someone from the old country.

"My God, Ma," Katie said, after Bridget ordered a soft-boiled egg from the woman who ran the B&B, "you're beginning to sound Irish." Katie, too, had begun to raise the tone at the end of her sentences.

Each morning, sitting on wooden chairs while eating breakfast they plotted their course. They weren't tourists, but on a mission. Bridget worried that if Delle Avenue didn't sell, everything would fall through.

Idealism of going to a perfect place died as Bridget read *The Irish Independent* with stories about the political problems of Taoiseach Bertie Ahern: Prime Minister, Taoiseach, new words for a new life. The talk of being tougher on drunk drivers, pollution, rising real estate problems, not enough schools were the same as back home.

Home.

Home was a place, a piece of land, wood hammered together where the family had played, fought, prayed, eaten, studied, worked, in other words, lived. Bridget thought a lot about the actions that made something home. Her home had been attacked from the outside. Her home was made up of people. Could she have half those people an ocean away?

Then she thought of coming home to find Peggy's house ransacked, the weeks her daughter hadn't dared leave the house. She thought of Jason's e-mails.

The answer?

Yes, she could leave Boston. Hopefully Jess and Aidan eventually would join them. Connor and Rachel would not. Jamie maybe. So be it. However, her stomach still knotted up.

They spent four days traipsing in and out of houses and flats, all priced at over a million Euros.

"We could rent," Bill suggested at a breakfast planning session.

"It has been so long since any of us paid anything normal, the idea of rent seems really strange," Bridget said.

Bill took his mother-in-law's hands in his. "Life will be different." When she nodded, he said, "I gotta go. I'm meeting a man who wants to sell his plumbing business."

* * * *

When the family boarded the plane back to Boston three weeks later, they had the answers to their questions. They also had answers to questions they hadn't know they'd had.

They would be able to find a place to live, although Bill had suggested they buy two handyman's nightmares – one for him and Katie, one for Peggy and his mother-in-law. They'd put an offer in on what he would call a duplex and the Irish called semi-detached and they prayed the money would be there. At last, he would own his own place and if his in-laws were next door, he'd live with it. He had never wanted to get away from them, just to lose the feeling of being beholden. The idea of redesigning a place from scratch was exciting.

There were jobs in banks, building societies and credit unions for Peggy. Katie had already interviewed for a job at Trinity. Peggy had reached the negotiation stage at the Irish League of Credit Unions.

He was still undecided whether to buy out Tom O'Malley's plumbing business or start one on his own. He was leaning toward the buyout, because Tom promised to work him through all the Irish and European Union regulations. He would let Tom know next week. Now all he had to do was to make sure Katie made up with Jess.

CHAPTER 81

Back in Boston, people traipsed through the flats. Katie and Bill's sold to the first people who looked at it. A mid-November closing was set. Mavis brought the papers for Bridget to sign. "The faster we do this, the better off we'll be. I suspect the market will be cooling off and soon."

Peggy's sold next.

As Mavis predicted, Bridget's flat was hard to sell. Unlike Peggy's, who with her imagination made the old-fashioned look retro chic, Bridget's just looked shabby. By the end of October no one who came through had even made an offer.

"We could reduce the price," Mavis said. She was attending a family Sunday lunch before yet another open house to encourage buyers. Helium-filled red, white and blue balloons were hovering over the table to be tied outside on the For Sale sign.

Katie and Bill hadn't come. Despite Katie's promise to Bill to make her peace with Jess, she hadn't. Rather than confront the problem by sitting down with Jess and Aidan for this meal, Katie had wheedled Bill into a final trip to Rockport for lobster to celebrate the sale of his business.

Some day, her daughter might learn to face problems head on, but Bridget doubted it. Still she admired Katie for her skill in appearing to agree while undermining. Bill had never caught on. Bridget was too loyal to her own flesh to tell him, although there were moments when she wanted to shake him and say, "Open your eyes."

"Or you could rent it," Jess suggested. "It'll be steady income on top of what you've made from the other two apartments."

What would she do if a tenant had a plumbing problem in the middle of the night? How could she guarantee the rent would be paid? "I can't take care of it so far away."

"I can," Aidan offered.

CHAPTER 82

Jamie showed up at Aidan's on a rainy Sunday afternoon. "Dad is impossible," she said as she settled herself among the scattered *Boston Globe, Washington Post* and *New York Times*. Aidan and Jess were in sweatshirts enjoying the rare Sunday when they both were home.

"And the news is ..." Jess said. She wondered what made Jamie nearly drown to visit them. The cousins never had much contact outside family gatherings. When Jess called Aunt Rachel and Jamie answered she would usually call for her mother without any chitchat. Jess hadn't made any effort either. It wasn't that she didn't like her cousin, it was just Jamie's interests were shopping, brand names and boys: Jess' were politics and history.

Jamie took off her sodden shoes. The walk from Harvard Square had been mostly puddles.

"He won't apply for the Irish nationality. If he doesn't, then I can't apply, you know, because I'm not, like, the child of an Irish national. It means I can't move over there. Mom backs him. She'd back him if he became a mass murderer."

Jess disappeared and came back with a towel and threw it at her cousin. "That's a bit of an exaggeration."

"Not much."

"So? What can we do?"

Jamie opened her mouth and closed it a couple of time as Jess and

Aidan waited.

"Can I, like, come stay with you guys?"

Aidan and Jess exchanged glances. Aidan motioned Jess into the bedroom. They had not made the bed. A basket of laundry stood in the corner next to an ironing board. The couple practiced just-in-time ironing. Iron it and put it on. Aidan ironed his own stuff and sometimes Jess'.

"I like just the two of us," he said. "She's your cousin and not a bad kid. You decide."

If Jess considered living with Aidan as a test, he had just earned an A. Then she wondered if he were testing her as well. "She's a bit of a whiner." The idea that he knew that they wanted the same thing flashed through her mind, so he was safe letting her make the choice. It wasn't that much of a conflict, yet it was a precedent. "Send her in. I'll talk to her."

Jamie entered. Jess led her cousin to the bed. They settled cross-legged and face to face. "You know Aidan and I are learning how to live together ..." She looked at her hands.

"That's, like, a no. You, like, don't want me around."

Jess didn't say yes, because you can't make love on the floor in the living room if your cousin is about to walk in, not that they did that. Floors were uncomfortable. What she wanted was the choice. "Look, if you were having mega problems with your parents, I'd say yes, but you aren't. Have you thought of living with some of your classmates?"

"Dad would never pay for it."

"Get a job."

Jamie pouted. "God, now you sound like Mom and Dad. If you want to go to Brandeis get a job, if you want more spending money, get a job."

Jess raised an eyebrow.

"I'm outta here." Jamie grabbed her shoes and stalked out without putting them on.

"Boy, will her feet be wet now," Aidan said.

Jess picked up the editorial pages of *The New York Times*. "I hope she won't hate me."

"I doubt it," Aidan said.

Although neither said it, both were pleased how they were making decisions and how what needed to be done seemed to get done seamlessly.

CHAPTER 83

All three apartments at 40 Delle Avenue were filled with packing boxes. On the top floor Bridget had emptied her kitchen cabinets. There was a pile for Goodwill and one with things to take. Before the moving company came, she was sorting a lifetime of possessions. No one wanted to spend money to ship things that they wouldn't need.

Peggy, dressed in her coat and scarf, watched her mother shovel through everything. She'd come upstairs to give her mother precise information about where she was going and what time she would be back. Someday, maybe she wouldn't have to do that, but now she was afraid that no one would know where she had been if she were taken again.

This house had been a cocoon all her life, but was anything wrong with a cocoon? If her mother could pull up stakes at her age, then she could do no less. In a way her cocoon was going with her. It might not be that bad.

Bridget hopped up on a chair to reach the top shelves.

"For God's sake, Ma, be careful."

"Careful, schmareful. You should be glad I'm so agile." She handed her a box. Back down, she opened it and pulled out two christening pewter cups, one with Connor's name and the other engraved with Desmond's.

Peggy picked one up. "I don't remember these."

"You weren't born."

"Did Katie and I have our own?" Peggy pulled off her gloves.

"Not from Aunt Marie who gave the boys these. She died before you girls existed." As if she were a robot, Bridget filled the tea kettle. "So many memories."

Peggy reached out and touched her mother. "How can you change like this; how can you throw this stuff away?"

Bridget didn't say anything for what seemed like a long, long time. "Memories aren't things. Memories aren't places. Memories are here." She put her hand over her heart. "Things and places trigger them, that's all. And that's how I can move us."

CHAPTER 84

The inside of Mission Hill Church seemed cavernous to many, but to Katie, the inside was the right size. Smaller churches were claustrophobic. She needed a big church to reach God.

She genuflected and entered a pew. Near the altar, Father Del'Allegro disappeared through a side door. He was new: she would never get to know him.

The smell of tired incense and candle wax filled the air as it had done for the thousands of times she had been in the church. At one time or another she must have been in each spot in every pew. She looked at the baptismal basin where she had become Christian. She could picture herself walking down the aisle, her hands in prayer mode to take her first communion.

Katie's face had been so innocent then, or so she thought. The face she wore now was barely recognizable as the same one, and she wondered how many other faces she wore hidden under her skin if she lived a long time.

When Bill found her holding her sagging jaw line with her thumbs in front of a mirror, he'd hugged her and said no matter how jowly or wrinkled she became he would love her.

He hadn't been the least loving right before she slipped out of the house 20 minutes ago. He'd been nasty in front of the movers who were tearing apart her life, shoving all her memories into a box to be shipped to God knows where. That wasn't fair. She knew. Dublin.

Other things, which they'd decided not to move, had been toted to Goodwill. It was like a burial of herself before she was dead. How people managed to move every few years, she had no idea.

At least some of the family would be together, not a plane ride apart. Her sister, nephew, mother, and husband would be close, albeit it not in the same house. The offers they had put in on the places they'd looked at had been accepted. At least Bill was content with next door as long as he was the owner. God, they had so much work to do to fix everything up, but then again, she and Peggy were looking forward to the decorating.

It was Jess who would be so far away, which was the reason that Bill had been so nasty. Katie still hadn't made the reconciliation phone call she'd promised him in return for a move to Ireland rather than Florida.

She knelt, crossed herself and began her rosary. When she finished, she sat back and looked around the sanctuary that she would probably never see again.

Different words on what she would say to Jess floated through her head. She liked none of them, because what her daughter was doing was immoral. When she threw that at Bill, he'd said, "Lovemaking is better than murdering and stealing. That's what our girl is doing, making love to the man who will be her husband. They're building their lives like we built ours." Only he said it at a high volume.

Last night she and Peggy had sat amid the chaos drinking tea. What else?

"I'm ready to leave. Me, the one who thought going downtown was a trip," Peggy said.

Katie wanted to ask if her sister would feel badly not being able to visit Jason's grave, but didn't want to raise the issue. At least Jess was alive, and although the idea had flashed through her mind that she would rather have her dead than dishonored, it was just that – a flash.

"At one point, I thought not being able to visit Jason's grave would bother me most," Peggy said as if she could read Katie's thought. "But I haven't been there since he died. He's not there. What still drives me crazy is what he had to do before he died: the killing, the violence. What a horrible way to spend his last days on earth."

Katie wondered if having a child who killed others wasn't harder to bear than a child who was sexually a sinner. Although she wasn't ready to admit she might have overreacted, she could at least mend whatever she could mend. The daughter of a seamstress can mend. The idea made her smile, but the smile lasted less than a second. Jess was still sinning; nothing would change that.

The priest came back onto the altar. He was dressed in jeans but still wore his Roman collar. A blue sweater that looked handmade was over his black shirt. The church was cold, or maybe it was just Katie that was cold.

He walked toward her. "May I help you?" His smile was warm, and she noticed his deep-set black eyes could barely be seen for the lashes.

Had he been a girl, Katie would have sworn they were fake. She shook her head. "No, thank you, Father. I just came in for a moment's peace."

How rude she sounded. "I didn't mean you Father ... you see ..." But what was her explanation? She wanted to hide from people tearing apart her life and putting it in boxes? She would be able to put it together an ocean away? This priest could be her son, yet she was stammering as if he were much older. She was older than Christ when he died, probably older than the Virgin Mary when she ascended into heaven, still a virgin, unlike her daughter.

The smile didn't go away. "If you need me, just knock at the door." He pointed.

"I better be going. There are phone calls I need to make."

"Ah, the phone. We're never free of it, are we?"

This time she smiled.

* * * * *

To pass into the second floor flat at 40 Delle Avenue, Katie had to squeeze by a giant roll of bubble wrap. The bubble wrap that ate Mission Hill she thought. No one was in Peggy's flat, but she went in anyway and picked up the phone. God, she didn't know Aidan's number, but Jess was probably still in class. She dialed Jess' cell.

"Hi, I can't take your call, but you know what to do." Her daughter's voice was as bubbly as the wrap. Why couldn't she have sounded miserable for the pain she caused Katie?

As Katie disconnected, her hands shook. To be afraid to speak on the cell phone to a child whom she had diapered, how stupid was that? And how stupid was she to expect her daughter to be pliant? She saw Jess grabbing her fingers so she could walk. Then when she could do it on her own, she wouldn't let her mother help. Jess had been like that all her life, once she could do something on her own. Lord help anyone who tried to help her.

Katie punched the redial button. After the message, "Jess, I wanted to let you know I love you. We're going to be at your Aunt Rachel and Uncle Connor's after tonight, and if you could stop by before we fly out and ..."

The space for the recording rang out. She hadn't had a chance to say, "I still don't agree with you."

CHAPTER 85

Peggy bunked in with Bridget their last five nights in Boston because the new owners had moved into the middle flat. Sean was staying with Rachel and Connor until June when he would move to Dublin, hopefully to start classes at Trinity in the fall.

Bill and Katie spent their last three nights with Rachel and Connor. This was their last night.

'I'm just as glad we'll be there to welcome your mother and Peggy when they fly in from Montréal," Bill said as they all sat in Rachel and Connor's living room. "It's good of Aidan to drive them to Canada." He stared at Katie.

"I'm glad you'll be there to take care of them," Rachel said. "It will seem so strange not having you here."

"No Sunday lunches," Connor said.

"We'll visit," Rachel said. "I always wanted to go to Ireland. Maybe kiss the Blarney stone. I wonder if it works for little Jewish girls."

The door opened and Jess and Aidan walked in.

"Hi all." Jess accepting Bill's hug. She then went and sat on the floor in front of her mother. "All ready for the flight?"

"As ready as we'll ever be." Katie spoke the first words to her daughter since the blow up. A cell phone didn't count.

"I bought a new umbrella," Bill said. "I'm destined to live in miserable climates."

Aidan had settled next to Bill. "Jess and I were talking. We were wondering if we could hold our wedding there sometime in the spring. It will be cheaper for us two to fly than for you all to fly over here."

Jess cocked her head. "Fall, darling, but nice attempt to move it up." She sat on the floor in front of her mother, who rested her hand lightly on her daughter's shoulder. Jess turned around and smiled. Katie smiled back.

"I think they call it autumn: maybe that's the Brits," Rachel said. "Are we invited?"

"Of course," Aidan said.

Everyone realized that times they were all together would be infrequent and would involve international flights. None of them said it. Some things were better left unsaid, including the apology that neither Jess nor Katie would ever make to the other. The most they would be able to say truthfully was that they were sorry for the pain they had caused the other, but neither felt they were wrong. They both could live with that.

CHAPTER 86

The last night before her drive to Montréal and then the flight to Dublin two days after the departure of Bill and Katie, Bridget lay in her marriage bed. The curtains were gone. The wallpaper had a clean cross mark where the crucifix had been. The new tenants were planning to paint in lieu of one month's rent. A lighter square marked where the picture of the Holy Mother had hung.

As she snuggled under the covers, she realized that now she would have a few of the experiences that she thought she never would have. Maybe she could even go to Rome and see Desmond. At 70 she had a new future. She was glad things had fallen into place so fast. Otherwise, she might have chickened out, but once she signed the first set of sale papers there was no turning back.

She reached out to touch Patrick's empty place. She had never taken over his place in the bed. "You wouldn't understand this, you Old Goat," she said to him. "And that's all right. I did what I had to do for the family. That part you'd understand."

It was enough.

EPILOGUE 2019

Bridget Flanagan lived another 10 years in Dublin. She became active in her local parish and made friends with several other widows. She had her chance to travel around Ireland, including kissing the Blarney Stone. She went to Rome to visit her son. The cause of her death was never determined. One day she did not wake up. She was found with a smile on her face.

Bill and Katie Kelly opened a new plumbing business which grew quickly. They often travel to Boston to visit with Jess, Aidan and their grandchildren.

Jess Kelly married Aidan Pelletier. They have a daughter and son. He continues to report for *The Boston Globe*. Jess opened her storefront legal practice with her friend Amy.

Connor Flanagan was elected to the U.S. House of Representatives. Rachel was never able to reconcile with her family. She went back to university for a masters in social work. Jamie grew out of her bratty teen-age phase. She became a physical therapist working with children who have problems like her sister. Ashley graduated from Simmons College and became a librarian in a small town in Maine.

All family members constantly look for bargain flights between Boston and Dublin.

ACKNOWLEDGMENTS

Much of this novel was written in real time then put aside. The final editing was done by my husband, Rick Adams. It is wonderful to have a writer/professional editor in the family. The photo of a triple decker was taken by William Jordan, Jr. Lori DeBoer, a Facebook friend, whose work I'd seen online, did the sketch. Deirdre Wait is my much-appreciated cover designer, not just for this work but for all my books.

ABOUT THE AUTHOR

D-L Nelson is a New England-born, Swiss writer. She makes her home in Geneva, Switzerland and Argelès-sur-mer, France along with her husband Rick Adams and dog Sherlock. Visit her website at www.donnalanenelson.com and her blog at http://theexpatwriter.blogspot.com. If you wish to contact her: dlnelson7@hotmail.com

Made in the USA
Lexington, KY
13 September 2019